# DINNER IN CAMELOT

JOSEPH A. ESPOSITO

# Dinner *in* Camelot

THE NIGHT AMERICA'S

GREATEST SCIENTISTS, WRITERS,

AND SCHOLARS PARTIED

AT THE KENNEDY WHITE HOUSE

*ForeEdge*

ForeEdge

An imprint of University Press of New England

www.upne.com

© 2018 Joseph A. Esposito

All rights reserved

Manufactured in the United States of America

Designed by Mindy Basinger Hill

Typeset in Fanwood

For permission to reproduce any of the material in this book,
contact Permissions, University Press of New England, One Court Street,
Suite 250, Lebanon NH 03766; or visit www.upne.com

Library of Congress Cataloging-in-Publication
Data available upon request

Hardcover ISBN: 978-1-5126-0012-4

Ebook ISBN: 978-1-5126-0255-5

5   4   3   2   1

I think this is the most extraordinary collection of talent,

of human knowledge, that has ever been gathered together

at the White House, with the possible exception of

when Thomas Jefferson dined alone.

PRESIDENT JOHN F. KENNEDY | APRIL 29, 1962

TO HOPE

# CONTENTS

*Illustrations follow page 42 and page 170*

# *Camelot*

JOSEPH ESPOSITO'S EVOCATIVE RENDERING of the famous Nobel Prize dinner at the White House in April of 1962 that symbolized the potential, the hope, of a truly forward-looking America so many of those of us attending innocently believed in, is enhanced in these pages by the author's exhaustive research. It has also deepened my understanding of that very special event when its host President John F. Kennedy famously remarked, "I think this is the most extraordinary collection of talent, of human knowledge, that has ever been gathered together at the White House with the possible exception of when Thomas Jefferson dined alone." We laughed. We were moved.

Why were my husband novelist William Styron and I invited? And why James Baldwin, who had lived with us in rural Connecticut for a year? We were young writers, not Nobel Prize laureates. Bill sat at a table with Robert Oppenheimer, Ralph Bunche, and Nathan Pusey. I sat with Albert Szent-Gyorgyi and other luminaries. Our Connecticut neighbor Fredric March and poet Robert Frost added vocal culture notes, but the stars were world-famous scientists, even one who had led a protest against President Kennedy outside the White House that afternoon and another who had been in the shadows for dubious reasons.

The personal and political backstories the author has presented of the Nobel Prize attendees are intriguing pieces of history. His descriptions of the many tables, including over-the-top flower arrangements and a unique menu served, struck me as cinematic.

I was charmed to be invited to dance by the man on my left: Albert Szent-Gyorgyi, to whom, when I was told that his office was in Woods Hole and he'd won the prize for his work on muscles (I assumed it was "mussels"), I began what must have seemed to him (embarrassing to me) a bizarre discussion on edible sea creatures. After dessert, tall Linus Pauling and his elegant wife Ava Helen got up to dance. Short Albert and I followed suit. It was apparently the first time anyone had decided to dance to the music of the select White House ensemble. Existing photographs confirm it was not all a dream.

I recall Bill's later humorous remarks about his distinguished tablemates and certain guests honored by being asked upstairs with us for a private gathering post-dinner. There Bill, full of antibiotics and champagne, sat in the presidential rocking chair and when the president arrived failed to rise quickly—*Bill's moment of embarrassment*—but our host pretended not to notice and sat on the couch with Robert Frost, whom he had chosen to read poetry at his inauguration. We writers were gratified by the president's obvious devotion to literature, beyond his own popular opus, *Profiles in Courage*. For Bill and me, it was the beginning of a sweet friendship with Jack and Jackie, following a sail off Edgartown they had promised that evening. Many meetings with Bobby and Ethel, to whom we'd been introduced there, later ensued in Washington and the Vineyard. By the '70s, we were especially close to Teddy Kennedy. Honoring my trip to Chile for Amnesty International, he facilitated a parole program for Pinochet's prisoners, with entry into the USA. At his invitation, I chaired the Robert F. Kennedy Memorial's Human Rights Awards, and (reciprocating!) he sailed over from Hyannis each summer bringing siblings, children, nephews, and nieces to camp overnight on our lawn, cook, play raucous games, and invade island beaches before sailing home, sometimes taking us and our kids along.

We need to remember what that night at the White House stood for. Can we, today or ever, re-create such Washington camaraderie, such promise of official appreciation of art and science, such trust in the future of a peaceful, moral, generous, just, welcoming America?

—*Rose Styron, June 21, 2017*

THIS BOOK is neither a biography of John and Jacqueline Kennedy nor a broad celebration of Camelot. It is a snapshot in time, one night in April 1962, in which American intellectuals were gathered for a memorable evening at the White House. Not only was the evening important in itself, and for what it symbolized, but it was significant because of the relationships that were formed at the dinner and how those relationships shaped the nation and the world in the years to come.

This Nobel Prize dinner, the largest of the Kennedy White House years, came at a time when the United States was at the height of its power. It can be argued that the world was different for many reasons after this time. One thing is clear: there never has been a gathering of such American intellectuals at the White House since. The value that we place on the contributions of artists, writers, scientists, and thinkers was at its apogee.

I was drawn to this story for several interconnected reasons. First, I met Senator John F. Kennedy in October 1960 in the waning days of the presidential campaign. Like so many, I was encouraged by him and his presidency. This childhood encounter stimulated my interest in government and politics, and subsequently I served in three presidential administrations.

Second, my wife, Hope Carter Esposito, is a direct descendent of James Hoban, the designer and first architect of the White House. I was drawn to the opportunity to further study the art and history of this most historic building in America.

And third and most important, I was mesmerized by the story of this dinner and what it represented. It remains a celebration of some of the most impressive qualities of this nation: research and thinking at the highest levels, often accomplished by people fleeing from tyranny and turmoil in other countries. This dinner also shows the United States at its finest and reminds us that we can again place a premium on civil discourse, consensus building, and recognition of serious achievement at the highest level.

This book is a paean to what America can be.

—*Joseph A. Esposito*

# KEY ATTENDEES AT THE DINNER AT THE WHITE HOUSE, APRIL 29, 1962

## THE KENNEDYS

*John F. Kennedy.* The youngest person ever elected to the presidency, the forty-four-year-old Kennedy brought a new sense of vitality to the White House. Although known for his style, political shrewdness, and wit, he was an interested student of history and took pride in his writing career, which included the Pulitzer Prize–winning *Profiles in Courage*. He had a modest interest in the arts, but supported his wife's enthusiasm and understood the power of symbolism.

*Jacqueline Bouvier Kennedy.* The First Lady had captivated Americans with her beauty and glamour, a marked change from previous presidential wives. Only thirty-two years old, Jackie Kennedy had a passion for the arts. She was responsible for the first interior renovation of the White House since 1902. This dinner followed closely on her popular televised tour of the White House, for which she had the opportunity to unveil new paintings and furnishings.

*Robert F. Kennedy.* Bobby Kennedy, thirty-six, was the attorney general and chief advisor to his older brother. Unswervingly loyal, the president could count on him to deal with thorny problems. He was in the midst of his increasingly acrimonious relationship with Vice President Lyndon Johnson. Robert Kennedy would develop relationships with others at tonight's dinner, including a close friendship with John Glenn, and work with James Baldwin on civil rights.

*Ethel Kennedy.* The fun-loving wife of the attorney general, the thirty-four-year-old Ethel Kennedy presided over raucous parties at her Hickory Hill home in nearby McLean, Virginia. At tonight's dinner, she would be the hostess at the table that featured two of the most interesting figures, the beleaguered physicist J. Robert Oppenheimer and the rising novelist William Styron.

## THE SCIENTISTS

*John Glenn.* The forty-year-old astronaut was the hero of the hour. He had become the first American to orbit the earth two months earlier and had been feted with a ticker-tape parade in New York City, which had even exceeded the tremendous celebration for Charles Lindbergh thirty-five years earlier. Glenn was becoming a close friend of the Kennedys, especially Robert Kennedy, who would encourage him to launch a political career that lasted until 1999.

*J. Robert Oppenheimer.* The brilliant scientist, known as the "Father of the Atomic Bomb," had seen his career decline since World War II and lost his security clearance after a dramatic hearing in 1954. The onetime wunderkind, now fifty-eight, had lost his swagger, but the invitation to dinner tonight represented the first step in a two-step process by the Kennedy administration to redeem him from spurious charges of disloyalty. McCarthyism had lost its potency.

*Linus Pauling.* Pauling, sixty-one, was a noted scientist and peace activist. Awarded the 1954 Nobel Prize in Chemistry, he barely missed receiving the Nobel Prize for Medicine, and later, in 1962, received the Nobel Peace Prize. He was ambivalent about Kennedy, recognizing his potential but disappointed by his lack of achievement on a nuclear arms ban. He had been critical of the president, picketing against him outside the White House a few hours before attending the dinner there.

*Glenn T. Seaborg.* A distinguished chemist, Seaborg, fifty, was currently chairman of the Atomic Energy Commission, which earlier had revoked Oppenheimer's security clearance. A longtime friend and colleague of Oppenheimer, Seaborg was interested in seeing his clearance restored. A Nobel laureate, he was the principal or codiscoverer of ten chemical elements, including seaborgium. He had worked on the Manhattan Project and eventually counseled ten presidents.

## THE WRITERS

*James Baldwin.* One of the few African-Americans at the dinner that night, the thirty-seven-year-old Baldwin was emerging as an important writer. Among his early works, *Go Tell It on the Mountain* and *Notes of a Native Son* were notable. Baldwin, who was also gay, wrote about race and alienation in American society. A close friend of William Styron, the onetime expatriate Baldwin would begin to have a louder voice in the civil rights movement.

*Pearl S. Buck.* Of all the Nobel laureates at the dinner, Pearl Buck was the only woman and the only American recipient of the award in literature. Buck, sixty-nine, had spent her childhood in China—she sometimes used her Chinese name, Sui Zhenzhu—and wrote most of her novels on Asia; perhaps her most famous was *The Good Earth*. She sat at Mrs. Kennedy's table at the dinner, and after dinner had an awkward discussion with President Kennedy about Korea.

*John Dos Passos.* The sixty-six-year-old Dos Passos was largely identified with his *U.S.A.* trilogy, written in the 1930s. William Styron, another guest at the dinner, had fallen under his spell as a college student, later saying that he was one who had "been valuable in teaching me how to write the novel." Dos Passos had been actively engaged in the Spanish Civil War, during which his friendship with Ernest Hemingway, honored at the dinner tonight, had soured.

*Robert Frost.* Frost, eighty-eight, was considered an American treasure. A four-time winner of the Pulitzer Prize, Frost had been featured at Kennedy's inauguration ceremony in 1961. The president had a high regard for the poet, asking him a few months after the dinner to take on an assignment in the Soviet Union. Frost, seated at the president's table at the dinner, was part of the select group to join the Kennedys in an after-dinner gathering in the family's private quarters.

*Katherine Anne Porter.* The seventy-one-year-old novelist and essayist was enjoying a unique experience the night of the dinner: her new book, *Ship of Fools*, had reached the top of the *New York Times* best-seller list that day. Porter arrived at the dinner with Pearl Buck. She was friendly with a number of people present, including James Baldwin, on whose demeanor that night she later reported.

*Rose Styron.* Rose Styron, in her thirties, recalls the dinner as a personal high point. She danced with Nobel laureate Albert Szent-Gyorgyi. More than a half-century later, she recounted the details of the intimate after-dinner cocktails in the Yellow Oval Room, at which the Styrons made plans for a sailing outing with the Kennedys and, indeed, launched a longtime friendship with the Kennedy family. She became a noted poet, writer, and activist in her own right.

*William Styron.* Bill Styron, thirty-six, was a rising American writer at the time of the dinner. His third book, *Set This House on Fire,* had attracted the attention of the White House. That and his friendship with writer John Marquand Jr. were probably responsible for his invitation. Styron's greatest works, *The Confessions of Nat Turner* and *Sophie's Choice,* lie in the future. Styron, affected by medication and drinking at the dinner, wrote a humorous account of the night.

*Diana Trilling.* "Di" of the "Di" and "Li" Trilling couple, the fifty-six-year-old writer, critic, and reviewer was known for her strong views. She was a staunch anticommunist. She knew many of the people at the dinner, including Oppenheimer, about whom she had written in the aftermath of the loss of his security clearance. She and her husband were invited to the after-party in the White House residence, and an account of the evening was published shortly after her death.

*Lionel Trilling.* Lionel Trilling, fifty-six, was a distinguished intellectual and critic who had taught for thirty years at Columbia University at the time of the dinner. He was a member of the group known as the New York Intellectuals and wrote for the *Partisan Review.* Among his books was the well-received *The Liberal Imagination,* first published in 1950. Trilling made a humorous, if not awkward, comment to Mrs. Kennedy in the receiving line that night.

THE PEACEMAKERS

*Ralph Bunche.* Along with James Baldwin, he was the most prominent African-American at the dinner. Bunche, fifty-eight, was an American diplomat who had received the Nobel Peace Prize in 1950 for his work on Israel. Active in both the United Nations and the civil rights movement, he was a distinguished scholar; he had achieved a doctorate in political science in 1934, the first African-American to do so at an American university.

*Ava Helen Pauling.* A former student of Dr. Linus Pauling, she had been his wife since 1922. Often known as "Ava Helen," the fifty-eight-year-old was a wide-ranging social activist, who had sent a letter to the First Lady nine months earlier protesting nuclear testing. She had joined her husband on the picket line earlier in the day and had a testy dinner conversation with White House aide Arthur M. Schlesinger Jr.

*Lester Pearson.* The attendance of "Mike" Pearson, leader of the Canadian Liberal Party, made the dinner a North American celebration. Pearson, sixty-five, had received the Nobel Peace Prize in 1957 for his work on the Suez Crisis. An ally of President Kennedy, he would be elected prime minister in 1963. He was accompanied at the dinner by his outspoken wife, Maryon, a polar opposite in temperament and outlook to the American First Lady.

## THE HEIRS

*Mary Welsh Hemingway.* The fifty-four-year-old journalist was Ernest Hemingway's fourth and last wife. Papa Hemingway, who had committed suicide nine months earlier, had been a Kennedy admirer, and the president admired him as well. Sitting to the president's left at dinner, Mary chided him on his Cuba policy. But her late husband would be honored in absentia, as actor Fredric March presented some of the Nobel laureate's unpublished work after dinner.

*Katherine Tupper Marshall.* Mrs. Marshall, seventy-nine, was the widow of General George C. Marshall, the war leader and subsequently secretary of state and then defense. He had received the Nobel Peace Prize in 1953 for creating and implementing the European Recovery Program (the Marshall Plan). She sat at the president's right at dinner that night. She said of the evening, "This is my last time out and it's been a wonderful climax for me. Now I can go back to my briar patch."

## THE PLANNERS

*Letitia Baldrige.* A former classmate of Jacqueline Bouvier, "Tish" Baldrige, thirty-six, had been social secretary to the US ambassadors in Paris and Rome. Now as White House social secretary she was heavily involved with dinners that became so notable during the Kennedy administration. She was fluent in French, as was the First Lady, and in Italian. She was called the "Doyenne of Decorum."

*Arthur M. Schlesinger Jr.* An anomaly among noted historians, Schlesinger, forty-four, never progressed beyond a bachelor's degree (from Harvard). He wrote a biography of Andrew Jackson, for which he received the Pulitzer Prize, and of Franklin D. Roosevelt. He was the son of a famous historian. A top White House aide, he was important both in selecting invitees to the Nobel dinner and in writing a draft of the president's speech for that night.

*René Verdon.* Born in France, Verdon, thirty-seven, held culinary arts positions for a quarter century before being selected by Mrs. Kennedy to be White House chef in 1961. He had been assistant chef at the Carlyle Hotel and the Essex House in New York City. His White House dinners were lavish and French oriented. He later wrote a cookbook on some of the foods prepared during his White House period, including the *filet de boeuf* Wellington served that night.

DINNER IN CAMELOT

# Heading to Dinner

BEADS OF PERSPIRATION streaked down the faces of the protesters as they moved along the sidewalk in muggy, eighty-degree weather one block away from the White House.[1] More than three thousand men and women had come to Lafayette Square the previous day, April 28, 1962, to picket in support of a nuclear test ban treaty. Fifteen months into the presidency of John F. Kennedy, the United States was locked into icy Cold War tension with the Soviet Union, and many Americans were uneasy about the prospect of global annihilation. The harrowing Cuban Missile Crisis was six months in the future.

The protesters descended on the nation's capital to influence the president to secure a stalled arms agreement with the Russians. An added incentive that weekend was that British Prime Minister Harold Macmillan, a key US ally on any such talks, was in Washington to confer with Kennedy. Those talks ended this afternoon as the prime minister left to visit Canada.

Now many were back for a second day, Sunday, one week after Easter, carrying signs such as "Stop" or, in the case of one young woman in bobby socks, "Women Strike for Peace." The latter sign identified the group that had organized the grassroots effort, which had demonstrated at the Washington Monument and in scores of cities around the country five months earlier. President Kennedy had viewed that Washington demonstration from the White House.[2]

The press paid attention today in part because of the appearance of Dr. Linus Pauling, a Nobel Prize winner and peace advocate, who unexpectedly joined the group for a second day. Because security for the Macmillan visit had pushed the pickets back from the White House, it would have been impossible for Kennedy to see Pauling.[3]

But the president was preoccupied anyway. After attending Mass at historic Holy Trinity Catholic Church in Georgetown, he was hosting Macmillan at a small farewell luncheon at the White House. Despite a quarter-century age difference, the two leaders had developed a fondness for each other. After lunch, they strolled around the South Lawn alongside two of Caroline Kennedy's ponies, Tex, three years old and dun colored, and the older Macaroni, a well-publicized roan-and-white gelding.[4]

Had the president glimpsed Pauling, he would have seen a six-foot-tall, blue-eyed man wearing a long-sleeve dress shirt and a necktie, and with a batch of pens lining his left breast pocket, as if ready for writing another critique to the president.[5]

Kennedy would have recalled a recent letter that Pauling wrote to him criticizing his lack of progress on banning nuclear tests, pointedly asking, "Are you going to give an order that will cause you to go down in history as one of the most immoral men of all time and one of the greatest enemies of the human race?" And there was more: "Are you going to be guilty of this monstrous immorality, matching that of the Soviet leaders, for the political purpose of increasing the still imposing lead of the United States over the Soviet Union in nuclear weapons technology?"[6]

That letter was written on March 1. Less than two months later, after having lunch in the park, the sixty-one-year-old Pauling grinned and sweated during his late afternoon shift. He was carrying a large rectangular poster with black-and-white printing that read: "Mr. Kennedy Mr. Macmillan / WE HAVE NO RIGHT TO TEST."[7]

The area of Lafayette Square was an obvious site for protesting on account of its proximity to the executive mansion. It might seem a peculiar spot otherwise, for it also bordered on two bastions of the American establishment: the large US Chamber of Commerce building and, across the street at the corner of H and Sixteenth Streets, the historic "Church of the Presidents," St. John's Episcopal Church, a small, yellow-and-white structure whose connections to power go back to James Madison.

And yet, the witnesses for peace might have been heartened had they attended one of the services at the church, the last of which ended at 12:15 pm, just as they were beginning their picketing. One of the readings for the day, the First Sunday after Easter, included a passage from Isaiah: "Lead out those who have eyes but are blind, who have ears but are deaf." The presence of the celebrant for that day, the Reverend Robert Smith from Tokyo, would have reminded them about the increasing interconnected nature of the world of the 1960s.

That notwithstanding, what makes Lafayette Square especially ironic as a site for peace protests is that the seven-acre park at the heart of it is a tribute to American war. Its corners have large statues memorializing four foreign generals who fought in the American Revolution: Kosciuszko, Lafayette, Rochambeau, and von Steuben. In the middle of the square facing the White House is an equestrian statue of American military leader—and president—Andrew Jackson.

Walking along the perimeter, Pauling was joined by his wife, Ava Helen, a longtime pacifist. Once a student in his "Chemistry for Home Economics Majors" class at Oregon Agricultural College, Ava Helen had been married to Linus for thirty-eight years. Although she deeply admired her husband, she had pushed the brilliant chemist toward social activism, heightening his awareness and joining with him on such issues as Japanese internment, women's rights, world federalism, and now, nuclear nonproliferation.

However, the Paulings had come from their home on Fairpoint Street in Pasadena, California, to the nation's capital not to protest, but to attend a White House event. President and Mrs. Kennedy had invited forty-nine Nobel Prize winners and other prominent intellectuals to dinner at the White House. Linus Pauling, whose political activism was monitored by Congress, including the House Un-American Activities Committee and the Senate Judiciary Committee, was criticized by both the Right and the Left for accepting the invitation. The Caltech scientist, however, believed in dialogue and saw no contradiction in accepting an invitation from someone he had so recently chided, and said so.[8] And evidently the president had no problem in inviting the dissident scientist, who was so blunt and public in his criticism.

The Paulings eventually left their fellow protesters and walked four blocks to the grand Willard Hotel at Fourteenth Street and Pennsylvania Avenue, where they were staying. Back at their air-conditioned room, he changed into his tuxedo and she into a chiffon gown and long white gloves. There was still a peek of sunlight left on this first day of Daylight Savings Time at 7:45 pm, as they joined a queue of distinguished guests entering the White House perimeter through the Southwest Gate.

The police checkpoint worked quickly and rather informally. Even when the controversial writer and longtime expatriate James Baldwin approached the guard station without an invitation or even identification, there was little problem; he simply showed the guard the inside of his tuxedo jacket, which had his name sewn in.[9]

A few guests entered through the Northwest Gate; and some, such as Samuel Eliot Morison, the noted historian, accompanied by his wife, Priscilla Barton Morison, and novelist Pearl Buck, had forgotten their invitation cards.[10] But under the keen observation of White House chief of police Ralph "Smokey" Stover, the guards—now experienced through a number of White House dinners this past year and a half—saw that the clearance system could adjust accordingly.

And so the Paulings were now standing in a much different line of people than they had been only five hours earlier. The group of mostly ordinary Americans who paced the nearby street that afternoon was concerned about what they considered an ominous future. This evening's group, according to one guest, Rose Styron, represented "a peak of American accomplishment and hope."[11]

White House social secretary Letitia Baldrige called this event the "Brains' Dinner" because of the intellectual stature of the guests.[12] Among the 175 guests, the largest dinner group during the Kennedy presidency, there were dozens of Nobel laureates—mostly scientists, but also Pearl Buck and two Peace Prize winners—as well as other prominent American writers, scholars, and college presidents.

They streamed into the vestibule and the grand, eighteen-foot-by-eighty-foot Cross Hall before queuing up for the reception line in the adjoining East Room. There they sipped drinks, from juice to martinis, and greeted one another, old friends and colleagues and new acquaintances.

Many guests were easily recognizable. There was the unmistakable eighty-seven-year-old, white-haired poet Robert Frost, who had struggled to read his poem at the inaugural ceremonies the previous year amid cold, wind, and midday sunlight. Now a group gathered around him as he spoke with John Glenn.[13]

At just forty, Glenn was the hero of the hour. Two months before, on February 20, he had become the first American astronaut to orbit the earth, a feat that sparked an outpouring of national pride and celebration not seen since the end of World War II.

This was not his first time at the Kennedy White House. He and his wife, Annie, had been feted by the president and First Lady shortly after his remarkable flight, just a few days prior to a massive ticker-tape parade in New York City on March 1, where the crowd of four million exceeded even that for Charles Lindbergh thirty-five years earlier.[14] And the attention continued; indeed, on the night of the White House dinner, Glenn was featured on an ABC television special, *60 Hours to the Moon*, narrated by Jules Bergman. Bergman, who had covered the flight, reported at the time that there was "a feeling of elation, a feeling of pride, and a feeling of achievement at Cape Canaveral."

Glenn, whose accomplishment was unprecedented for its sheer reach, had one of the easiest commutes to the dinner. In those days, guests could actually drive onto the White House property, and John and Annie Glenn made the six-mile trip from their house on North Harrison Street in Arlington, Virginia, in a few minutes in their Studebaker.

A newsreel camera caught a few of the diners being dropped off by cars, smiling and observing the growing crowd. Among them were the only political leaders at the dinner: Vice President Lyndon Johnson and "Lady Bird" Johnson and Attorney General Robert Kennedy and Ethel Kennedy. These two men, longtime foes, would be seated at adjacent tables, with an opportunity to keep an eye on one another.

Also easily spotted at the reception was the lean J. Robert Oppenheimer, who was likely puffing on either his ever-present pipe or a cigarette, and his wife, Kitty. Mary Welsh Hemingway observed Kitty as "the liveliest and prettiest of the few wives" present.[15] Anyone speaking with Oppenheimer would be attracted to his deep blue eyes; one adversary, Roger Robb, once characterized him as having "the iciest pair of blue eyes I ever saw."[16] Many of those familiar with him over the years would also have carried a mental picture etched in their minds of him with his trademark, brown porkpie hat. The hat was gone, as was his onetime swagger. The brilliant physicist known as the "Father of the Atomic Bomb" had spent the last eight years in political purgatory after he lost his security clearance. Tonight represented his release, if not officially then at least symbolically.

Dr. Glenn T. Seaborg, a Nobel laureate in physics and the new chairman of the Atomic Energy Commission, was there with his wife, Helen Griggs Seaborg, who was once secretary to the late Ernest O. Lawrence, another Nobel winner and a key Manhattan Project leader. Seaborg—whose predecessor, Lewis Strauss, had orchestrated the public humiliation of Oppenheimer—had a question to ask his longtime friend and former colleague. That would have to wait until after dinner.

Looking around the room, Seaborg would have seen five colleagues who had joined him at a dinner for science and military leaders hosted by President Eisenhower four years earlier. Among these were the outgoing president of the National Academy of Sciences, Dr, Detlev "Det" Bronk, and his wife, Helen. A noted biophysicist and college leader, he had one other unusual claim to fame: his ancestor Jonas Bronck was an early Dutch settler in New York and was responsible for the name of the borough known now as the Bronx.

Seaborg also would have quickly glimpsed Pauling. Fresh in his mind was the letter that Pauling had sent to the president nine weeks earlier, a copy of which was sent to Seaborg, which chastised Kennedy for his stalled progress on a nuclear test ban. Deeply enmeshed in the nuclear geopolitical chess game, he surely would have remembered the tone, which chided the president.

There were other tensions under the three huge Bohemian chandeliers and between the two large, serene portraits of George and Martha Washington in the East Room. Scanning the room, Oppenheimer might have been anxious to see Pauling there, though it was obvious that he would be invited. They were once close friends and colleagues at Caltech in the 1920s. Indeed, Oppenheimer had given a large prized mineral collection to Pauling, which came to dominate his office. For his part, Pauling had taken to wearing the distinctive type of hat that Oppenheimer wore. But they had become estranged after Oppenheimer made a bumbling pass at Ava Helen in 1929.[17] As part of the rupture, Pauling jettisoned the hat and adopted his own trademark hat, a ubiquitous black beret.[18]

The Pauling-Oppenheimer breach was known to the White House staff. In fact, White House files indicate that the atomic scientist was "to be invited, *if* Pauling regrets," and another note says that this was the president's wish.[19] But the president, apparently interested in ensuring that Oppenheimer would attend, later relented, and both men were present this night.

Most, of course, were delighted to be here. Among them were the younger, rising writers James Baldwin and William Styron. Both in their late thirties, they were good friends, having met in Europe in the 1950s; in fact, Baldwin was then living in a small cottage on the Styrons' six-acre property in Roxbury, Connecticut, where they discussed issues ranging from writing to race relations. The latter issue was notable because each had grandparents affected by slavery—Baldwin by bondage and Styron by slaveholding.

Both writers' works involved race. Baldwin's included *Go Tell It on the Mountain* and *Notes of a Native Son,* while Styron would later produce a controversial novel, *The Confessions of Nat Turner*, dealing with early nineteenth-century slavery. But it was Styron's most recent book—his third—*Set This House on Fire*, which had impressed the White House staff.

Baldwin, short and thin with large eyes and an ever-present gap-toothed grin, would have stood out as one of the two most prominent blacks at the dinner, with the Nobel Peace laureate Ralph Bunche being the other. Baldwin was exuberant at the reception, mingling with people and smoking his favorite Marlboro cigarettes.

The lives of these two writers from different backgrounds would subsequently intersect with the Kennedys. In Baldwin's case tonight marked the start of a testy working relationship with Robert Kennedy, whose interest in the civil rights movement would define his term as attorney general and later, as a presidential candidate. For Bill and Rose Styron, this would be the first of many friendly occasions with President and Mrs. Kennedy, Robert and Ethel Kennedy, and even Edward Kennedy and their families. For Styron, this relationship would begin with a small gathering upstairs in the Yellow Oval Room in a few hours.

The literary critic Diana Trilling, there with her husband, the essayist, professor, and also literary critic Lionel Trilling, spotted a number of friends, including Baldwin, Styron, and writers John Dos Passos and Katherine Anne Porter.[20] Porter, who had sought an invitation to a White House dinner the previous year, was rewarded on a day of great professional success: her new novel, *Ship of Fools*, had just become the number one *New York Times* best-seller after only three weeks, supplanting J. D. Salinger's *Franny and Zooey*.[21]

Diana Trilling also chatted with her friend Arthur M. Schlesinger Jr., the historian and presidential aide, who seemed to be an anomaly among the excited crowd. Likely clutching a martini, his favored drink, "He appeared to be self-conscious," she recounted, "as if borne down by his official White House duties." He had been part of the planning, including the invitations list, for the dinner.[22]

The Trillings were known to be passionately opinionated. One Trilling friend had responded to the question about the Trillings' Manhattan apartment, "Do they have a view of the river?" by saying, "Oh, yes, the Trillings have an opinion about everything."[23]

Diana, a staunch anticommunist, certainly had a view about fellow diner Robert Oppenheimer. Writing in the *Partisan Review* in the aftermath of the Oppenheimer security-clearance hearing in 1954, she judged him to be naïve in his youthful understanding of the Soviet threat, but clearly the victim of the political winds of McCarthyism.[24] Diana Trilling and many others that night understood the toll that the events of the past eight years had taken on him.[25]

Surveying the room, the chain-smoking Lionel Trilling also had relationships with others present, perhaps none as oddly fractious as that with Robert Frost. These two influential men of letters approached the world differently. Trilling had attended a lecture of Frost's in 1946 on which he later wrote that the poet frequently "makes himself the buffoon—goes into a trance of aged childishness." More bizarre, though, was a speech that Trilling gave at a birthday celebration for Frost at the Waldorf-Astoria in 1959. While Frost extolled the virtues of rural America, Trilling favored the city—and that colored Trilling's assessment of the celebrated poet. Shockingly, he said, among other critical things at the dinner: "I regard Robert Frost as a terrifying poet."[26]

Trilling had been widely criticized for his attack on Frost and felt the need to patch things up. But Frost was gracious, saying, "Not distressed at all. Just a little taken aback or thrown back on myself by being so closely examined so close by. . . . You made my birthday party a surprise party."[27]

While the reception was taking place, the president was meeting upstairs for drinks with four men selected for the Nobel Prize the previous year. Those four were Dr. Georg von Békésy, the recipient in physiology or medicine; Dr. Melvin Calvin, chemistry; and Dr. Robert Hofstadter and Dr. Rudolf Mossbauer, who shared the physics prize. Joining them were Vice President and Mrs. Johnson, the ambassador from Norway, the wife of the Swedish ambassador, and the counselor from the Swedish embassy: Norway and Sweden, of course, being the sites of the Nobel ceremonies.

At 8:20 pm the United States Marine Band struck up *Hail to the Chief*. The Color Guard presented the honors toward the East Room, and President and Mrs. Kennedy advanced down the staircase into the Cross Hall and a few steps over to the East Room. Both were smiling broadly.[28]

The youthful first couple was tanned, recently returned from their nine-day Easter vacation in Palm Beach. The six-foot-one president always attracted attention, with his distinctive appearance and shock of reddish-brown hair. He wore a small, blue boutonniere on his left lapel positioned to the left of his ever-present short, triangular pocket handkerchief. But most eyes were focused on Mrs. Kennedy. She was stunning, wearing a long celadon green jersey gown that was draped over her left shoulder—a creation of her favorite designer, Oleg Cassini. Completing her wardrobe were green shoes and green earrings.[29]

Both were greeted with applause.

"Jack and Jackie actually *shimmered*," William Styron recalled. "You would have had to be abnormal, perhaps psychotic, to be immune to their dumbfounding appeal. Even Republicans were gaga."[30] Diana Trilling was impressed, too: "She was a hundred times more beautiful than any photograph ever indicated."[31]

It was, indeed, an electric moment for many, who were excited, even overcome, by being invited to the White House and honored for their achievements. Some cried, according to Pearl Buck. "One felt a wave of love and admiration flow out from us toward the spectacular couple," she said.[32]

The guests now positioned themselves in a receiving line in the East Room, in alphabetical order, to be announced to their hosts. After being presented to the first couple, each was greeted with small talk, which served as an official prelude to the evening's program. Some of it was casual banter. More than half of the guests had been introduced when the line reached Dr. and Mrs. Oppenheimer, who were immediately followed by Dr. and Mrs. Pauling. Clearly this was to be a dramatic part of the evening. The conversation between the controversial physicist and the president was not recorded, but that between the president and the controversial chemist and peace activist was.

Most guests were aware of the Paulings' picketing earlier in the day, and surely many were curious about how the encounter would go. Despite the picketing and the recent letter, the president was a gracious politician with an appreciation for irony. He also understood that alliances shifted and that there was usually a distinction between politics and personal enmity. "Dr. Pauling, how do you do. You've been around the White House a couple of days already, haven't you?"[33] Before introducing Pauling to Mrs. Kennedy, he added, "Dr. Pauling, I hope that you will continue to express your opinions."[34]

Mrs. Kennedy, ever the protective wife and mother, took leave of her usual public graciousness. Fixing her brown eyes on the scientist thirty years her senior, she said in her characteristic low voice, "Dr. Pauling, do you think that it is right to walk back and forth out there where Caroline can see you, so that she asks 'What has Daddy done wrong now?'" There was a little laughter to break the tension.[35]

Fresh in Mrs. Kennedy's mind was the stern letter that *Mrs. Pauling* had sent nine months earlier. "Your children, like all other children in the world, are laying down in their bones, along with the calcium, Strontium 90," she had written, adding, "I urge you to use your influence to safeguard your children as well as all of the children of the world by keeping the United States Government from resuming nuclear testing under any circumstances."[36]

The next two honored guests in line also were peace advocates, but in different ways. Lester Pearson, known as "Mike," and his wife, Maryon, were the only guests from Canada. He was the leader of the opposition Liberal Party, a friend of Kennedy's, and soon to be Canadian prime minister. He had been awarded the 1957 Nobel Peace Prize for his work on the Suez Crisis.

Following them was Clarence Pickett and his wife, Lilly. Pickett, seventy-seven, had *also* been protesting near the White House earlier in the day.[37] No stranger to presidents—he had worked closely with his fellow Quaker, Herbert Hoover, as well with Franklin Roosevelt and Harry Truman—Pickett was the executive secretary emeritus of the pacifist American Friends Service Committee (AFSC). The AFSC, part of the current White House demonstration, had received the 1947 Nobel Peace Prize for its cumulative efforts in peace advocacy as well as humanitarian assistance.

Then came people such as influential Harvard president Nathan Pusey and his wife, Anne; labor lawyer and civil rights activist Joseph Rauh—added to the guest list by the president—and his wife, Olie; Arthur and Marian Schlesinger;

and Dr. and Mrs. Seaborg.[38] Now the Styrons were announced. Bill Styron, who admired the president, met the Kennedys for the first time. The First Lady said to him in the receiving line, "Hi there! You're a friend of John and Sue's," referring to her old friend novelist John P. Marquand Jr. and his wife.[39]

The president and Mrs. Kennedy put the Trillings at ease. Mrs. Kennedy told Lionel that her stepsister Nina Gore Auchincloss was a devoted former student at Columbia. "She never says anything unless you say it's all right for her to say it," she reported. He couldn't remember her, but Lionel, by now inebriated, said, "Wait till I tell you what they said about you at Vassar."[40]

Finally, the reception line wound its way to the end as Dr. Chen Ning Yang, a Nobel physicist, and his wife, Chi LiTu, were announced. Dr. Yang then joined the president and Mrs. Kennedy for a large-group photograph with all the other Nobel winners in the East Room along the east wall in front of a large portrait of Martha Washington painted by Eliphalet Frazier Andrews. The official photograph, taken by White House photographer Cecil Stoughton, shows the president sitting beside Mary Welsh Hemingway and Katherine Tupper Marshall, widows of laureates Ernest Hemingway and George Marshall. They and the four recent winners and Mrs. Kennedy sat in the front row, and the remaining Nobel guests stood in three rows behind them.

Other guests—many spouses, additional eminent scientists, writers, university presidents, and influential Americans—preceded the laureates to their dining locations. They had been greeted by Tish Baldrige and provided information on their seats, to which they would be escorted by a small army of social aides.[41] Mrs. Kennedy was always engaged in the seating arrangements and would move around names with veteran social staffer Sanford "Sandy" Fox, who used his calligraphy skills to create an attractive table-by-table seating plan with place cards at each setting.[42]

The guests had much to think about as they moved down the historic hall, past the Green Room—some stopping at the Blue Room for their dinner seating—while others continued past the Red Room and then into the large State Dining Room. Those who passed by the Red Room might have caught a glimpse of the official presidential portrait of Theodore Roosevelt painted by John Singer Sargent; Roosevelt was the first American to be awarded a Nobel Prize, the Peace Prize, in 1906. As such, he was an integral part of this growing fraternity of distinguished figures.

With the introductions over, these men and women were about to embark on an evening of exquisite dining, spirited—sometimes awkward—conversation, literary entertainment, and even impromptu dancing led by Linus and Ava Helen Pauling. Few could have imagined how the lives of so many people that night would be interconnected in the decades to come. They were about to participate in what was arguably the dinner of the century.

# CHAPTER ONE

# America in Transition

THE SUN ROSE AT 5:59 AM on this first day of Daylight Savings Time. Most of the tenants in the eleven-story, half-century-old apartment building located at 35 Claremont Avenue in New York's City's Morningside Heights neighborhood were still asleep. But on the first floor Lionel and Diana Trilling were rushing about their stylish, book-lined, first-floor residence, dressing and packing.[1] They knew this would be a long, but notable day, starting with a nearly four-hour train trip to the nation's capital, then changing clothes at a friend's house, having dinner at the White House, and finally making a late-night return.

One of New York's most prominent literary couples, "Li" and "Di" would be joining a group of writers, scientists, and scholars in paying tribute to Nobel Prize winners from the Western Hemisphere. The Trillings, both fifty-six, would be comfortable interacting with these intellectuals, many of them friends and colleagues. They also were expecting to enjoy this time with the president, who shared their liberal, but strongly anticommunist views.

Lionel was the better-known half of the couple. Long associated with the once left-leaning *Partisan Review*, he was a professor of English at Columbia. His most prominent book, *The Liberal Imagination*, provided a balanced postwar perspective on liberalism. Published twelve years earlier, it was a best-seller that remained popular and influential. "And," according to one modern critic, "it changed the role of literature in American intellectual life."[2]

His marriage to Diana Rubin in 1928 turned out to be a bumpy one, but she admired his intellect. Different in temperament from her husband, she was a tough, acerbic writer, one of the few prominent women writers of the period. The British novelist Martin Amis, who wrote an essay on her in the 1980s, said of the experience: "Whenever I announced my intention of going along to interview her, people looked at me with trepidation, a new respect, a certain holy dread," he said. "I felt I was about to enter the lion's den—or the den of the literary lioness, which is often just as dangerous."[3]

Train travelers at the time departed from the majestic old Pennsylvania Station, a Beaux Arts structure created by the legendary architectural firm of McKim, Mead and White. The Trillings would have known about this firm because it also had created the master plan for Columbia University in the early 1890s. They would come across another magnificent example of their work that evening; McKim, Mead and White was responsible for the restoration of portions of the White House in 1902—including rooms that the Trillings would be visiting.[4]

As light streamed into the cavernous waiting room, the Trillings walked on the pink marble floors as they passed two large statues of Pennsylvania Railroad magnates Alexander Cassatt and Samuel Rea, sculpted by Adolph A. Weinman. Weinman had also designed the popular Winged Liberty or Mercury dime and Walking Liberty half-dollar coins, still in wide circulation in 1962; Lionel probably had a few jingling in his pocket.

On this particular morning, a streamlined GG1 locomotive of the Pennsylvania Railroad awaited the couple to pull their run on the Midday Congressional. The temperature had already soared to its daytime high of eighty degrees on this unusually warm spring day as the train departed at 11 am. The passengers in the fluted stainless-steel cars painted in Tuscan red with gold trim would make their way past Newark, Trenton, Philadelphia, Wilmington, and Baltimore before arriving midafternoon at Washington's Union Station; they would follow the same route that Amtrak would in the decades to come.

After getting settled in her coach seat, Diana Trilling was not feeling well, and that made her anxious. Another of her migraine attacks had hit, and she had taken a cocktail of medications to address it. After swallowing one of the tablets, the pink one, she panicked, realizing her supply was low. Worrying about tonight's big event, would she run out if new attacks came later?

"I got nervous: suppose I passed out in the middle of the dinner party?" she recalled. "My headache was becoming quite severe, and I was alarmed because, if it followed its usual pattern, by eight o'clock I'd be very sick and by nine I'd be throwing up."[5]

We don't know how she passed those anxious hours on the train; but if she and Lionel were typical of well-educated train travelers on a Sunday train from Manhattan, they likely were clutching a copy of the *New York Times*, the "Gray Lady" that was enjoying its undisputed dominance of American journalism. In fact, it was must-reading for the largely Jewish liberal circle of thinkers and writers known as the New York Intellectuals, with which they were associated. Perhaps both read the newspaper during the trip, exchanging sections or—if Diana's headache was too overwhelming—Lionel may have commented on portions to her.

The newspaper was not much different in appearance than it would be a half-century later, but it was heavier and larger. What they would have seen in the newspaper's 474 pages would prepare them for what would be part of the conversations at dinner that night. The *Times* provided a snapshot of the nation and world during this period that was on the cusp of major transitions.

The train ride presented enough time to become acquainted with the events of the city, nation, and world as reported that day in the newspaper of record. Foremost was the lead story in the upper-far-left first column of the eight-column paper: an article reported that President Kennedy and Prime Minister Macmillan had decided to delay a summit meeting with the Soviet Union "because," as E. W. Kenworthy wrote, "there was virtually no prospect of useful results." A photo of the president, whom they would be seeing in a few hours, was prominently displayed, as he was conferring with the prime minister and other officials.[6]

Addressing the concern that Pauling and his fellow protesters were picketing at the same time—in Washington—the article noted that Macmillan expected that there would be no movement on a nuclear test ban treaty until both the United States and the Soviet Union completed a new round of testing.[7] But anyone reading that newspaper that morning would have read about much more, reflecting the prominence of the discussions and concerns about nuclear testing. In fact, a photograph of Pauling holding aloft a "WE HAVE NO RIGHT TO TEST" sign was part of almost an entire page of related stories on page twenty-nine. The caption and article accompanying the photograph noted that the chemist-turned-activist would be at the dinner that night.[8] The Trillings might have thought about that photo. Certainly it would prime them for what might come in a few hours.

The other articles on that page in the first section dealt with some of the preparations being undertaken at Christmas Island, a fifty-two-square-mile Australian territory in the Indian Ocean. Among those assisting was a contingent from Los Alamos, the birthplace of the atomic bomb.[9] It was there in the

New Mexico settlement that two of the dinner guests that night, Dr. J. Robert Oppenheimer and Dr. Isidor I. Rabi, had held such prominent roles. Rabi had been awarded the Nobel Prize for Physics in 1944. Both men were present at the Trinity test explosion in the desert in July 1945.

Both scientists, along with hundreds if not thousands of others associated with the Manhattan Project, had done their job well. In an adjacent article on the same page, a wire-service story reported on how accurate the subsequent aerial bombs had been. "With few exceptions, they have been on or satisfactorily close to the aiming point," the article stated and then noted that just "two known misses have been reported publicly."[10]

Oppenheimer and many of the scientists had immediately realized the horrific potential that was created by their work. At the moment of detonation of the bomb at the Trinity test site, the man who was the driving force behind it recalled a line from the *Bhagavad Gita,* the Hindu work: "Now I am become death, the destroyer of worlds."[11]

As the years wore on, more people around the world grew increasingly anxious about the potential horror. Protests such as those occurring in April 1962 were being replicated around the world. In the *New York Times* that day, the Trillings and more than one million readers could learn about three thousand protesters in Tokyo who even urged redefining relations with the United States as a result of the administration's nuclear position.[12] They also could read about protests near the American Embassy in London and a report that three of the four national Indian newspapers criticized new us nuclear tests.[13]

There was an article addressing New York Senator Kenneth B. Keating's argument that the United States should withhold foreign aid from those countries which criticize us nuclear policy and focus foreign aid money on "those nations which share our view of the world crisis." Keating was a Republican, but a liberal one.[14]

The issue of nuclear testing was prominent and growing. That afternoon Adlai Stevenson, the United States ambassador to the United Nations, appeared on his regularly scheduled television program; and his guest, the head of the us Arms Control and Disarmament Agency, commented on nuclear testing and recent discussions in Geneva, Switzerland.[15] These discussions involved seventeen nations, including the United States, Great Britain, and the Soviet Union.

You could not get away from the topic that day if you were exposed to newspapers, television, or radio. In addition to breaking news stories, there was extensive analysis of the current and anticipated tests, testing in general, and the superpower "propaganda war" in the "Review of the Week" section. The section was led by a front-page article, complete with a map that explained the nuclear detonation that had taken place the day before on Christmas Island. There also had been a blast on Friday, as well as the most recent underground explosion in Nevada. Additional tests were soon to begin on Johnston Island, an atoll in the North Pacific.[16]

This action was the administration's response to the Soviet Union's resumption of tests the past fall after a three-year hiatus. When Nikita Khrushchev turned down an offer to develop a new ban, Kennedy acted. The president succinctly stated the position of the United States: "If they [the Russians] persist in rejecting all means of true inspection, then we shall be left with no choice but to keep our own defensive arsenals adequate for the security of all free men."[17]

The impact of resumption was enormous. An armada of one hundred ships was massed in the Pacific to support the us effort. Protests against the tests, predictably, came from the Soviet Union as well as in the form of demonstrations at home and abroad.[18] Many would see all this as a further escalation of a continuing dangerous arms race.

In yet another article, Max Frankel, then a young reporter in the Washington bureau, discussed how an aggressive propaganda war was being waged by the two superpowers.[19] But public concerns were increasing as the amount of radiation from this proliferation of tests continued to grow, as John W. Finney reported in yet another piece, in his nuclear energy beat.[20]

To all this the *Times* editorialized that Kennedy was correct in reentering the testing, placing the blame squarely on the Soviet Union. "The United States has done everything in its power to arrest the grim nuclear armament spiral on which we have embarked," the paper's editors argued. The administration's position, then, was a matter of self-defense as well as a strategy to bring the prickly Khrushchev to the bargaining table.[21]

Train 121 sped its way down the East Coast, sometimes at a speed of eighty miles per hour. Looking out the window of the train, the Trillings and their fellow passengers would have seen such sights as the Lower Trenton Bridge over the Delaware River near Trenton, which underscored the state capital's manufacturing heritage with the sign "TRENTON MAKES, THE WORLD TAKES." Soon they crossed the river again, this time over the nearly century-old Connecting Railway Bridge. Diana might have chosen to keep her focus on the interior of the car because she had long suffered from acrophobia.

They now entered Pennsylvania, passing through the deteriorating neighborhood of North Philadelphia before arriving at the Quaker City's Thirtieth Street Station around 12:35 pm. A majority of the passengers who weren't continuing on to Washington would be stopping here, the nation's fourth-largest city at the time. They were nearly at the halfway point of their trip.

Diana and Lionel ate the lunch they had purchased at the Tip Toe Inn, a popular delicatessen on the Upper West Side at Broadway and Eighty-Sixth Street. Stopping there en route to the train station, they would have seen a menu that listed, among other things, sandwiches ranging in price from sixty-five cents to $1.80, which the restaurant touted as "a meal in itself." The Trillings, notably Diana, were trying to save money, so they chose to avoid the dining car as well as the more expensive parlor car; they would, however, splurge on a sleeper returning home late that night.[22]

A long train ride encourages daydreaming. The Trillings were a compatible and devoted—but often difficult—couple, even with each other. What glued them together was a life of the intellect. A former student of Lionel's who knew the couple well reflected: "They were passionate about everything: people, ideas, books, our time, the past, tendencies, trends, transitions, tectonic shifts."[23] They also were in step in their political liberalism and strong anticommunist views. Over the years, they wrote, debated, and helped shape public views on most of the major issues before, during, and after World War II. For Lionel, these positions were often built on Hebraic tradition or ethic, as essayist Louis Menand later argued. But such a perspective was somewhat secular based ("a concern with right conduct"). Although Jewish—in fact, the first Jew to receive tenure at Columbia's English department—Lionel was standoffish in his religious identity.[24]

Diana and Lionel met at a Midtown speakeasy named Mario's on a cold Christmas Eve in 1927. She remembered that night vividly, even recalling what she was a drinking at the time: a gin, grenadine, and apricot mix known as a "bullfrog." Both were recent college graduates—she from Radcliffe and he from Columbia—and she was immediately attracted to him. Their marriage two years later created an intellectual partnership. He introduced her to a wide range of literature, but profited from her talents. "Lionel taught me to think; I taught him to write," she said.[25]

He also absorbed her into a stimulating, but harsh intellectual orbit. Lionel's friends "were not easy companions, these intellectuals I was now getting to know," she later wrote. "They were overbearing and arrogant, excessively competitive; they lack magnanimity and often lacked common courtesy."[26]

That afternoon on the train that would deliver them to a highlight of their public lives Diana glanced over at her husband of now more than thirty years. He was a small, white-haired man who exuded grace. He suffered from bouts of depression and often was frustrated and lacked self-confidence. He smoked too much and easily became inebriated, something he would be after six martinis later that night. He also was a brilliant intellect, an attribute that she greatly admired, and a partner who had been very supportive of her writing career. In turn, she edited his material and provided a sounding board.

Lionel was often contradictory. Although most of his career was spent at Columbia, he didn't like the university; although he had spent decades teaching at this research university, he didn't like working with graduate students; and although he was primarily an essayist and critic, he saw himself as a novelist.[27]

Lionel Trilling didn't even like his given name, saddened that he did not have a more common one. "He bitterly envied the friends of his youth who went forward to meet their destinies armed with names so much sturdier than his," Diana recalled.[28]

Diana's life was completely intertwined with his and, despite her literary achievement, largely at *The Nation*, she was usually seen as Mrs. Lionel Trilling. While that may have amused—perhaps even chafed—her, she accepted it; and in fact, after his death in 1975, she would work to burnish his image for the next two decades. Her attachment to him would become crystallized later in life, as she wrote in 1993: "I sometimes think that what I miss most is the companionship of his mind."[29]

As the train rumbled into Delaware, there would have been much more for the Trillings to consider in the day's newspaper. While the tense Cold War rivalry between the United States and the Soviet Union dominated the news, there were other, sometimes related stories. In the first section, for instance, there were articles on NATO and its role in nuclear talks, West Berlin's concerns about Soviet intentions, whether American rock and roll and jazz are welcome in Russia, Austria and Norway's quest to join the European Economic Community (now the European Union), prospects for more open elections in Poland, and issues related to the health of Spanish leader Francisco Franco.

Also covered were recent developments in the aftermath of the ending of the seven-year civil war in Algeria; separate reports on various issues in Saudi Arabia, Jordan, and Israel; and political and economic updates from India, Pakistan, Japan, and Hong Kong.

Of special interest to tonight's dinner guests was an article on Latin American policy and the role of Kennedy confidante Richard Goodwin. Goodwin, then thirty years old, was a bright lawyer, speechwriter, and policymaker. A former law clerk to Justice Felix Frankfurter, he quickly burnished his foreign policy credentials, helping launch the Alliance for Progress, meeting with Che Guevara, serving as a White House aide on Latin American issues, and now serving as a deputy assistant secretary for Inter-American Affairs at the State Department. Goodwin had also helped plan this dinner; in fact, he suggested the idea of inviting Nobel laureates to a special event.[30] In a few hours he would be hosting a table directly between the two tables where Diana and Lionel were seated.

The nugget of the story in the *Times* was that Goodwin and his superior, assistant secretary Edwin M. Martin, appeared to have achieved a modus vivendi in moving forward on Latin American issues. This was the latest development in an evolving relationship between the two men, who had both come to their jobs recently and needed to iron out any potential difficulties as a result of Goodwin's influence in the White House. The article, written by seasoned foreign correspondent Tad Szulc, was entitled "US Closes Rift on Latin Policy."[31]

The major external challenge to US policy in the Western Hemisphere, and one that had been simmering since 1959, was Cuba. The United States had fumbled badly in its attempt to unleash Brigade 2506 one year earlier; the result was the fiasco that become known as the Bay of Pigs invasion. That night at the Nobel dinner, Mary Welsh Hemingway, seated next to President Kennedy, would grill him on his Cuban policy. There were two reports on Cuba in the paper, one from Havana and the other from Miami. The Havana-filed article recounts that anti-Castro demonstrations were dispersed with some people arrested. This was the first notable demonstration in Cuba since September 1961.[32] The other article reports the apprehension of Cuban exiles that the United States was shifting to a policy of coexistence toward the communist government. No goods were being provided to rebels, and in fact, the Coast Guard was preventing supplies from reaching Cuba. Concern was raised that Dick Goodwin was using the Brazilian government as a go-between to work with Fidel Castro and his regime.[33]

Anxiety over communism was ever present in the United States, and the Trillings were among those who shared that concern. Only a few years after Wisconsin junior senator Joseph McCarthy's campaign against communism, there were various manifestations of the need for popular vigilance. One example was Loyalty Day. In the aftermath of the Red Scare after World War I, May 1 was identified as Loyalty Day to supplement the May Day or International Workers' Day commemoration of the Far Left. In the mid-1950s, Congress, once again alert to outside threats, enacted a law officially recognizing it. And so, the previous day, the last Saturday before May 1, saw Loyalty Day parades in Manhattan and Brooklyn.

The parades were organized by the Veterans of Foreign Wars. The governor and mayor attended the parade marching down Fifth Avenue, and they were joined by city and veterans' officials as well as "organizations representing the dispossessed of countries now under communism," the newspaper reported.[34]

National security was an issue very much in the forefront in 1962. Defense spending was increasing, and more and more money was being channeled toward missiles and space-related programs. On the front page of the business section were two stories under the banner headline: "The Advent of the

Space Age Changes the Pattern of Defense Spending." The 1963 federal budget request by the Kennedy administration provided funds for Atlas, Titan, Nike-Zeus, Minuteman, and other missiles. The paper further reported that aircraft, missile, and space-related contracts awarded by the US government reached 11.5 billion dollars in 1961.[35]

In a hint of the growing significance of the Sunbelt states, it noted that one-quarter of these defense contracts were filled by California firms. And there were ripples throughout the economy; one article reported with awe: "Last Sunday's *Los Angeles Times* carried twenty pages of help-wanted advertisements from most of the big companies in the defense business. But they weren't for Rosie the Riveter. They were mostly for Egbert the Engineer—servosystem engineers, thermodynamics engineers, propulsion engineers, and a score of other categories."[36]

In a further harbinger of what was coming—and what would form an important part of the public's perception of the space program—a NASA center in Houston was in the planning stages. Construction work for the 1,700-acre facility was expected to begin in five months, with an anticipated cost of ninety million dollars. This would be part of a larger regional enclave devoted to providing material for space- and defense-related programs.[37]

⚬═⚬⚬

Shortly before 1:30 pm, train 121 passed through the small town of Elkton, Maryland. The Trillings and the other passengers that day were now firmly below the Mason-Dixon Line and, officially if not somewhat ambiguously, in the South. And to many northerners that raised the prominent issue of race relations, including integration and racial justice. During the past decade, there had been racial confrontations in the Deep South, with one notable example being the bus boycott in Montgomery, Alabama, in 1955–1956, highlighting the leadership of Rosa Parks and Dr. Martin Luther King Jr. Another significant event occurred when President Eisenhower was compelled to send troops to integrate Central High School in Little Rock, Arkansas, in 1957.

There would be many dramatic developments in the coming years of the 1960s, such as the infamous Stand in the Schoolhouse Door by Governor George C. Wallace at the University of Alabama. Wallace, seeking to prevent black students from enrolling, was true to his mantra: "Segregation now, segregation tomorrow, segregation forever." The following year would see the violent confrontations in Birmingham, Alabama. But through it all, there was the uplifting defiance and promise that was exhibited by the famous March on Washington in August 1963. Even so, social tensions would remain unresolved for years to come, as seen by the urban riots of the late 1960s and continuing through various incidents and inequities even into the twenty-first century.

The previous day's paper reported on one recent racial issue, part of a continuing effort to impede integration: an initiative by the segregationist New Orleans Citizens Council to encourage greater northern migration of blacks by providing free transportation out of the region.[38] There had been some precedent albeit with a different, more spontaneous approach. The Great Migration began about the time of the World War I and had continued onward as blacks left their rural roots in the Deep South and relocated to such cities as Chicago, Detroit, Philadelphia, and New York, where they transformed Harlem. One of these people seeking a better life forty years earlier was James Baldwin's stepfather, who left New Orleans for Harlem.

The Census Bureau reported that nearly 1.5 million blacks left the South for opportunities in other regions in the 1950s, and as writer Claude Sitton reported, today that amounted to an out-migration of four hundred people per day for the decade. The largest black out-migration came from Mississippi, Alabama, South Carolina, North Carolina, and Georgia—each with more than two hundred thousand. Ultimately, there were six million blacks who left the South over a half century, sometimes achieving modest success but often being further frustrated. The Citizens Council wanted to further encourage that movement.[39]

The *Times* cites New Orleans as "one of the better-integrated, more tolerant cities of the Deep South." There appeared to be little support for the relocation effort in the city, including among blacks. Black leaders had called the plan "a cruel joke" because upending people without clear opportunities available in the new locations would be foolhardy.[40]

A roundup of newspaper editorials from Alabama, Florida, North Carolina, South Carolina, and Virginia seem to argue, albeit grudgingly, its lack of sound public policy. One representative editorial, from the *Richmond Times-Dispatch*, says that "this plan to ship colored people out of the South offers no solution. Dumping unemployed Negroes in the North causes a certain amount of embarrassment there, but these people are our responsibility, unless they choose to leave on their own initiative."[41]

The *Times* ran two cartoons lampooning the effort, including one that satirically imagined the Citizens Council's "travel agents" beside a promotional sign that read: "Specialists in Human Traffic / Ask Us About . . . Cuba Auschwitz Buchenwald Siberia."[42] The paper editorially chided the effort, noting that cities in the North were "already burdened with heavy unemployment problems of their own." And continued, "Where any state seeks to export its dependent families, the responsibility for support should become that of the National Government and not of the particular area to which people are sent without work or the prospect of finding it."[43] Maybe the gulf between the North and South was more nuanced than it appeared.

An article that provided an interesting insight into the status of black performers appeared in a front-page story in what was the arts-and-culture section. Highlighting a current Broadway comedy, "Purlie Victorius" (with Ossie Davis and Ruby Dee), and an off-Broadway musical, "Fly Blackbird," Harold Taubman says, "The Negro serves notice that he is through being patronized by the theatre."

Taubman, a drama critic, adds: "If he is eager to accept the responsibility and the risk of being judged without benevolent paternalism or elaborate discussion, it is because he insists on the privilege to be himself, to speak his own mind and to express his deepest feelings without resort to pretense and evasion." Citing the work of James Baldwin and others, he continues, "The spirit of Negro affirmation is in the air. It is getting into print."[44] More will be said about this later.

While the conversation about an education achievement gap between the haves and have-nots would become more pronounced later in the twentieth century, there was an article on "A Wide Gap in Excellence," which coincidentally focused on one of the guests at the dinner at the White House that evening. Dr. Lee A. DuBridge, the Caltech president, told a conference focusing on high school achievement that scores for incoming students at his institution on the College Entrance Examination Boards between 1951 and 1961 showed notable achievement. And yet, a professor at the University of

Oklahoma at the conference argued that lesser high schools—ones that did not feed into Caltech—presented more troubling trends.[45]

There were other interesting glimpses into the future in that day's paper. Perhaps the most ominous—at least in hindsight—was a front-page story on US Special Forces advisers working with ethnic Rhade people in Vietnam's Central Highlands. Two thousand Rhades were being trained to defend "against the Communist guerillas, who are known as the Vietcong." In the years to come, of course, the Vietcong would enter into common parlance in the United States as the Vietnam War grew steadily and then exponentially by the end of the decade.[46]

Closer to home, Gay Talese, then a thirty-two-year-old reporter, wrote about the work started at Flushing Meadows Park in Queens in preparation for the World's Fair that would begin in two years. Two hundred buildings would be constructed, some of which might be erected by the end of the summer. The great 1939–1940 World's Fair on the same site—and still fondly remembered for its peek into the world of tomorrow as well as its trademark Trylon and Perisphere—might have given pause to readers who also recalled it as preceding a cataclysmic war. Would anxious Americans, with a douse of superstition, be wondering if this upcoming exposition would presage catastrophe as well?

But excitement was pervasive as a new generation of New Yorkers and millions of others would get an opportunity to sample world cultures, technological advances, and perhaps a fantastic, highly positive view of what was in store for humanity. There would be differences with this new fair,[47] Talese reported: "While some cities have charged the 1939 Fair with being too zany and possessing traits of a freak show, the tone for the Fair in 1964 is expected to be cultural and sophisticated, a spokesman said."

Continuing through the news of the day, there was an article, perhaps the first ever in this paper, on a building complex in Washington that would become a legend and a symbol. Architecture critic Ada Louise Huxtable reported on the controversy generated by the proposed Watergate along the Potomac River.

The news was that the presidentially appointed Fine Arts Commission objected to the height, the encroachment on open space, and the increased population in the city's Foggy Bottom section that this construction would bring. Referring to the prospect for "chaotic disharmony," the commission argued that the Watergate "will begin to erode and destroy the qualities that give Washington its particular beauty." Still, construction began the following year on what would become an eight-year project.[48]

There was some domestic political news with future implications as well. Richard Nixon, defeated for the presidency by Kennedy in 1960, was running in the upcoming June primary for the Republican gubernatorial nomination in California.[49] He would win the nomination, but famously lose the general election to incumbent Governor Edmund G. Brown. Across the country in New York State, New York City Mayor Robert F. Wagner declined to run for the Democratic gubernatorial nomination in a bid to face incumbent Nelson Rockefeller in the November general election.[50] Rockefeller would be reelected and then seek the Republican nomination for president in 1964, but of course, the events of November 22, 1963, and a conservative tide led by Barry Goldwater upended the political calculus.

While waiting for the train at Penn Station, Diana and Lionel spotted an acquaintance, novelist James T. Farrell. Farrell, fifty-eight, was a prolific writer probably best known for his trilogy of novels entitled *Studs Lonigan*, published in the 1930s. Diana recalled him being seedy and disheveled that morning, and her immediate reaction was a twofold horror. She said, "My God, has he been invited to the White House, too? But an even worse thought was that we were going to have to ride all the way down to Washington with him, and it was going to be terrible."[51]

Soon Diana's fears were allayed, at least having to ride with him, and they parted. But Farrell was, indeed, going to the same dinner at White House. He too spent several hours passing the time en route to the nation's capital, and perhaps he also might have been interested in what the *New York Times* reported that day. Jim Farrell was a literary man with a strong socialist and even Trotskyist bent to his politics. His Studs Lonigan character was turned into an average movie in 1960, starring Christopher Knight, Frank Gorshin, and Jack Nicholson.

It is not unreasonable that Farrell would have focused on the arts-and-culture section, including information on the rich array of plays, films, and television programs that were offered that day in his adopted hometown (he was a native Chicagoan). Many of the productions have now become dramatic and musical classics, and the stars began notable careers or continued to burnish them.

Appearing on Broadway was *Camelot* currently starring William Squire, Patricia Bredin, Robert Goulet, and Robert Coote. Chronicling the magical time of the mythical King Arthur and the Knights of the Round Table, this play would become synonymous with most descriptions of the Kennedy administration. The Kennedy image of Camelot, on the day of this Nobel Prize dinner, might have been vaguely hinted at, but was something that would not come about until later.[52]

Among the other plays and performers that were on the Great White Way were the drama about Thomas More, *A Man for All Seasons,* with Paul Scofield and the musical *How to Succeed in Business without Really Trying* with Robert Morse. Margaret Leighton, starring with Shelley Winters, was appearing in *The Night of the Iguana.* Other plays and their performers were Walter Matthau in *A Shot in the Dark,* Diahann Carroll in *No Strings,* and Anna Maria Alberghetti in *Carnival.*[53]

There were yet other well-known stars and plays on Broadway, such as Zero Mostel in *A Funny Thing Happened on the Way to the Forum,* Jason Robards Jr. in *A Thousand Clowns,* Henry Fonda and Olivia de Havilland in *Gift of Time,* and twenty-five-year-old Robert Redford in *Sunday in New York.*[54]

The films that were showing included: *El Cid* with Charlton Heston and Sophia Loren; *Judgment at Nuremberg* with an all-star cast of Spencer Tracy, Burt Lancaster, Richard Widmark, Marlene Dietrich, Judy Garland, Maximilian Schell, and Montgomery Clift; *Cape Fear,* a thriller with Gregory Peck, Robert Mitchum, and Polly Bergen; *Never on Sunday* with Melina Mercouri; *Sweet Bird of Youth* with Paul Newman and Geraldine Page; and two other classics: *West Side Story* and *La Dolce Vita.*[55]

❧

The Pennsylvania Railroad train sped through the Maryland suburbs for the last forty minutes of its trip from New York to its scheduled arrival in the nation's capital at 2:45 pm. The Trillings and Farrell might have thought about their long-anticipated dinner that awaited them. They also might have reflected on the city that they were about to enter. Washington, DC, with a population of a little less than eight hundred thousand people, was on that day the nation's ninth-largest city. It also had experienced a great boom during the New Deal and World War II years. With the end of the war, Washington had become a key power center in the world, and it was gradually emerging as a great city.

The United States of 1962 had a population of 186.5 million (compared with about 325 million today). It was still a nation dependent on heavy manufacturing, with its industrial strength unrivaled and its unions strong. The Eighty-Seventh Congress, which convened in January 1961, was solidly in the hands of the Democrats, who had more than 60 percent of the members of both chambers. President Kennedy, of course, was a Democrat as well. Although Democrats enjoyed enviable superiority, there were challenges to the president's power, notably from conservative southern Democrats who were staunchly opposed to integration and civil rights legislation. While partisanship was typical in Washington, there also were instances of bipartisan work, especially on foreign policy, something far different from the political climate of the early twenty-first century.

As the Trillings disembarked at the increasingly dilapidated fifty-four-year-old Union Station, about one mile from the White House, the reality surely hit them: they would be going to dinner with the glamorous (and intellectually compatible) young president and his attractive, culturally literate wife. And they would be joined by the greatest intellectuals of America at midcentury, with the nation at the height of its influence and basking in its attainment of becoming a great superpower.

Diana had hoped for this opportunity. When it had been announced a few weeks earlier that there would be such a dinner, she was envious of those who would get a coveted invitation. And yet, she recalls that "even as I was saying it, a quick wonderful thought ran through my head that perhaps we were going to be invited."[56]

Now the Trillings were going to a friend's house to change and get ready for the evening. Packed in Diana's luggage was her new $250 dress, which she described as "an all-seasons dress, champagne colored, made of moiré taffeta printed in soft orange and green flowers."[57]

The Kennedys' other guests had arrived from all over the country. One-fifth of them had come from California, then as now a center of advanced scientific research. Many of the literary people had come from the New York area. They now all funneled either through the White House gates on foot or by car through the driveway at the North Portico. Among those being dropped off by car were Vice President Lyndon Johnson and his wife, Lady Bird, and Attorney General Robert Kennedy and his wife, Ethel—and the Trillings. Coming in from the North Portico, they ascended a few steps, walked past a gaggle of photographers, and went through the doors of the Entrance Hall, a large foyer.[58]

By the time the Trillings joined this now growing group, Diana's headache had vanished. Looking over the mansion's fountains and flowers and then the assembling people, she was nearly overcome, saying, "It was like nothing I had ever witnessed, and it made my heart pound with excitement."[59]

## CHAPTER TWO ⇥

# Camelot at Midpoint

BY THE SECOND YEAR of the Kennedy administration, many Americans and others around the world were already beguiled by the style and glamour of the young occupants of the White House. The allure began with the inauguration, which included five inaugural balls and a lavish preinaugural gala produced by Frank Sinatra and featuring many stars. The dinners, the performances, the fashion, and the energy that followed would become synonymous with the myth that came to be known as Camelot.

But those living through that brief era from January 1961 to November 1963 had not yet come upon an easy handle to identify what they were observing. Some fortunate few, such as those at the Nobel dinner, experienced this elegance directly, while most learned about it through newspaper, magazine, and television accounts. And just as those thirty-four months seemed to suggest a new era—the New Frontier—for supporters of the administration, the promise was erased suddenly and dramatically one afternoon in Dallas, Texas.

The idea of Camelot was born after the tragic death of the president. In fact, the now storied image began to be crafted at 8:30 pm on the rainy evening of Friday, November 29, 1963. It was articulated over the next five-and-a-half hours. And this took place a mere four days after the funeral of John F. Kennedy.

Jacqueline Kennedy, her emotions clearly raw after the horrific ordeal that she had experienced, wanted to unburden herself from her grief as well as begin an effort to tell her story of those whirlwind White House years with Jack. "I kept saying to Bobby, I've got to talk to somebody, I've got to see somebody. I want to say this one thing. It's been almost an obsession with me."[1] That "somebody" turned out to be political writer Theodore H. White, who would be the widow's amanuensis as well as the conduit for the most enduring political myth of the twentieth century.

Mrs. Kennedy had asked White to come to Hyannis Port. It was a sudden request, one that caught the gnomelike, forty-seven-year-old off guard. White was an old China Hand, once closely associated with *Time* magazine mogul Henry R. Luce. But he had achieved recent prominence for his book *The Making of the President 1960*, a favorable treatment of candidate Kennedy, and one that earned him a Pulitzer Prize. More important, White was a Kennedy admirer, so much so that he was seen as an "honorary Kennedy."

White arrived from New York by car because the downpour that day prevented him from flying. There he found Mrs. Kennedy surrounded by several friends and advisors. White recalled: "The chief memory I have is of her composure; of her beauty (dressed in black trim slacks, beige pullover sweater, her eyes wider than pools): and of her calm voice and total recall."

After discussing the events of the past week in gruesome detail, Mrs. Kennedy got to the point: she wanted the world to know about the specialness of the Kennedy White House and to put a name to it, and it would be taken from Broadway.

*Camelot*—the story about King Arthur and a magical time in England—had been performed at the Majestic Theater in New York since a few weeks after the 1960 presidential election and was nearing the end of its slightly more than two-year run at the time of the president's death. The play, originally starring Richard Burton as King Arthur and Julie Andrews as Queen Guinevere, reached a wider audience through its vinyl record on the Columbia label. One of those who listened and enjoyed the record was the late president.

Mrs. Kennedy likened the Kennedy era to King Arthur's, and recited to White those classical lines: "Don't let it be forgot / That once there was a spot, / For one brief, shining moment / That was known as Camelot." She explained to the enraptured White that this was a unique time, implying that no presidential predecessor could match it. "There'll never be Camelot again," she said.[2]

White took copious notes and, in a complete lapse of journalistic ethics, allowed the grieving widow to amend and approve a draft article that he prepared. It came out in the December 6, 1963, issue of *Life* magazine, and "Camelot" now had a new meaning, one that has been more strongly identified with the 1,036 days of the Kennedy presidency than with King Arthur.[3] Ironically, the writer of the original work—actually a series of books completed in the 1930s and 1940s—on which the *Camelot* play was based was T. H. White, a British writer who was not related to Theodore H. White. And the real editor of the magazine article was Jacqueline Kennedy.

In the years to come, Teddy White reconsidered the myth that he helped to create. In a memoir published in 1978, he called it "a misreading of history. The magic Camelot of John F. Kennedy never existed. Instead, there began in Kennedy's time an effort of government to bring reason to bear on facts which were becoming almost too complicated for human minds to grasp." He added that a more accurate appraisal of Kennedy and his advisors presented us with a challenge: "What kind of people are we Americans? What do we want to become?"[4]

❦

Bound together in this modern-day Camelot legend was youth and glamour. Nearing the midpoint of the Kennedy years in the spring of 1962, the first couple had already set a tone of style and entertaining that was unprecedented for the presidency and clearly a departure from the previous two postwar administrations. Kennedy was the youngest elected president, taking over from the oldest president. Mrs. Kennedy was only thirty-one when she entered the White House; Mamie Eisenhower was sixty-four. They were the first president and first presidential spouse born in the twentieth century. But it was more than youth and, as the president would say in his Boston accent, "vigor" that set the new first couple apart. There was this extraordinary polish, learned through well-bred families, money, private boarding schools, elite colleges, travel abroad, and intellectual curiosity.

While neither the president nor First Lady was an egghead, they appreciated arts and artists, books and writers, and music and musicians. They also understood that symbolism was a critical tool of leadership. Jacqueline Bouvier Kennedy was the cultural connoisseur of the couple. She attended Miss Porter's School and then Vassar College before spending a year in Paris, which left her, as she recalled, "with a love for Europe that I am afraid will never leave me."[5] When she returned home, she completed her bachelor's degree in French literature from The George Washington University.

Her initial job, "Inquiring Camera Girl," for a local newspaper in Washington, DC, gave her an opportunity to take photographs and write on a modest scale. She was engaged when she met the quite-eligible Congressman Kennedy at a Georgetown dinner party in 1952. The following year they married when she was twenty-four years old. She had a strong interest in languages, notably French; art of all types, but especially French; and history, especially French history. One writer later said, "Her elegant Continental tastes were revealed in her fashion, decorating, and cultural interests."[6] Being the hostess at the nation's most famous living museum became a natural role for her, and one that she came to enjoy.

First Ladies have come to be known for their causes: Eleanor Roosevelt for her promotion of social justice, Lady Bird Johnson for highway beautification, Nancy Reagan for her antidrug campaign, and Barbara and Laura Bush for reading literacy. Jackie Kennedy channeled her passion for art into restoring the interior of the White House and adding historic paintings and antiques that underscored America's rich heritage.

The White House was designed by Irish-born architect James Hoban and completed in 1800 in time for John Adams to be the first president to occupy it. As a result of the extensive damage from the War of 1812, Hoban rebuilt it and then added a north and south portico in the 1820s.

The presidency of Theodore Roosevelt was a watershed for the structure. First, it became known as the White House, replacing the earlier names of "President's House" or "Executive Mansion." But more important, Roosevelt initiated a major renovation under the direction of McKim, Mead and White. Perhaps the two most significant changes were the creation of what would become known as the West Wing presidential offices and the significantly expanded State Dining Room.

A half century later President Harry Truman added a balcony and made other changes, but the most important renovation of the late 1940s and early 1950s was to strengthen the structural soundness of the building. Repair work was badly needed. As Truman's secretary wrote after the renovation was completed: "The work necessitated by the crumbling of foundations which could have at any minute collapsed all of the floors of the White House, consisted of removing the entire house inside of the outside walls, and building an entirely new house inside the old walls." The $5.8 million was well spent.[7]

With the structure better secured, the opportunity was ripe for enhancing the old mansion's beauty. From the outset of the Kennedy administration, the First Lady was actively engaged in the upgrading the art of the White House and promoting its history. In the first year, she helped create the Office of the Curator to catalog the mansion's art and antiques; form the Fine Arts Committee to acquire new artworks and review the extensive White House interior renovations; establish the independent, nonprofit White House Historical Association to help promote the heritage of the building; and initiate a White House guidebook.[8] The First Lady also was responsible for redesigning the White House grounds, notably the Rose Garden, done under the supervision of Rachel Lambert "Bunny" Mellon.[9]

Two months into the Kennedy administration, Mrs. Kennedy selected young Lorraine Waxman Pearce to be the first curator. Although they had never met, the First Lady appointed her on the strength of her graduate work at the notable Winterthur Program in Early American Culture and on the recommendation of Henry Francis du Pont.[10]

Du Pont had transformed the family estate at Winterthur, near Wilmington, Delaware, into a public museum. An octogenarian at the time and a leading figure in American art, he would become the chairman and the major force of the Fine Arts Committee. "The day he agreed to be chairman was the biggest red-letter day of all," Mrs. Kennedy said.[11] Other members on the committee were notable figures in the fields of arts, antiques, and society. Assisting them was a Fine Arts Advisory Committee, which included prominent museum directors and curators as well as historians, such as Dr. Lyman H. Butterfield, the editor of the Adams Papers, and Julian P. Boyd, the editor of the Jefferson Papers.[12] Later in 1961, the Fine Arts Committee set up yet another committee to seek out new artwork for the White House.

Congress passed a bill that became Public Law 87–286 in September 1961. This legislation rebranded the historic building as a museum and emphasized the role of historic preservation. With this new law and the support of a high-powered group of leaders in the art world, the First Lady was now in a stronger position to continue the most complete restoration of the interior of the White House in its history.[13]

At this same time Mrs. Kennedy explained her plan to the public and solicited support for it. The September 1, 1961, issue of *Life* magazine featured a cover story on the restoration. In the twelve-page article, accompanied by photographs of some of the new treasures acquired for the White House, the First Lady explained her motivation and goals. She was interested in finding and returning pieces that once were in the White House, such as a chair from the Lincoln Bedroom, and obtaining pieces which would help enhance both the grandeur and history of the building. To date, fifty pieces had been acquired, some through donations while others were purchased.[14]

In the end, the Kennedy restoration—the new artwork, returning and acquiring antiques, painting, and various other examples of refurbishing—focused primarily on the public rooms of the first floor. Those rooms would form the perimeter of the evening for the Nobel dinner in 1962. Among these were the State Dining Room and the Blue Room, the sites used for the actual dinner, and the East Room, the venue for the evening's literary presentation that followed.

Perhaps the most conspicuous, the State Dining Room, took on a more French Empire–style appearance, but included examples of American, British, and even Chinese art. The room, forty-eight feet long and thirty-six feet wide, was repainted antique white. The chandelier and sconces were gilded. Three paintings by George P. A. Healy were hung: one of Abraham Lincoln above the fireplace and paintings of Daniel Webster and Thomas Jefferson above serving tables.

Some new decorations were loaned by individuals, such as a coromandel, or folding screen, from the Chinese K'ang Hsi period, while others were simply repositioned from other rooms. The key people in refurbishing the State Dining Room were Du Pont, noted French designer Stéphane Boudin, and American socialite and designer Dorothy Mae Parish (Mrs. Henry Parish II), more widely known as "Sister" Parish, who also was a member of the Fine Arts Committee.[15]

While most of the guests at the Nobel dinner would be seated in the State Dining Room, some would be in Blue Room, with Mrs. Kennedy presiding as the hostess. This room also was extensively recast in the renovation. As White House records note, "The opening of the newly hung Blue Room represents a major effort on the part of the F.A.C. [Fine Arts Committee] to return it to the period of President Monroe, who ordered the Empire furniture and bronzes for it in 1817 after all the previous furnishings had been destroyed by [the] fire of 1814."[16] Mrs. Kennedy later noted, "The Blue Room was Boudin's masterpiece."[17]

The Blue Room is an elliptically shaped formal parlor. Located at the center of the south view of the White House, it has six doors. The room was repainted in cream and received a blue, pink, and gold Savonnerie carpet that complemented the blue curtains. A new chandelier was added; again, in an effort to revert to the Monroe era, it approximated the original. Gilt chairs purchased by Monroe were reacquired. This became a Monroe room; and his portrait, painted by Samuel F. B. Morse in 1819, was there. Also included in the room were portraits of the four presidents who preceded Monroe and the two who followed him, including another Healy portrait, this one of Andrew Jackson.

For most of the guests at the Nobel dinner and for other special occasions, the room that was used for a formal program was the East Room, the largest room in the mansion. Minimal changes were made here during the Kennedy renovation. Birch-colored paneling was added, a new red carpet was laid, a few pieces of furniture were added, and portraits of three First Ladies—Julia Gardiner Tyler, Sarah Childress Polk, and Ellen Axson Wilson—were added.

The East Room, which has seen so much history before and since, is adorned by three huge Bohemian chandeliers and a copy of the famous Gilbert Stuart painting of George Washington. That painting, with its huge ninety-five-inch length befitting the stature of the great general and president, was the one that Dolley Madison saved from fire and the British invasion in 1814.

By early 1962, the new White House was ready to be unveiled. Perhaps timing its broadcast by the White House and CBS network executives as a special gift to the American public, Mrs. Kennedy narrated a televised tour of the historic mansion on Valentine's Day. The urbane journalist Charles Collingswood was her cohost, and the president joined the one-hour broadcast at its end. The First Lady was delighted with the work that had been done, and her husband, beaming, was clearly proud of her efforts.

Eighty million people—30 percent of all Americans at the time—watched the black-and-white broadcast, as the White House was opened to the people; and the First Lady was later given an honorary Emmy. The reviews were admiring. In an extensive and gushing front-page article the next day, the *New York Times* called her "a virtuoso among guides" and went on to say that Mrs. Kennedy's "vivacious scholarship was fully as vital as the visual pageantry."[18] An Associated Press report said, "It was informative, entertaining television at its very best and credit is due largely to the easy, authoritative commentary by Mrs. Kennedy."[19] Notably, she became the first woman to host a network documentary.

❦

While Mrs. Kennedy had extensive and fairly sophisticated artistic tastes, the president had rather ordinary cultural preferences, suggested by his collection of scrimshaw folk art and an enjoyment of maritime paintings.[20] Still, he took an interest in his wife's artistic pursuits and supported them. He was intellectually curious and read extensively—and rapidly—particularly biography and history, with a fondness for British history for insights and even Ian Fleming's James Bond books for enjoyment. Among other twentieth-century writers that Kennedy enjoyed was the prolific biographer and novelist John Buchan. Journalist Hugh Sidey reported that Kennedy's favorite work was a biography of nineteenth-century British prime minister Lord Melbourne written by Lord David Cecil.[21] Mrs. Kennedy would purchase books for him at the Savile Bookshop in Georgetown.[22]

Kennedy was a writer. His expanded senior thesis was published as *Why England Slept* in 1940. The book, which discussed British appeasement policy in the 1930s, was aided by editorial help from Arthur Krock of the *New York Times*, who also came up with the title.[23] He also benefited from a foreword written by *Time* publisher Henry Luce. But it was Kennedy's work, and it sold very well.

A more significant book, however, was *Profiles in Courage*, a discussion of eight United States senators who took courageous stands that placed their political careers in peril. While questions were raised, then and later, about the extent to which aide Theodore Sorensen or others assisted with the book, *Profiles in Courage* established a reputation for the Massachusetts senator as an author. At age thirty-nine he was awarded the Pulitzer Prize for Biography in 1957, the first American political figure to receive a Pulitzer in that category since Albert J. Beveridge in 1920.

Kennedy also wrote various articles over the years, beginning with covering the United Nations meeting in San Francisco for the Hearst newspapers in 1945. During his senatorial career in the 1950s, he wrote articles for *Foreign*

*Affairs, Atlantic Monthly, America, The New York Times Magazine,* and a number of popular magazines.[24] In 1961 Pearl Buck—the organization's president—sent him a membership card for the Authors Guild, which identifies itself as "the nation's oldest and largest professional organization for writers."

The president took pride in his writing and enjoyed thinking about history and its application to current events. He saw a common cause with historians, relishing his Senate assignment from 1956 to 1959 to chair a special committee to select the five greatest us senators. In a speech to the Mississippi Valley Historical Association during that period, he said: "But I would ask the historian to appreciate a bit more fully the role of the politician—of his frequent stand against these groups and masses and trends that might otherwise be shaping our history."[25] He consulted with historians and scholars, and he enjoyed interacting with them.

In addition to his curious mind and often probing intellect, the president had an astute political sense and an understanding of what has come to be known as political "optics." As such, he was very much a partner in bringing a sense of a European salon to the White House. While obviously not an unbiased source, Ted Sorensen wrote of his boss's achievements in this field: "The White House became both a showplace and a dwelling place for the distinctive, the creative and the cultivated."[26]

This focus on honoring intellectual achievement was seen immediately when Kay Halle, a journalist and Kennedy friend, drew up a list of "creative Americans" to invite to participate in the inauguration. A telegram of invitation sent to 168 distinguished people, including Nobel and Pulitzer Prize winners, read, in part: "During our forthcoming administration we hope to seek a productive relationship with our writers, artists, composers, philosophers, scientists and heads of cultural institutions."[27] Each person also was invited to contribute to a book for President Kennedy, which he read with interest.[28]

Kennedy also launched the Presidential Medal of Freedom, recognizing the contributions of Americans in diverse fields; that program, which has subsequently honored more than five hundred scientists, artists, and government officials, would gain considerable luster over the next half century.

⌐━━←

Armed with a strong interest in the arts and history—and with an effort under way to refurbish the White House—the Kennedys were keen to entertain and do so in royal style. During the preceding Eisenhower administration there were, of course, state dinners, including those for Queen Elizabeth of Great Britain, British prime minister Winston Churchill, and Soviet leader Khrushchev.

In all there were fifty-eight dinners for chiefs of state and heads of government during the eight years that President Eisenhower and Mamie Eisenhower occupied the White House.[29] While some of these events were quite formal, including white-tie dinners, the menu was usually very traditional American food; the dinner for Khrushchev in 1959, for example, included roast turkey, sweet potatoes, and cranberry sauce. Luncheons for special groups might include sliced turkey, broiled chicken, or filet of sole.

Mrs. Kennedy had a vision of grandeur for the White House, and that was reflected in the dinners and special events that marked the Kennedy years. The official entertaining, notably dinners, had five characteristics: a guest list of distinguished Americans and often even non-Americans; men and women accomplished in a wide range of fields; high fashion, especially highlighted by the Oleg Cassini–designed dresses of Mrs. Kennedy; impressive after-dinner entertainment; and superb cuisine, usually French inspired.

The first dinner that President and Mrs. Kennedy held was an intimate one for seven, including columnist Joseph Alsop and family friend Franklin D. Roosevelt Jr., two days after the inauguration.[30] Over the next three months, it appeared that the plan was gradually to ease into entertaining, focusing on small dinners for intimates and small-to-medium-sized lunches for visiting dignitaries. This latter group included Prime Minister John G. Diefenbaker of Canada, Prime Minister Keith Jacka Holyoake of New Zealand, Prime Minister Tage Erlander of Sweden, Prime Minister Harold Macmillan of Great Britain, Chancellor Konrad Adenauer of the Federal Republic of Germany, Prime Minister Constantine Caramanlis of Greece, and President Sukarno of Indonesia.

By April 1961 the White House was beginning to expand its official entertaining, increasing the size and elegance of the events. There were luncheons for Prime Minister Hayato Ikeda of Japan, President Ibrahim Abboud of Sudan, Prime Minister Jawaharlal Nehru of India, and others. But the most notable meals over the next year—up until the time of the Nobel dinner—were a luncheon for an American-born princess; a dinner for the Pakistani president held at George Washington's home at Mount Vernon; a dinner for the governor of Puerto Rico, with one of the world's greatest musicians performing; and a sparkling dinner for the Shah of Iran, also featuring a memorable musical performance.

It was clear that the social program at the White House was reaching a new level—inviting a larger number of people, experimenting with new approaches such as holding a unique state dinner *away* from the White House, and showcasing outstanding musical talent and culture. While Mrs. Kennedy was actively engaged in these social events, the two linchpins were social secretary Letitia Baldrige and executive chef René Verdon. And supporting these special events—as well as the overall operation of the White House—was the veteran chief usher, James Bernard "J. B." West.

"Tish" Baldrige had a history with Mrs. Kennedy and an impressive résumé when she was appointed White House social secretary in early 1961 at the age of thirty-five. She and the First Lady had attended Miss Porter's, the elite all-girls boarding school in Farmington, Connecticut, where they were acquaintances. Baldrige then went on to study at Vassar and the University of Geneva. She was social secretary to Ambassador David Bruce in London and then Ambassador Clare Booth Luce in Rome before becoming director of public relations at Tiffany and Co. in New York. She was fluent in both French and Italian.[31]

The hard-charging, six-foot-one-inch tall, blond-haired Baldrige become known as the "Doyenne of Decorum" because of her regal commitment to social convention and grace. But she also could be difficult to deal with. Mrs. Kennedy eventually grew weary of Baldrige's personality. She told Arthur Schlesinger in 1964 that "so much of her energy was rather extra that I—now that I think of it, she really made me tireder than I'd had to be. Because she'd send you so many extra things that you really didn't have to answer. And on weekends, she'd keep sending folders down until I stopped it."[32] The First Lady also disapproved of Baldrige's "White House-itis," as she called it, which was a haughty sense of her position. Lorraine Waxman Pearce, the White House curator, also suffered from "White House-itis," according to Mrs. Kennedy.[33]

Still, Baldrige was very good at what she did, and she was vital in pulling together luncheons, dinners, and other special events for the Kennedys for more than two years until she departed in June 1963. It was Baldrige who coordinated the guest lists, archived the acceptances, and oversaw the logistics. She also served as Mrs. Kennedy's chief of staff—a less-demanding job than it is today, but still one with important and broad responsibilities.

René Verdon was the first executive chef at the White House. Chefs in previous administrations were either individuals known to the first family or were readily available military people or civilians who had some culinary background. The Roosevelts were served by Henrietta Nesbitt, the family's housekeeper at Hyde Park, who by most accounts had mediocre culinary skills. The chef during the second Eisenhower administration was a Navy chef.

The son of bakers, Verdon was born in Pouzauge, France, and apprenticed at several French restaurants in the 1930s and 1940s. He worked his way up through several Parisian restaurants and even served aboard the French steamer ss *Liberté*. He then was assistant chef at the Carlyle Hotel, where the Kennedys had an apartment, and the Essex House in New York in the late 1950s. Verdon was thirty-six years old when appointed to his White House position.[34]

At the outset, though, the president was presented with a problem related to the hiring of Verdon and his Italian deputy, Julius Spessot—they were both European citizens, and the appearance of foreign chefs in charge of food at the White House might cause a political problem. Kennedy addressed that by having the Secret Service expedite us citizenship for the two men. That solved the problem, but Spessot was soon replaced by a pastry chef, Ferdinand Louvat, who also was French.[35]

Verdon immediately attracted attention for his French culinary skills. His first meal was a luncheon for British prime minister Harold Macmillan on April 5, 1961. The menu included trout en gelée au Chablis, filet of beef au jus and artichoke bottoms Beaucaire, asparagus with sauce Maltaise, and meringue mold glacée. In a front-page story, *New York Times* food critic Craig Claiborne discussed the chef's background as well as this inaugural culinary event, which was judged a big success: "Verdict: Bravo." Verdon also had the distinction of having a photograph of himself in his kitchen run on the front page.[36] Expectations for culinary excellence at the White House had been substantially raised. Verdon earned good press during his tenure. After he clashed with the Johnsons over cultural differences in food tastes, he resigned in 1965.[37] The *Washington Post* was prompted to editorialize, "The resignation that truly signals the end of the Kennedy era is that of Chef René Verdon."[38]

In May 1961, in the month following the initial Verdon luncheon, the Kennedys entertained Prince Rainier III and Princess Grace of Monaco. Although it was a small event—only nine guests—it attracted attention because of the storybook tale of the young and radiant Philadelphia-born actress Grace Kelly, who became a European princess. Baldrige said this event was originally supposed to be a lavish dinner, but it was downgraded to lunch by the First Lady owing to "a bit of jealousy, perhaps" because Kelly and John Kennedy may have dated when they were both single.[39]

What followed were various social events, but there were three significant dinners over the next year in the run-up to the Nobel dinner. The first was in July 1961, and it was held in honor of President Mohammad Ayub Khan of Pakistan. Mrs. Kennedy seized on a venue offer presented to her by Baldrige and the superintendent of Mount Vernon, George Washington's iconic estate on the Potomac River. One hundred and thirty-seven guests, mostly American and Pakistani government officials, would participate in this state dinner at Mount Vernon.

There were huge logistical issues, notably transporting the guests, food, dishes—in fact, everything needed for the dinner. Four boats, including the presidential yachts *Honey Fitz* and *Sequoia,* left from the pier at the Naval Weapons Plant in Southwest Washington, DC, beginning at 6:10 pm and sailed up the river to Mount Vernon, giving the guests a breathtaking view on a warm and pleasant evening.

Guests dined on a main course of Poulet Chasseur under a large tent on the lawn of the historic property. They listened to the National Symphony Orchestra perform selections from Mozart, Debussy, Barber, and Gershwin.[40] And they heard President Kennedy praising Ayub Khan and saying optimistically that "I have seen a most particular manifestation of your country's willingness to commit itself for the cause of freedom." While the president was being diplomatic to a Cold War ally, both Ayub Khan and Pakistan still had a long way to go.

Another historic dinner took place five months later in honor of the governor of Puerto Rico, Luis Muñoz Marín. What made this White House event so

President Kennedy, Vice President Johnson, John Glenn, and others in the Oval Office after the astronaut's orbital flight in 1962. *Source:* John Glenn Archives, The Ohio State University

Table setting in the State Dining Room. President Kennedy always sat at table seven when the round tables were used. Among those joining him at this table tonight were Mary Welsh Hemingway, Katherine Tupper Marshall, and Robert Frost. *Source:* Robert Knudsen, White House Photographs, John F. Kennedy Presidential Library and Museum, Boston

Table setting for the table hosted by Jean Kennedy Smith in the State Dining Room. The inscription on the fireplace was written by John Adams and added during Franklin Roosevelt's presidency. *Source:* Robert Knudsen, White House Photographs, John F. Kennedy Presidential Library and Museum, Boston

Table settings in the Blue Room. Mrs. Kennedy hosted table seventeen, which included John Glenn, Canadian political leader Lester Pearson, and Pearl Buck. *Source:* Robert Knudsen, White House Photographs, John F. Kennedy Presidential Library and Museum, Boston

One of the table settings in the Blue Room. *Source:* Robert Knudsen, White House Photographs, John F. Kennedy Presidential Library and Museum, Boston

## DINNER

Puligny Montrachet
Combetter 1er Cru    *La Couronne de l'Élu Victoria*
1959

*Filet de boeuf Wellington*
Château Mouton    *Pommes Chipp*
Rothschild    *Fonds d'artichauts Favorite*
1955    *Endive Meunière*

Piper Heidsieck    *Bombe Caribienne*
1955    *Petits-fours assortis*

The White House
Sunday, April 29, 1962

The dinner menu with food prepared by chef René Verdon and his staff.
*Source:* Robert Knudsen, White House Photographs, John F. Kennedy
Presidential Library and Museum, Boston

Guests gathered in the Red Room, pictured here, and the Green Room after dinner.
*Source:* Robert Knudsen, White House Photographs, John F. Kennedy Presidential
Library and Museum, Boston

President and Mrs. Kennedy, Mary Welsh Hemingway, Fredric March, and Katherine Tupper Marshall in front of a painting of Martha Washington in the East Room. *Source:* Robert Knudsen, White House Photographs, John F. Kennedy Presidential Library and Museum, Boston

special was the after-dinner performance by the incomparable cellist Pablo Casals, who was making an encore appearance more than a half century after entertaining President Theodore Roosevelt in 1904. Casals, a native of Catalonia, Spain, was also giving his first American performance in thirty-three years.[41]

Casals, then eighty-four years old, was well known in Puerto Rico, playing there often and even launching a Casals Festival in 1956. Both his mother and his second wife, sixty years younger, were natives of Puerto Rico. The Puerto Rican connection, according to Baldrige, was a way to invite Casals to the White House without upsetting the cellist's concern that the United States had been associated with Spanish dictator Francisco Franco.[42]

On November 13, 1961, Casals appeared in the East Room along with Mieczysław Horszowski, a pianist, and Alexander Schneider, a violinist, both of whom often played with the virtuoso. Casals scored a front-page photograph in the *New York Times* the next day. Harold C. Schonberg, the music critic, wrote that the event "was one of the few occasions where a program of serious chamber music, lasting almost an hour, has been presented in these surroundings."[43]

Schonberg added, "The concentration on serious music last night was an indication of one aspect of the New Frontier. President and Mrs. Kennedy have been highly responsive to cultural elements in the American musical scene, and have been making efforts to raise the standard not only for the White House but also for Washington."[44]

Among the 153 guests were many American composers and musical directors, including Leonard Bernstein, Aaron Copland, Gian Carlo Menotti, Eugene Ormandy, Walter Piston, and Leopold Stokowski. Others present were the actor Harry Belafonte, more representatives from the music and arts world, and even Alice Roosevelt Longworth, in a nod to history when Casals visited the Roosevelts more than a half century before. As would be the model for the Nobel dinner, the large number of guests required that two rooms, the State Dining Room and the Blue Room, be used for dinner, with the President and Mrs. Kennedy each hosting one of the rooms.[45]

Mrs. Kennedy's attire that night at the white-tie dinner was a Cassini creation: a chartreuse three-piece outfit with an embroidered shell, long skirt, and a short evening jacket. High fashion intersected with haute cuisine as executive chef Verdon served *filet de boeuf* Montfermeil as the main course.[46]

Over the next five months, there were a number of lunches and dinners, but none was as memorable as that held for Mohammad Reza Pahlavi, the Shah of Iran, and his wife, Empress Farah Diba, on April 11, 1962. Although this was not a large dinner, the White House rolled out the red carpet for an important Middle East ally. President and Mrs. Kennedy met the Shah and his entourage at Washington National Airport upon their arrival and traveled back to the White House with him in a large motorcade.

The dinner that evening was largely restricted to government officials, including congressman and future president Gerald R. Ford. There also were three college presidents, several reporters and editors, and others associated with Iran and its oil interests. The following day the Shah addressed Congress.

The White House selected Jerome Robbins and his contemporary ballet company as the evening's entertainment in the spacious East Room. The seventeen dancers performing several selections, including Debussy's *Prelude to the Afternoon of a Faun,* presented a memorable production. Their appearance was rivaled by the two foremost women of the evening, the American First Lady and the Iranian empress. The empress wore an exquisite gold Dior gown complemented by a diamond tiara. Mrs. Kennedy wore another Cassini creation and was turned out with a new hairdo, a brioche. Both couples upheld a regal style, and the White House was again the focus of the best of American culture.[47]

❦

In November 1961 Dick Goodwin sent Mrs. Kennedy a memorandum suggesting a special event. "How about a dinner for the American winners of the Nobel Prize," he asked. "So far this year they have all been scientists, giving you a good chance to switch from the Arts to the Sciences."[48] And so the process was put in motion to have a dinner honoring Nobel laureates. Over the next five months, Mrs. Kennedy, Goodwin, Arthur M. Schlesinger Jr., Schlesinger assistant Antonia "Toni" Chayes, Baldrige, the First Lady's aide Pamela Turnure, Edithe Rowley of the social office, and others worked on the myriad of details required to stage such a White House dinner. Although not a state dinner or one honoring a prominent foreign leader, this dinner would be the largest and most consequential of the Kennedy presidency.

A crucial challenge for this dinner and for those White House dinners to come was identifying a guest list. In that memo to Mrs. Kennedy, Goodwin also suggested, "Perhaps you might even want to ask the Zulu who won the Peace Prize and the Yugoslav who won the prize for literature."[49] He was referring to Albert Lutuli from South Rhodesia and Dr. Ivo Andric of Yugoslavia; their selections were announced in late October. Goodwin was clearly reacting to the publicity that each man had recently received.

While the idea of honoring Nobel laureates remained focused on the sciences, the dinner evolved into a celebration of those from the Western Hemisphere. In the end, it was the American winners plus one Canadian, Lester Pearson. Why the worldwide scope was whittled down is unclear, but logistics surely had something to do with it. There also were no other winners from the Western Hemisphere. It was discovered that the one laureate from South America, Lucila Godoy Alcayaga (pen name: Gabriela Mistral), who had received the 1945 prize for literature, had died nearly five years before.

The list of Nobel awardees was compiled, their addresses were secured, and invitations were prepared. Accompanying them would be wives—the sole female laureate was the widowed Pearl Buck—Kennedy relatives, White House staff, college presidents, selected members of the press, and a wide range of American scientists and literary figures.

This group of Nobel laureates stretched back to awardees of 1934: Dr. Harold C. Urey, who had received the award for chemistry for his work on radioactive isotopes, and Dr. William P. Murphy, who was honored for his work related to anemia. Also attending were the most recent recipients, who met with the president before dinner.

The us Nobel honors had been most prominent in the fields of physics, chemistry, and physiology or medicine, and the representation that night reflected it. Their achievements spanned the spectrum of scientific work. For instance, Dr. Rabi worked on radar and nuclear magnetic resonance; Dr. John F. Enders was the "Father of Modern Vaccines," instrumental in the development of the polio and measles immunizations; and Dr. Seaborg was pivotal in identifying ten new chemical elements. Few areas of scientific achievement of the century were untouched by these men.

There was still an international flavor to the group. Some of the honorees were émigrés from Austria, Canada, China, France, Germany, Italy, Russia,

Spain, and Switzerland. Pearl Buck had grown up in China and lived there for more than thirty years. Buck received the 1938 Nobel award for literature for her work on China, notably *The Good Earth*.

Some guests who were suggested by outsiders found their way to the dinner. Katherine Anne Porter's publisher at the Atlantic Press Monthly Press, Seymour Lawrence, recommended her to Arthur Schlesinger in letter in November 1961. He said, "I don't know how these things are arranged but I am sure that Katherine Anne Porter would consider it an honor to be invited to one of the President's receptions."[50] He referred to her forthcoming book, *Ship of Fools*, which was scheduled to be released in May 1962. Actually, it was out in April and rocketed to number one on the *New York Times* best-seller list on April 29.

R. Sargent Shriver, President Kennedy's brother-in-law and director of the Peace Corps, received a letter from a relative of his who endorsed Katherine Tupper Marshall for a White House event. She was the widow of the late George C. Marshall, a Nobel peace laureate. William H. Shriver Jr. started his letter by saying, "A thought on public relations." Saying that Mrs. Marshall would love to visit the White House and meet the Kennedys, he added, "This is all my idea and, if you think it should end right here, so be it."[51] It did not: it was passed along, Baldrige put the notation "Nobel" on the letter, and Mrs. Marshall sat next to the president at the dinner.

It is clear from the Kennedy archives that Schlesinger had a major role in identifying the guests. Toni Chayes, Schlesinger's assistant, provided him with a compilation of the Nobel winners through research conducted with the Library of Congress, and information from the inauguration files, science advisor Dr. Jerome Wiesner, and even from the president's physician, Dr. Janet G. Travell, on "the medical people." The president also was involved; he drafted a handwritten note to Schlesinger saying that Goodwin should be invited, which he was.

In March, Schlesinger wrote to Goodwin and updated him on the guest list. Recommendations by Goodwin and Mrs. Kennedy were acknowledged; Schlesinger, Wiesner, and Goodwin were included; a prioritized list of "literary types" and scientists were identified. He also noted that Goodwin's friend and Martha's Vineyard neighbor William Styron was ranked high, "so you should not be too unhappy."[52]

A longer list had been winnowed down. Now there were eighteen literary figures, ranked in order of priority and with correspondingly ranked alternates. There also were seven scientists and seven alternates. Appended to the science list was J. Robert Oppenheimer, who required the most vetting. His name was probably generated by Schlesinger or perhaps even by his friend and national security advisor McGeorge Bundy. But he had two hurdles to clear. First was that the president's approval was needed, and second was that Oppenheimer was to be invited only if Linus Pauling, with whom he was somewhat estranged, declined. In the end, the president did approve, and it was finally agreed that Pauling and Oppenheimer should both attend.[53] With these hurdles surmounted, the redemption of J. Robert Oppenheimer was under way.

The highest priority among the literary figures was Baldwin; the specific alternate for him was black writer Ralph Ellison, author of the important book *Invisible Man*. Among those on the preferred list who were invited and attended were Van Wyck Brooks, John Dos Passos, James T. Farrell, Robert Frost, and Lionel Trilling. Among those on the alternate list, Samuel Eliot Morison, the historian and the first alternate, and Katherine Anne Porter were the only ones fortunate enough to be invited and attend the dinner.

Those on the two lists who either were eventually not invited or declined, in order of precedence, included E. E. Cummings, John Hersey, Archibald MacLeish, Reinhold Niebuhr, J. D. Salinger, Carl Sandburg, Upton Sinclair, John Steinbeck, Thornton Wilder, W. H. Auden, Arthur Miller, Tennessee Williams, Truman Capote, Robert Penn Warren, Saul Bellow, Eudora Welty, and Lillian Hellman.[54]

Salinger declined with no reason given.[55] Carl Sandburg regretfully replied that he had another commitment. One surprise invitee, probably advanced by Mrs. Kennedy, was children's book illustrator Ludwig Bemelmans, the creator of the Madeline series. In what was surely the most amusing reply to Baldrige, Bemelmans said he was forced to be in Ireland and, if not there, "they would do awful things to me." He included a drawing of an Easter bunny.[56]

Faulkner was one of the Nobel winners who declined. He was in the final months of his life and was living in Charlottesville, Virginia; he was quoted as saying, "Why that's a hundred miles away. That's a long way to go just to eat."[57] It might have been interesting—perhaps awkward—had Faulkner attended. Baldwin and Faulkner had a spirited disagreement over the methods and speed used for desegregation. Faulkner, a son of the South, was an incrementalist, placing a premium on the concern for order; while Baldwin was impatient for racial progress. After Faulkner made comments that he found disturbing, Baldwin responded with an article entitled "Faulkner and Desegregation" in *The Reporter*, a liberal biweekly publication.

Although Faulkner and a number of others declined, many others were willing—even eager—to journey a considerable distance for the special evening. Many came from California. Nine were members of the University of California faculty. Kennedy relished being able to one-up the Soviet Union's poor showing in Nobel honors, boasting at Berkeley five weeks earlier: "Your faculty includes more Nobel laureates than any other faculty in the world—more in this one community than our principal adversary has received since the awards began in 1901."[58] Several of those men joined him at the White House for this memorable dinner.

Some of these Californians likely came on a transcontinental flight aboard the new and popular workhorse narrow-body jet, the sleek Boeing 707. Some, such as the Trillings, came by rail, then in its waning days and several years before its resuscitation by Amtrak. But regardless of how they arrived, they came from all points of the United States and even from Ottawa, in the case of Pearson. Dr. Selman A. Waksman, the discoverer of streptomycin and a Nobel laureate, sent a telegram from Haifa, Israel, saying he and his wife, Deborah, would cut short their trip to Israel and India to attend.[59]

All seven of the preferred scientists were invited and six accepted. Those who attended were Dr. Detlev W. Bronk of the Rockefeller Institute, Dr. Lee A. DuBridge of Caltech, Dr. James R. Killian and Dr. Julius A. Stratton of the Massachusetts Institute of Technology, Dr. George B. Kistiakowsky of Harvard University, and Dr. Alan T. Waterman of the National Science Foundation. Only Dr. James B. Conant, a former Harvard president and Manhattan Project leader, wrote "regret extremely that previous engagements" present a problem.[60]

Because of the relationship between Norway and Sweden and the Nobel prizes, diplomats from both countries were invited. Perhaps the most intriguing of those who did not make the final cut was famed but controversial aviator Charles A. Lindbergh; however, he would attend a White House dinner for French cultural official André Malraux two weeks later.

Tish Baldrige called it the "Brains' Dinner," which confused executive chef Verdon, who exclaimed, "We are not serving brains for that dinner." In the end, although she anticipated "wacky old professors," she was surprised that the guests "included a goodly number of well-dressed, fun-loving swingers."[61] And Verdon put together another culinary feast with *filet de boeuf* Wellington as the main course.

Elmer "Rusty" Young, the White House chief floral designer, selected a bountiful garden's worth of flowers for the evening. In a memo the day before the dinner, he identified the arrangements: "Baskets of White and Yellow Freesia, White Sweetpeas, White, Yellow, Red and Orange Single Ranunculus, Red and Lavender Anemone, Blue and Yellow Iris, White Marguerite Daisies, Blue Leucocoryne, Yellow and Orange Gerberas, Red and Yellow Tulips, Gypsophila, and Cream Narcissus with Orange Centers."[62] As was the usual protocol, Young was now busy arranging the flowers as the guests were entering the White House. The head butler and his small group of associates were scurrying about with the last-minute touches for the dinner.

The china was now set. The phalanx of vermeil flatware was perfectly aligned at each setting. The place cards with the presidential seal and the name of each guest elegantly written in calligraphy were placed at each of the one hundred seventy-seven settings. The beautifully refurbished and exquisitely decorated White House was now ready for the arrival of the largest and most prestigious social gathering of the Kennedy years. It would be, as Carl Sandburg said, "an event of a lifetime."[63]

# CHAPTER THREE ☞

# Poetry, Prose, and Politics

THE GUESTS PROCEEDED down the Cross Hall, women in their long gowns and men in their black tuxedos, as some were escorted by the smartly dressed social aides toward the southwest corner of the White House to the State Dining Room and others to the Blue Room in the center of the mansion, directly facing the South Portico. Excitement must have been high as the many well-known scientists and writers—and their spouses—surely wondered whether they would be seated near the president or the First Lady.

More than two-thirds entered and took their seats in the State Dining Room.[1] Once used as an office for President Thomas Jefferson, this room had been used for entertaining for more than a century and a half.[2] It had been enlarged and now measured forty-eight feet long and thirty-six feet wide. With renovations undertaken three times in the twentieth century—during the administrations of Theodore Roosevelt, Truman, and now Kennedy—the State Dining Room was one of the most impressive rooms in the White House, if not in America. In fact, Mrs. Kennedy said that it had "the most architectural unity of any room in the White House."[3]

As 127 people filed in, their eyes were immediately attracted to a massive electroplated gilded chandelier in the center of the room and the large full-length portrait of a seated Abraham Lincoln by G. P. A. Healy. Along the north and east walls were five doors, three public and two used for the meal servers, who were now swiftly and efficiently moving from table to table, tending to their duties.

Guests were making their way to their assigned seats at one of thirteen small round tables, most of which had ten place settings and chairs. These tables were numbered, and the most conspicuous was number seven, in the center of the room; as usual, this is where President Kennedy sat, with the Healy portrait and a historic mantel and fireplace framing his silhouette. Finishing his duties in the receiving line, he arrived after many of the guests were already seated.

While the president welcomed guests to his table, there also were hosts for each of the other tables, either a relative of the president or a representative of his administration. Among the former group were the president's sister and brother-in-law, Jean Kennedy Smith and Steve Smith, and his sister-in-law and wife of Robert Kennedy, Ethel. The staff hosts were Lady Bird Johnson, wife of the vice president; press secretary Pierre Salinger and his wife, Nancy Joy; White House aides Richard Goodwin and Arthur Schlesinger and his wife, Marian; and science advisors doctors James Killian, Jerome Wiesner, and Glenn Seaborg, who also was a Nobel Prize winner.[4]

The place of greatest prestige, however, was to be seated at the president's table, and those five women and four men who found themselves there had a night of proximity and conversation that would last them for the rest of their lives. The seats of honor were reserved for the widows of two Nobel laureates, Katherine Tupper Marshall on the president's right and Mary Welsh Hemingway on his left.

Mrs. Marshall had been married for twenty-nine years to George C. Marshall before he died in 1959. Marshall's distinguished army career was followed by service as secretary of state and then defense; his work on the European Recovery Program (the Marshall Plan) earned him the Nobel Peace Prize in 1953. At age seventy-nine, Katherine Marshall was eight years older than the president's mother, Rose Fitzgerald Kennedy.

Prodded by his relative Billy Shriver, Sargent Shriver's intervention on behalf of Mrs. Marshall was apparently enough to work its way into the social secretary's queue and make her a proxy for her famous late husband. That night she admitted, "When they first called me I said, 'I'm such an old lady I could never go.' I've been away from here so long I don't know any of the people, except from the newspapers. But I bought myself a dress so I could come." And there she was. When informed by a White House staffer that she would be seated at the president's table, she expressed surprise, saying, "Now isn't that a nice young man?"[5]

As the others were being seated at this special table, the French wines were poured into American-made crystal glasses. Mrs. Marshall would immediately see the ivory and celadon green Truman china that had been set. This service may have reminded her of the president who was a great admirer of her husband and who had appointed him to his two cabinet positions. Made by Lenox and introduced in 1951, the china has a center design of the Great Seal of the United States surrounded by forty-eight stars. Coincidentally, the official image of the Great Seal is in the possession of the State Department, and that too would have reminded her of General Marshall and his tenure there.

But even more special and personal for Mrs. Marshall, her husband was to be honored in a few hours. The actor Fredric March would be reading from Secretary Marshall's 1947 speech outlining the Marshall Plan. The general, were he still alive, might have been embarrassed by this. He refused to write a memoir and shunned displays of intimacy, public or private; even his stepson and President Roosevelt called him "General." Mrs. Marshall, however, was very proud of him; while he felt constrained from writing about himself, she was not, and wrote of him in her book *Together: Annals of an Army Wife.*[6] Tonight, whether Mrs. Marshall recalled it or not, there is no evidence that she was upset that John Kennedy, when a congressman, had accused her husband of the defeat of Chiang Kai-shek and the communist takeover of China.[7]

On the president's left was Mary Welsh Hemingway, a generation younger and much different from the reserved Katherine Marshall. Mary Hemingway, Ernest Hemingway's fourth and last wife, was a journalist when she first met him in 1944. Shortly after meeting her, Hemingway, still married to Martha Gellhorn, told Mary Welsh Monks, also married, "I don't know you, Mary. But I want to marry you. You are very alive. You're beautiful, like a May fly."[8]

Mary was attractive and personable, and like Ernest's second and third wives, was a journalist. She edited the *American Florist* magazine and then worked on the society page of the *Chicago Daily News.* Anxious for a more challenging position, she moved on to become a war correspondent, first for London's *Daily Express* and then for Henry Luce's Time Inc., posted mostly in London and but also in Paris.[9] She covered a number of the most important events of the late 1930s and 1940s in Europe, including the appeasement at Munich, Hitler's annexation of Czechoslovakia, Normandy at the time of the D-Day invasion, and the liberation of Paris.[10]

Two years after meeting her, the burly writer, already world famous, did marry the petite, blue-eyed, light-haired woman.[11] Thus began a tempestuous fifteen-year marriage, during which they lived for many years in Cuba, and that ended with Hemingway's suicide in July 1961.

It would be unlikely to find two more different women than the widows Marshall and Hemingway. While Katherine Marshall was the dutiful help-mate of a paragon of rectitude, Mary Hemingway was an earthy, driven former war correspondent and the wife of a philandering, hard-drinking writer. Mary herself liked a good time. Once reflecting on her World War II stay in the City of Light: "I was like a cat in heat."[12]

But Mary Hemingway shared a special role with Mrs. Marshall because her husband also would be honored this evening. In fact, the evening's literary entertainment would be mostly centered on Ernest Hemingway. Mary Hemingway, the executor of Ernest's estate and the keeper of his flame, was pleased when social secretary Letitia Baldrige wrote to her to say that a selection from Hemingway's 1927 short story "The Killers" would be read. This Nick Adams tale involved a murder plot of a Swedish boxer—an odd choice for Nobel laureates. Mrs. Hemingway had something else in mind. She provided the White House and Fredric March with an unpublished manuscript that would become part of *Islands in the Stream*, which was eventually released in 1970.[13]

Mary Hemingway differed from Katherine Marshall in that her husband had a relationship with President Kennedy, albeit from a distance. The author and the politician had a mutual respect for each other, but they never met. Both had been awarded a Pulitzer Prize in the 1950s, so there was a writer's kinship between them. Kennedy, who relished his role as writer, perhaps paid Hemingway the ultimate compliment in setting up his book *Profiles in Courage* by saying, "This is a book about that most admirable of human virtues—courage. 'Grace under pressure,' Ernest Hemingway defined it."[14]

By the mid-1950s, Hemingway was arguably the most famous American writer. He had been awarded the Nobel Prize for Literature in 1954. Among his many notable books were *The Sun Also Rises* and *A Farewell to Arms* from the 1920s; *To Have and Have Not* and *Death in the Afternoon* in the 1930s; *For Whom the Bells Toll* in 1940; and *The Old Man and the Sea* in 1952.

As part of his outreach to artists and writers, Kennedy invited Hemingway to his inauguration in January 1961. But the writer, physically ailing and suffering from depression, replied from the Mayo Clinic, where he was being treated for morbid hypertension: "I must restrict certain activities."[15] However, the Hemingways joined millions of Americans in watching the proceedings on television. It moved Ernest Hemingway so much that he gushed in another communication to the president: "Watching on the screen I was sure our President would stand any of the heat to come as he had taken the cold of that day. . . . It is a good thing to have a brave man as our President in times as tough as these are for our country and the world."[16]

While watching the inauguration, Mary had little reason to anticipate how much would happen over the next year and a half and how much the president would be involved. When Papa Hemingway committed suicide less than six months later, Kennedy issued a statement: "Few Americans," he said, "have had a greater impact on the emotions and attitudes of the American people than Ernest Hemingway."[17]

Soon after, William Walton, a friend of President and Mrs. Kennedy as well as Mrs. Hemingway, asked the president to allow Mary Hemingway to travel to Cuba to retrieve her husband's papers.[18] This, in the immediate aftermath of the Bay of Pigs invasion and the even icier relationship between the two governments, represented a major intervention on the part of the president.

Now she was seated next to the president and having dinner with him, and her late husband would soon be honored. And yet, she had a disagreement with Kennedy, and that would present some tense moments at the table.

Seated next to Mary Hemingway was Nobel laureate Dr. Carl D. Anderson. The fifty-six-year-old physicist had received a award in 1936, when he was only a few years removed from having earned a doctorate from Caltech. He had now been associated with this scientific mecca for nearly forty years.

Dr. Anderson's early research was on the positron, but he also studied X-rays and cosmic and gamma rays. In an interesting twist, Dr. Anderson's parents were Swedish, and the young scientist was humbled by being able to give his Nobel speech in Stockholm in December 1936.[19] He and his wife, Lorraine, had traveled from San Marino, California, for tonight's dinner. Mrs. Anderson was seated at a nearby table directly in front of the fireplace and the Lincoln portrait and next to the president's brother-in-law and family business and political operative Stephen Smith.

If Dr. Anderson looked straight ahead beyond tables five and six and toward the South Lawn, he would see three fifteen-pane windows. Had he been able to see into the night that obscured his view, he would have spied magnolia trees brought to the White House by President Andrew Jackson. This was also the area where the president's Marine helicopter landed on the south grounds and where there was a shed for Caroline Kennedy's ponies. But he would mostly see blackness at this point.

Looking around the room, Dr. Anderson would have spotted an impressive array of historic furnishings as well as many of his peers. Perhaps to his surprise—given his heritage—seated on his left was the wife of the Swedish ambassador to the United States, Agnes Charlier Jarring. She was quite familiar with Washington—her husband, Gunnar, had been the ambassador since 1958. He was not present, however, and she represented him. It was especially appropriate tonight because Mrs. Jarring, fifty-three years old, had a scientific pedigree herself; she once worked in a laboratory, and her father was an astronomer and longtime professor at Lund University, about three hundred miles from Stockholm.

The ambassador's wife, often known as Lilla Jarring, wore a distinctive floral dress. She was one of thirteen people to meet with the president on the second floor of the White House before dinner; four 1961 Nobel laureates were part of this group, as was her husband's colleague from the Swedish embassy, Count Axel Lewenhaupt, a veteran diplomat and the embassy's counselor.

While we don't know whether Dr. Anderson's speech in Stockholm came up at the dinner discussion, she would have been pleased to have learned that during his remarks he had praised her country and his ancestral homeland: "The characteristic idealism of Sweden continues to express itself in the admirable way in which she is making use of her unique opportunity, through the annual awards of the Nobel Prizes, to foster international good will and promote the development of science throughout the whole world."[20]

A fellow European sat at her left—another Nobel awardee and the only Frenchman at the dinner, the poet Alexis Leger. Leger, dapper and mustachioed at seventy-four, had received the prize for literature in 1960. He was also known by his pen name, Saint-John Perse. Leger, who was born on the Caribbean island of Guadeloupe, moved to France when he was a boy. There he served for many years as a French diplomat. He was a close friend of the late United Nations Secretary-General Dag Hammarskjöld, who like him also disliked French president Charles de Gaulle.[21] Years later, *Le Monde* identified Leger's *Amers*, published in 1957, as one of the "100 Books of the Century."

Leger attended with his wife, Dorothy Millburn Russell Leger, an American. They were living in Georgetown, about fifteen minutes from the White House, but also had a house in the south of France. In less than two weeks, they would return to the White House for the lavish dinner honoring French cultural leader André Malraux, complete with a concert by violinist Isaac Stern. Tonight, Mrs. Leger was seated at press secretary Pierre Salinger's table.

Seated to the left of Alexis Leger was Maryon Elspeth Pearson, wife of the Canadian Liberal Party leader. In what might be considered an anticipation of the future, when Lester Pearson would become prime minister in 1963, she was seated at President Kennedy's table and he was in the Blue Room next to Mrs. Kennedy. When Mrs. Pearson ascended to this position, she would be the polar opposite in temperament of the American First Lady.

Maryon, who was sixty on this night, was known for her biting personality. In fact, there were compilations of such quotes as: "Behind every successful man is a surprised woman."[22] "Mike" Pearson had been stationed as a delegate in London at the beginning of World War II, and Maryon joined him there for a year beginning in mid-1939. It was during that time that Joseph P. Kennedy, the president's father, served as ambassador to the United Kingdom and young Jack was finishing up his work at Harvard University.

Tonight, Maryon Pearson had one of the best seats. Not only was she directly opposite the president, but she faced him when he later delivered his memorable remarks. She also had an unimpeded view of the great oil painting of Lincoln. This massive work, measuring 73 ¾ by 55 ⅝ inches, was a subset of George Peter Alexander Healy's larger work, *The Peacemakers*. The painting is of a pensive Lincoln, seated on a wooden chair with his right hand on his chin and his elbow on his right leg. Although unseen in this portrait, he is listening to his top military strategists, generals Ulysses S. Grant and William T. Sherman and Admiral David D. Porter. This scene took place in March 1865 on the steamboat *River Queen*, at City Point, not far from Richmond.

In the recent renovation, the Lincoln painting was moved to the State Dining Room in place of a landscape by George Inness. Situated as it was, Lincoln seemed to be keeping watch over the assembly of people below. Directly beneath the painting is a mantle and stone fireplace that included two sentences written by John Adams in 1800 and placed there by Franklin Roosevelt: "I pray

Heaven to bestow the best of Blessings on this House and on all that hereinafter inhabit it. May none but honest and wise Men ever rule under this roof."

❦

This was the table for celebrated poets, as Leger was complimented by the presence of Robert Frost, the poet laureate of Vermont and a four-time winner of the Pulitzer Prize for Poetry. He was seated to the left of Maryon Pearson. A renowned champion of rural America and New England, Frost was in the last year of his long life.

His relationship with John Kennedy began, interestingly enough, the night of his eighty-fifth birthday at the Waldorf in 1959, where he received that awkward rebuke from Lionel Trilling. At a news conference that evening, Frost implied an endorsement for the Massachusetts senator's anticipated presidential candidacy.[23] Two weeks later, Kennedy sent a letter to Frost, in which he extended birthday greetings and joined the poet in extolling the virtues of New England. "I only regret," the senator gushed, "that the intrusion of my name, probably in ways which you did not entirely intend took away some of the attention from the man who really deserved it—Robert Frost."[24]

Frost's absence from Vermont prevented him from voting for Kennedy in 1960, but after visiting his good friend Stewart Udall, soon to be the new interior secretary, Frost sent a telegram to the president-elect that began: "GREAT DAYS FOR BOSTON, DEMOCRACY, THE PURITANS AND THE IRISH." Reflecting his elation at Udall's appointment, he added, "YOUR APPOINTMENT OF STEWART UDALL OF AN OLD VERMONT RELIGION [Udall was a Mormon] RECONCILES ME ONCE FOR ALL TO THE PARTY I WAS BORN INTO."[25]

The poet was forty-three years older than the president—in fact, he was a contemporary of Kennedy's grandfather—but the two developed a rapport. At the behest of Udall, Kennedy floated the idea of Frost delivering a poem at the inaugural ceremony. On December 13, less than two weeks after Frost's telegram, Kennedy formally invited him.[26]

The next day, Frost accepted. His telegram read: "I MAY NOT BE EQUAL TO IT BUT I CAN ACCEPT IT FOR MY CAUSE—THE ARTS, POETRY, NOW FOR THE FIRST TIME TAKEN INTO THE AFFAIRS OF STATESMEN."[27] The poet and the president talked about the poem, Kennedy suggested something new, while Frost demurred. Kennedy then asked about "The Gift Outright," a poem originally composed in 1935 but not made public until six years later—though he asked for a minor revision.[28]

Frost did come up with a new poem, "Dedication," but the conditions at the podium forced him to revert to "The Gift Outright," which he knew by heart. Frost's performance was a huge success, despite his bumbling, and it had the effect of boosting the aged poet's popularity. "Frost's fame penetrated to a new level," his friend Harold Curtiss said. "People on the street suddenly recognized him. He could no longer go into a restaurant without someone asking for his autograph or wanting to shake his hand."[29]

Before leaving Washington after the inauguration, Frost visited the president and provided some counsel: "Be more Irish than Harvard. Poetry and power is the formula for another Augustan Age. Don't be afraid of power."[30] Kennedy wrote at least two letters to Frost in the next few months, one congratulating him on being named to a prestigious lectureship at the Hebrew University in Jerusalem, and the other thanking him for sending copies of the inaugural poem.[31]

Then one month before the Nobel dinner, President Kennedy attended a ceremony in the White House in which Frost was presented with a gold medal authorized by Congress. The president said in very brief remarks, "We are proud of Mr. Frost and his interpretations of what we feel is the best of America. And therefore I present this award to our very good friend."[32]

Later this evening, Frost would be honored by being part of a small, select group that would convene in the Yellow Oval Room with President and Mrs. Kennedy. And that summer, the president would dispatch America's leading poet to the Soviet Union on a special mission. More about that later.

○═══◦─

Muriel Barnett Beadle had traveled to the dinner with her husband, George Wells Beadle, the chancellor of the University of Chicago. Muriel Beadle had something in common with Mary Hemingway: she was a writer and former newspaper reporter. Now, at forty-six years, she had moved from the fashion and women's desk at the *Los Angeles Mirror* to writing books. Her first book, published the previous year, was a light account of the couple's time at Oxford University. She went on to write a number of books in several fields.[33] The *Chicago Tribune* called her "an amusing, shrewd and observant writer."[34]

Dr. Beadle, who was seated at the next table hosted by Lady Bird Johnson, was a geneticist who had won the Nobel Prize for Physiology or Medicine in 1958. Like so many others at tonight's dinner, "Beets" Beadle had taught at Caltech, only assuming his administrative position at the University of Chicago the previous year.[35]

Muriel Beadle was seated next to the final guest at the president's table, Dr. Rudolph L. Mossbauer, a German-born physicist whose time briefly overlapped the Beadles' at Caltech. At thirty-three he was a 1961 Nobel co-awardee in physics, and as such he joined Lilla Jarring, seated directly across from him, at the predinner conversation with the president. Like Dr. Anderson, Dr. Mossbauer worked on gamma rays. He was responsible for identifying the Mossbauer effect, which deals with gamma ray absorption.

Dr. Mossbauer and his wife, Elisabeth Pritz Mossbauer, had an unusual and humorous encounter as they were joining the president in the Yellow Oval Room before dinner. It seems they were unable to catch the White House elevator, as it kept going up and down. Then they spotted four-year-old Caroline Kennedy playfully operating the elevator.[36]

Now Mrs. Mossbauer sat in the Blue Room at the table hosted by Attorney General Robert Kennedy. The Mossbauers were arguably sitting with the two most powerful political figures at the dinner, the Kennedy brothers, and neither of the Mossbauers was an American citizen. Of the Nobel Prize winners at the dinner tonight, three were not Americans, and two of those—Leger and Mossbauer—were at the same table with the president.

⊂═⊷

As the president surveyed his table and those throughout the State Dining Room, he could be satisfied that he, his wife, and their staff had brought together an impressive—perhaps unprecedented—array of scientific and literary minds. And although the gold-colored wooden chairs with four interior spindles at the back may not have been as comfortable as desired for his persistently painful lumbar area, he was relaxed and refreshed after returning from his Easter vacation in Palm Beach, Florida. It promised to be an enjoyable evening.

He had been president for fifteen months. This was an eventful period. In the soaring eloquence of his inaugural address, he had said, "Let every nation know, whether it wishes us well or ill, that we shall pay any price, bear any burden, meet any hardship, support any friend, oppose any foe to assure the survival and the success of liberty."

Dick Goodwin, the Kennedy aide who had helped plan the dinner this evening, was among those who were inspired and had high hopes. "As I stood in that bitter-cold, iridescent day—sun glistening from the marble, the snow scattered from the unobstructed heaven—it seemed as if the country and I were poised for a journey of limitless possibility," Goodwin recalled.[37]

But even the new president recognized the magnitude of the task ahead of him. In his first State of the Union address, only ten days into his presidency, he said: "Life in 1961 will not be easy. Wishing it, predicting it, even asking for it, will not make it so. There will be further setbacks before the tide is turned."[38] He was right: the first year was challenging. In April 1961 Kennedy sought to implement a muscular Western Hemisphere policy when he approved the Bay of Pigs invasion in Cuba, which was planned by his predecessor. But in the end, he was unwilling to live up to the rhetoric, as the United States reneged on its commitment to the rebels. The president, embarrassed by the ensuing fiasco, was forced to shoulder the blame, saying, "There's an old saying that victory has 100 fathers and defeat is an orphan."[39]

There had been other foreign policy worries. The United States was slowly becoming engaged in the war in Vietnam, as the new administration continued a mindset from the previous administration that a domino theory in Asia was, indeed, something to consider.

But the biggest challenges came in Europe and with the Soviet Union. During a disastrous summit in Vienna with Soviet premier Nikita Khrushchev in June 1961, the Russian leader tested and then upstaged the new president. Two months later, the Berlin Wall was erected, precipitating a crisis of superpowers reminiscent of the blockade and airlift of the late 1940s. Added to this was the Soviet resumption of nuclear tests.

In America, racial tensions continued in the South, particularly in Alabama. Especially troublesome were the attacks on the Freedom Riders, a biracial group from the North seeking to integrate buses. One of the few bright spots for the new administration in 1961 was astronaut Alan Shepard's space launch, allowing the United States to begin to catch up with the Soviets in the Space Race.

By the end of the first year of the Kennedy administration, the promise was great but the accomplishments were few. One skeptical journalist, writing in the *American Scholar*, commented on the concept of the New Frontier, saying, "The phrase, with its implicit suggestion of dramatic initiatives and a sharp break with the past, arouses false hopes and distracts attention from both the problems the new Administration faces and the way in which it proposes to meet them."[40]

The second year began to show more potential, beginning with the First Lady's televised White House tour. While this event had nothing to do with public policy, it provided a valuable public relations boost. Mrs. Kennedy personally captivated the nation while unveiling a White House that allowed more people than ever before to connect with this symbol of American democracy.

And then in February, John Glenn orbited the earth, the first American ever to do so. Glenn instantly became a national hero and, shortly after, a Kennedy family friend. He sat at Mrs. Kennedy's table tonight.

Despite these bright spots, the president encountered two recent challenges, one foreign and one domestic. The foreign policy issue was the renewal of us atomic testing in the Pacific, the situation that had prompted demonstrations and caused Linus Pauling to picket the White House before tonight's dinner.

The domestic challenge was United States Steel Corporation—then a heavy manufacturing powerhouse—boosting the price of its product. While such an action might seem newsworthy but not calamitous today, the president saw it differently in 1962. At an April 11 news conference, he said, "If this rise in the cost of steel is imitated by the rest of the industry, instead of rescinded, it would increase the cost of homes, autos, appliances, and most other items for every American family. It would increase the cost of machinery and tools to every American businessman and farmer."[41]

And there were other implications. "It would add," he said, "an estimated $1 billion to the cost of our defenses, at a time when every dollar is needed for national security and other purposes."[42] The president stewed: "My father always told me that all businessmen were sons of bitches, but I never believed it until now." He said this privately, but the comment soon became public.[43]

Although the profane comment was quickly met with anti-Kennedy political buttons saying "S.O.B. Club," US Steel quickly gave in to the president's aggressive response and rolled back the increase.[44]

With that crisis resolved, the president and First Lady left on April 18 for a nine-day Easter vacation in Palm Beach. He returned on Friday, two days before the dinner, tan and rested. Since then his schedule had been light. He met with baseball slugger Roger Maris, held meetings with Prime Minister Macmillan, and attended the White House Correspondents and News Photographers Association dinner at the Sheraton-Park Hotel with Macmillan in attendance and Benny Goodman entertaining.[45] At the Friday night event, the president couldn't avoid poking fun at his steel industry adversaries. Speaking of the several performers present, he said, "I have arranged for them to appear next week on the United States Steel Hour! [a popular, long-running television series of the time]."[46]

⌐⛧⊸

If the president was looking forward to a relaxing night with the Nobel laureates, he surely did not reckon on the prospect of that enjoyment being constrained by the woman on his right at dinner, Mary Hemingway. They had not previously met, but as their mutual friend Bill Walton noted, "They did know about each other and they were terribly interested in each other."[47]

The keeper of Ernest's flame surely appreciated the gracious gestures that the president had made toward her late husband. But there was a problem, and it was Cuba. She had lived with Ernest in Cuba for years, and was not pleased with the president's policy.

Soon after the table introductions were made and everyone was settled, Mary recounts, "I suggested to our host that the US government's position toward Cuba was stupid, unrealistic, and worse, ineffective, especially—sotto voce—since the Bay of Pigs fiasco."[48]

The president had not expected this assault. He fidgeted with his tie. Mary Hemingway said he was "looking irked and impatient." The president tried to shift his attention to Katherine Marshall, but Mary continued: "I could jump into Cuba, you know," she told him. "The Cubans liked my husband, and I know Fidel."[49]

In fact, Ernest loved Cuba, where he had lived off and on from 1940 until his death. He was well respected there, and the Cubans all knew his book-lined home—"Finca Vigia"—outside of Havana. Following a brief absence shortly after the revolution, he was warmly greeted by Cubans at the airport, where he kissed the blue, white, and red flag.[50]

Ernest was elated by the departure of Cuban dictator Fulgencio Batista, who was forced to flee in the early morning hours of January 1, 1959. Wishing Castro well, Hemingway said, "The Cuban people now have a decent chance for the first time ever."[51]

But the US government was cool and then hostile to the new regime; this was the policy of the Eisenhower administration and, now, Kennedy. President Kennedy was not interested in discussing a change in Cuban policy tonight or in offering an olive branch to the communist leader. He tried to pivot away from the topic. "Have you read Katherine Anne Porter's *Ship of Fools?*" he asked. The author, whose book was the literary work of the moment, sat a few tables away, next to Ernest's onetime friend Dos Passos. Mary said that she hadn't read the book, and then persisted, "If I talked to Fidel . . . "

"You are rated politically unreliable," the president snapped. "You haven't checked M.I. 5," Mrs. Hemingway replied.[52]

This conversation was going nowhere. In fact, the president later called Bill Walton at home to complain, "Well, your friend Mary Hemingway is the biggest bore I've had for a long time." He added that "she never cracked a smile or a joke." And, "If I hadn't had Mrs. Marshall, I would have had a terrible night." What the president didn't know, Walton recalled, was that she was there with Walton when the call came; she was a guest at his house on P Street.[53]

Reflecting on all this years later, Walton conceded that "she bombed like mad." But he said, "I think she was just out of her mind nervous. She'd been a widow about a year then and she was not used to this. It was really too much for her."[54]

The president's discomfort didn't affect her, as she explained in her memoir: "I had never been a knee-deep member of any political party." An outspoken and fiercely independent person, she might actually have been even more agitated to learn that Dick Goodwin had asked the FBI to check out the honored guests. No problem, the FBI, reported—we already have.[55]

The most important part of the evening for Mary Hemingway would be the introduction of an unpublished work of Ernest's as the main part of March's presentation. Despite whatever disagreement she might have had with the president's policy, she was not hostile to him personally. A few years later, she presented the Ernest Hemingway Personal Papers, a great literary trove, to the new John F. Kennedy Presidential Library and Museum.

There were, of course, other conversations at table seven as the meal progressed. Mary Hemingway asked Dr. Anderson a question that may have crossed the minds of others that night: "If an enemy were to bomb this room at this moment, how much, do you think, of our technological knowledge would be lost?"[56]

Dr. Anderson had an easy answer: relatively little. "As you may have observed," he said, "most of us fellows here are elders. All those young scientists, working away in our laboratories, already know what we learned; they'll go forward with their research."[57]

Meanwhile, Katherine Marshall kept the conversation on a much lighter note, certainly offering a counterpoint to Mary Hemingway: "Oh, Mr. President, you don't have to worry a thing about me. I'm so happy to be out of my briar patch."[58] With years as the wife of a military man and public official, she knew when to be diplomatic.

❦

Despite the exquisite meal and the many conversations, both lively and sometimes uncomfortable—as well as routine small talk, the highlight of the dinner came when the president rose at his table to deliver his remarks. The original comments, prepared by Arthur Schlesinger, were dry and more of a testimonial to Alfred Nobel.

This first draft focused on Nobel and ended with a three-paragraph toast, quoting Benjamin Franklin. The final, delivered remarks added humor and introduced another Enlightenment thinker, Thomas Jefferson, to the discussion.

As the president stood at the table, he was handed a long, fixed microphone by a member of the White House domestic staff. His remarks were heard in the State Dining Room and broadcast into the adjacent Blue Room. He began by referring to Lester Pearson, who was seated next to the First Lady. The Canadian leader and Nobel laureate, he said, "informed me that a Canadian newspaperman said yesterday that this is the President's 'Easter egg-head roll on the White House lawn.' I want to deny that."

The audience laughed, and he moved on to the most memorable line of the evening—indeed, the comment that most people who know of this dinner readily recall. He said, "I think this is the most extraordinary collection of talent, of human knowledge, that has ever been gathered together at the White House, with the possible exception of when Thomas Jefferson dined alone." The president was emphatic about the importance of the dinner. "I regard this as the most distinguished and significant dinner that we have had in the White House since I have been here, and I think in many, many years," he said.

While the reference to Jefferson dining alone was an intriguing statement and has often been cited in subsequent years, the premise is faulty. The fact is that the third president rarely dined alone. He was quite social and regularly invited members of Congress, their wives, and others to the executive mansion. He was actively engaged in planning the dinners and, in fact, kept a running guest list.[59]

But the Jefferson allusion was well received. President Kennedy then went on to talk about the great success that had been achieved by researchers, writers, and peacemakers from the Western Hemisphere and how their many advances had been justly rewarded by so many Nobel prizes. The eleven-paragraph remarks, which ended with a toast, included a hope that young people in the United States and the hemisphere would be encouraged by these men and women of such accomplishment.[60]

There was still much more of the evening to enjoy, including the literary program provided by Fredric March. For a select few, including Robert Frost, the conversation would continue in that informal gathering in the private residence. For those at the president's table, the evening was a once-in-a-lifetime event. But it also was turning into an amazing evening for many others, with so many gifted people meeting and sharing in conversations throughout the State Dining Room and the Blue Room. For a number of them, this night would have important implications for the future.

## CHAPTER FOUR ⟨⟨⟩⟩

# America's Queen and
# America's Hero

THIRTY-YEAR-OLD CLINT HILL, the agent in charge of the Secret Service detail for Mrs. Kennedy, was routinely assigned to watch over her at state and formal dinners. Hill, who had joined the elite service four years earlier, was initially disappointed to be assigned to this detail. He had worked directly for President Eisenhower, visited four continents with him, and experienced events that a boy from rural North Dakota could only dream about. He believed that he worked at the heart of the American government.

But as soon as the election was decided, he was called into the office of Urbanus Edmund ("U. E.") Baughman, the longtime head of the Secret Service, to be told of his new assignment: the First Lady's detail. His initial reaction: "Why me?" Considering it a comedown, with visions of attending meaningless tea parties, he had a strong reaction: "I was devastated."[1]

Three days after the election, on November 11, 1960, Hill visited the president-elect and Mrs. Kennedy at their home located at 3307 N Street in the Georgetown section of the nation's capital. He quickly realized that a new era had dawned, but could not anticipate what it would mean. "None of us realized it at the time, but we were being swept into Camelot," he recalled.[2] And his life would never be the same.

The past sixteen months had been a whirlwind for Hill. He had traveled with the Kennedys on their triumphant visit to France and Mrs. Kennedy's excursion to Greece. He saw his first ballet, and he played touch football with the Kennedy family at Hyannis Port. And one month ago, Hill had returned from a successful trip that the First Lady undertook to India and Pakistan, with a few other brief stops in Europe and the Middle East.

By the end of the trip, this once skeptical agent was won over by Mrs. Kennedy. Sitting with her, he later recounted that he wanted to tell her, "Everything you do impresses me. The way you handle yourself with such grace and dignity without compromising your desire to enjoy life and have fun. You don't even realize the impact you have, how much you are admired. . . . Just by being yourself. No politics. No phoniness. Just you being you."[3]

By April 1962, millions of Americans were captivated by the glamorous, thirty-two-year-old First Lady. Using the Secret Service code names, so too was agent Hill, known as "Dazzle," as he watched over "Lace."[4] Her story was unique among American First Ladies.

⚬━⥤

Jacqueline Lee Bouvier, like her husband, grew up as a Catholic in a socially prominent family. As a youth, she attended balls, loved riding horses, and developed an enjoyment of history and languages, especially French. Her childhood was also marked by family financial challenges and by the excesses of her father, John Vernou "Black Jack" Bouvier. Her parents divorced in 1940 when she was eleven years old, but she still had the trappings of an upper-class life: attendance at New York's prestigious Chapin School; Holton-Arms School in Bethesda, Maryland; Miss Porter's School in Farmington, Connecticut; and then on to Vassar College, one of the Seven Sisters elite women's colleges, located in Poughkeepsie, New York.

The nation caught its first glimpse of her when she had just turned twenty-four. In July 1953, one month after her engagement to the eligible Massachusetts senator, she landed on the cover of *Life* magazine. The photo, taken by Hy Peskin and destined to become an iconic image, showed the happy couple perched on Kennedy's beloved twenty-six-foot sailboat, *Victura*.[5] The weekly magazine was at the height of its popularity, and its millions of readers were given a foretaste of the vast amount of media attention that Jacqueline Kennedy would attract over more than forty years.

Less than two months later, on September 12, one of the most spectacular fairy-tale weddings in twentieth-century America took place in Newport, Rhode Island. Eight hundred guests attended the wedding Mass at St. Mary's Roman Catholic Church; hundreds of others waited outside. Twelve hundred guests, literally a "who's who" of politics and society, participated in the reception at the bride's stepfather's estate, Hammersmith Farm. A photograph of the newlyweds appeared in the *New York Times* the following day: not in the Sunday society pages, but on the front page. "The ceremony far surpassed the [spectacular] Astor-French wedding of 1934 in public interest," the accompanying article said.[6]

While the young couple received print and broadcast attention over the next several years, the beginning of the intense interest came during the 1960 presidential election campaign. Mrs. Kennedy was really introduced to the nation over three stages: the campaign and the gala inauguration; her trips abroad, which showed her to have an international following; and the widely watched White House tour two months before the April 29 dinner.

She was rapidly becoming what today would be considered a superstar, in some ways surpassing her husband, who despite his charisma and wit remained a political figure. When the First Couple visited France in June 1961, the president said in jest but with some significance: "I am the man who accompanied Jacqueline Kennedy to Paris."[7] The First Lady's hairstyle, clothes, and even the naming of newborns "Jacqueline" were some of the manifestations of her rapidly growing popularity. Not surprisingly, she became the most admired woman in America in 1962, supplanting humanitarian and former First Lady Eleanor Roosevelt.[8]

Looking back over more than a half century, how can this phenomenon be explained? Certainly, there was youth and glamour, especially in marked contrast to recent First Ladies. Bess Truman was sixty years old and Mamie Eisenhower was fifty-six years old when their husbands became president. Neither was especially fashion conscious.

Nor were these postwar First Ladies college educated. In contrast, Mrs. Kennedy had studied at Vassar, spent a year at the Sorbonne in Paris, and received an undergraduate degree from The George Washington University, located only a few blocks from the White House. She loved languages, art, literature, and history. She also was a writer, artist, and photographer. She had traveled extensively as a young woman and developed a certain sense of worldliness at an early age. Remarking about a trip to Europe in 1948, a friend and fellow traveler remarked, "Jackie had taken her education seriously. She had learned and memorized her European history beforehand, and read more than guidebooks. . . . Young, educated, and interested, but it was more than preparing because we were there, she wanted to know even more."[9]

Miss Porter's School in Farmington, Connecticut, which the future Mrs. Kennedy attended for three years in the 1940s, was then a finishing school for upper-class girls. Manners were an important element in molding a young woman. Her classmate there and later White House social secretary Tish Baldrige commented on her "beautiful manners, posture, and grace of carriage," all traits that the school would take pride in promoting.[10]

In sum, Jackie Kennedy was a determined, multitalented woman who reflected quiet elegance. But her popular image as a vibrant role model certainly was enhanced by having two very young children, a first since Grover and Frances Cleveland welcomed a daughter to the White House in 1893.[11] And despite these attributes and personal status, a great deal of Mrs. Kennedy's popularity rested on her being the first presidential spouse to be highlighted on, as well as use, the growing medium of television. She was extremely photogenic, just like her husband, and could employ her strengths to attract a wide audience of followers. Her status as a celebrity was greatly enhanced by her recent televised White House appearance. Indeed, it elevated her to the status of a queen in the minds of many Americans.

⊂═⊷

Even a queen has a public and private persona. And that was the case with Jacqueline Kennedy. Whereas the First Lady exhibited a strong and engaging presence, the wife and mother was more guarded, as demonstrated by her curt but amusing response to Linus Pauling in the reception line this evening when she scolded him for picketing the White House and upsetting four-year-old Caroline.

She was keenly aware of the national and international spotlight, and by and large, she adapted herself. But listening to the oral history interviews she did with Arthur Schlesinger in 1964, she does not hold back in her criticism of some of the leading people of the day. She said that "Martin Luther King is a really tricky person" and "a phony"; she was annoyed about his "orgies"; and she was upset with what she called his joking about the president's funeral and saying that Cardinal Richard Cushing "was drunk at it."[12]

Mrs. Kennedy also repeated columnist Joe Alsop's dim view of her husband's predecessor: "'Eisenhower would be the worst president of the United States with the possible exception of James Buchanan.'" She was critical of both President and Mrs. Eisenhower.[13]

She also grew weary of Tish Baldrige, who worked with her in planning this dinner and many other social engagements. In addition to pushing her too hard with the media and giving her a barrage of folders of papers, Baldrige fell prey to what Mrs. Kennedy called "White House-itis," self-absorption in the mystique of serving at the most important address in the nation. "Tish," she said, "loved to pick up the phone and have 'White House calling' or 'Send all the White House china on the plane to Costa Rica' or tell them that they had to fly string beans in to a state dinner." This syndrome was a big deal to the First Lady, calling it "The Poison of the Presidency."[14] Despite her demure image, Jacqueline Kennedy had an independent intelligence and made up her own mind.

Of course, candid views on friends and foes are not unusual for people, whether for those in the public arena or not. Mrs. Kennedy, however, was a complex figure, much different at times from what the media reported on and promoted as "Jackie." Pearl Buck, who sat across the table from her at the Nobel dinner, said, "She is, of course, an enigma, and totally unpredictable." She went on to add presidential pal and assistant David Powers' assessment: "Just when you are sure you know her, be careful."[15] And J. B. West, who worked closely with her as chief usher—and had served at the White House since 1941—compared her to previous First Ladies, saying she "had the most complex personality of them all."[16] At the dinner tonight, examples of this would be seen, as she was quiet and reserved during the meal but gregarious and fun loving in the smaller setting afterward.

How much of her upbringing accounted for her complicated nature, only she knew. While she had all the trappings of an upper-class upbringing, her family life was challenging. She adored her father, who was a philandering, unstable alcoholic. The family had financial difficulties that were much improved by her mother's remarriage. The relationship between her mother and father after their divorce in 1940 was acrimonious.[17] Pearl Buck, who later studied her family history, said, "Jacqueline grew up with her heart torn in three directions, her father and the Bouviers, her mother, her stepfather."[18]

Perhaps not surprisingly she was guarded about her public role, saying, "I can't stand being out front. I know it sounds trite, but what I really want is to be behind him [President Kennedy] and to be a good wife and mother. I have no desire to be a public personality on my own."[19]

Mrs. Kennedy did not have many close friends. Perhaps her closest confidante was her younger sister, socialite Lee Radziwill. She had a good, but not close, relationship with her husband's siblings, although her bond with Robert Kennedy was strong. Many of the people with whom she interacted during the White House years were men from the art world, who assisted with her restoration project.[20]

For those who did know or had met her, what stood out in addition to her intelligence and determination was her quiet voice—sometimes almost a whisper—and her wit and sense of fun. J. B. West recalled, "Relaxed and uninhibited, she was always popping up anywhere, wearing slacks, sitting on the floor, kicking off her shoes, her hair flying in every direction. We all had fun along with her."[21]

Even the ever-professional Secret Service agent Clint Hill was brought into the web of fun. Recounting a trip to the Kennedy house in Middleburg, Virginia, he remembers how she asked him to join her in the back seat of the car to sneak a cigarette. "She was like a giddy teenager," he said, "who was getting away with something, and I was her cohort in crime." This became a standard practice.[22]

⌐═✦⌐

Mrs. Kennedy could be playful, but she was very serious about her role in upgrading the White House and making it a historic and beautiful mansion that stirred pride in Americans. Her interest stemmed from a visit to the White House as an eleven-year-old on an Easter vacation. "From the outside," she said, "I remember the feeling of the place. But inside, all I remember is shuffling through." When she visited in the 1950s when her husband was a senator, she was struck by the "interior remoteness."[23] Her priority, her "project," as First Lady would be to enhance the 160-year-old executive mansion and to add the artwork and furniture to return it to an earlier, original appearance and make it a world-class living museum.

One of those rooms, an original one built by James Hoban, was the Blue Room, where she was now serving as the hostess. The thirty-by-forty-foot oval room has six doorways. This room had been used mostly for weddings—President Grover Cleveland was married here—and for receptions. Once red, the chamber was painted blue during the Van Buren presidency and had shown various shades of the color ever since.[24] At one time this room served as an entrance to the White House.

During her television documentary, Mrs. Kennedy said of the room, "It's the most formal room in the White House. It's really not used for anything except for receiving lines, so all it needs is a table and some beautiful chairs, more to look at than to sit in."[25] One use during the Kennedy years was to place the principal White House Christmas tree here.[26] But tonight, for the largest dinner of the Kennedy years, it was pressed into service as the second dining room. Five tables were set up, surrounded by the same stiff, gilded chairs also being used in the nearby State Dining Room.

In addition to its distinctive color, the Blue Room is easily identified by its French Empire appearance, a European style of the early nineteenth century. In the aftermath of the War of 1812, President Monroe rehabilitated the damaged White House and surreptitiously—to avoid political criticism—added furnishings from Europe.[27] Some of the key pieces landed in the Blue Room, and the recent restoration reflected its appearance during the Monroe presidency.[28]

In considering how to go about restoring the White House, Mrs. Kennedy said, "When I first moved into the White House, I thought, I wish I could be married to Thomas Jefferson because he would know best what should be done to it."[29]

In the end, she had to settle for guidance from the Fine Arts Committee, which she assembled and which was chaired by Henry Francis du Pont. She also relied heavily on the noted French designer Stéphane Boudin. She later said, "I learned more about architecture from Boudin than from all the books I could have read."[30]

But interestingly, the impetus for restoring the Blue Room came to Mrs. Kennedy from reading an article in *Gazettes des Beaux Arts,* a monthly French art magazine, from 1946.[31] And so with her arts committee searching for antiques and cajoling donations, and with her working directly with Boudin, the Blue Room was returned to its earlier period style. Among the gems, which this night's guests were able to admire, was a gilded pier table highlighted by numerous carved olive branches and a mirrored back. It was created by Pierre-Antoine Bellange in approximately 1817.[32] Amazingly, the table had been turned into a sawhorse in a White House carpentry shop before being recovered. Atop the table is a somewhat crude bust of George Washington reminiscent of Caesar, which was done by Giuseppe Ceracchi, an eighteenth-century Italian neoclassical sculptor. It was rediscovered by Mrs. Kennedy's art sleuths in a White House men's room.[33]

The table and bust were now positioned where Monroe had placed them. Above them is a full-length portrait of George Washington in military uniform. The 82-inch by 57-$^{15}/_{16}$-inch painting was done by Ecuadorian Luis Leonardo Cadena in 1877 and was a gift from the Republic of Ecuador. The painting, table, and bust were set between two doors, which led into the similarly impressive Red Room, another parlor.

Also prominent in the room is a nineteenth-century cut-glass and gilded-wood French chandelier and blue silk drapes and valences. A Louis Moinet gilded mantel clock of the Roman goddess Minerva was another original purchase made by Monroe.

Among the other paintings in the room are Rembrandt Peale's famous 1800 portrait of Thomas Jefferson and a portrait of James Monroe by the artist and inventor of the telegraph, Samuel F. B. Morse. When the room was completed, Mrs. Kennedy was initially overwhelmed by its appearance, but later she called it "Boudin's masterpiece" and applauded the resultant "sense of state, ceremony, arrival and grandeur."[34]

Tonight, the First Lady would be showing off the new Blue Room to an important group of guests. The art connoisseur would be the hostess for that next several hours; she was equally adept at fulfilling both roles. Tish Baldrige said of her boss, "She knew how to receive guests, and how to make conversation with princes, ambassadors, and potentates of all kinds when they came to call on her family."[35]

⊙━⊷

Jackie Kennedy's turn as First Lady came at just the right time. This was the era of the Washington salon. Since the end of World War II and in the years in which the United States was claiming its role as a global leader, powerbrokers were meeting in the nation's capital to discuss the great issues of the day in intimate settings. Many of these dinner parties took place in Georgetown, about two miles from the White House. The participants were government officials, journalists, thinkers, and socialites. This was, in many ways, the epicenter of the postwar Establishment.[36]

Many of these elite opinion makers lived only blocks from one another. Among them were the Alsop brothers, Joe and Stewart, both influential columnists; former secretary of state Dean Acheson; diplomats Averell Harriman, Charles "Chip" Bohlen, and George Kennan—all deeply immersed in the Cold War and the geopolitical combat with the Soviet Union; *Washington Post* publisher Philip Graham and his wife, Katherine; and editor Ben Bradlee, then at *Newsweek* and soon to become a legend at the *Post*.

Looking back, the writer Gregg Herken referred to these people as the "Georgetown Set," and John and Jackie Kennedy were part of it. So much so that when the official inaugural events ended on the early morning of January 21, 1961, the new president capped off the momentous day by visiting Joe Alsop for food and a nightcap.[37]

Neither President Truman nor President Eisenhower was part of this group. But with the elevation of one of their own members to the presidency, it ensured that these intellectuals and their views would be represented in the White House. As Katherine Graham, who had become friendly with Senator John Kennedy in the 1950s as a result of parties and dinners, said, "There is a thrill to knowing someone of your generation who runs for, and actually becomes, president."[38] In fact, Graham, who would become a dominant powerbroker in the years after her husband's death in 1963, said of her social circle on Inauguration Day: "Everyone was a little delirious with excitement."[39]

A biographer of the Alsop brothers added, "There was a new spirit in the city, a political and social ferment, as well as the prospect of imaginative leadership in the executive branch. Georgetown was once again fashionable."[40]

In retrospect, the years of the New Frontier may have been the final gasp of a wealthy, well-educated Eastern elite. But for three years the concept of a refined salon, attracting some of the brightest American minds, reached its apogee. And the impresario, the madame of the soirée writ large, was Jacqueline Bouvier Kennedy. Her salon was the most famous address in the nation.

☞⸙⸜

One-third of tonight's dinner guests, fifty of them, had been escorted by several well-groomed, white-gloved social aides to the Blue Room this evening. If any of them were disappointed by not being in the same room for dinner with the president, they were quickly elated to see Mrs. Kennedy hosting the center table, one of five round tables. As they entered, they could glance at the antiques and paintings and admire the white fireplace, flanked by Louis XVI andirons, and the mantel, which was installed in 1902. They could also peer out one of three windows that faced the South Lawn.

Vice President Johnson was hosting another table, next to the one with Attorney General Robert Kennedy. Peering to his left, the president's younger brother could keep his foe in sight, should he be interested in doing so. But all eyes were on Mrs. Kennedy and the star-studded group that was assembled with her.

There at what social secretary Tish Baldrige identified as table seventeen for the event, Mrs. Kennedy was joined by five men and four women, each of whom was notable in their own field. But especially well known were Pearl Buck, the only female Nobel laureate present; Lester Pearson, the Canadian Liberal Party leader; and Fredric March, the actor who would be the presenter of this evening's literary entertainment. Their table—as well as the other tables in the Blue Room—was set similarly to those in the State Dining Room with two exceptions: the dinner service was the china with a golden corn motif with a thick blue border and an eagle in the center from the Benjamin Harrison presidency, and the cushions on the gold-backed chairs were blue.

The most notable of the guests at Mrs. Kennedy's table, perhaps equaling the star power of the First Lady at this moment, was astronaut John Glenn. He was clearly the American hero of the hour. Glenn, the photogenic crew-cut Marine lieutenant colonel, had captivated the nation with his orbit of the Earth two months before. His Mercury flight took him around the globe three times in a little under five hours; that was enough to raise him up to a level of instant-hero frenzy not seen since Charles Lindbergh's solo transatlantic flight thirty-five years before. Indeed, Glenn later said of Lucky Lindy, "I couldn't say why, but he inspired in me a feeling of kinship."[41]

Glenn's splashdown near Grand Turk Island in the Caribbean on February 20 set off a round of celebration. Three days later, he and Annie Glenn met with President Kennedy at Cape Canaveral, where the astronaut received NASA's Distinguished Service Medal and the president examined the recovered Friendship 7 capsule, which was less than seven feet long. He and the president rode together in a parade at Cocoa Beach, Florida. Glenn went on to Washington, DC, where there were more commemorations, including an address to Congress and a parade. The fanfare then shifted to New York City, where a ticker-tape parade on March 1 attracted four million people.

Very quickly Glenn forged a relationship with the Kennedys, the president and First Lady as well as Robert and Ethel Kennedy. By the summer, the Glenns would be joining in the frivolity at Hickory Hill parties and go water-skiing with Jackie Kennedy at Hyannis Port. The link between the Glenns and Kennedys, especially Robert and Ethel, would grow so rapidly that one enterprising novelty manufacturer issued a political button which yoked the Kennedy administration to the astronaut, identifying the astronaut as "The New Frontier Man of the Year."

There would be many happy and sad times that the two families would share over the next half century. But tonight was at the beginning of that relationship.

What the Kennedys, the country, and indeed the world were learning was that John Herschel Glenn Jr. embodied the "right stuff" which seemed to exemplify the virtues of small-town America. He was raised in New Concord, Ohio, a town in eastern Ohio of approximately one thousand people in the 1920s. Glenn would speak with pride of his hometown, stressing its patriotism and the residents' sense of duty. "Love of country was a given. Defense of its ideals was an obligation. The opportunity to join in its quests and explorations was a challenge not only to fulfill a sacred duty, but to join a joyous adventure," he recalled.[42]

New Concord, he said, "formed my beliefs and my sense of responsibility. Everything that came after that just seemed to follow naturally." He could have added that he was also a humble and religious man.[43]

He attended Muskingum College in his hometown. At the beginning of

World War II, Glenn, like John F. Kennedy and millions of other men, volunteered for military service after the Japanese attack on Pearl Harbor. He also married his childhood sweetheart, Annie Castor, who was seated tonight at the next table beside Vice President Johnson. He entered the Navy, soon became a Marine, fought as a combat pilot in World War II, and compiled an even more notable record in the Korean War; in the two wars he flew 140 combat missions. Not surprising, he was heavily decorated for his service.[44]

Glenn understood that a cross section of service experience would help his advancement in the Marines; and after the Korean War, at age thirty-two, he became a test pilot.[45]

In the wake of the Sputnik shock in 1957 and with the heightened concern that the bitter Cold War rivalry needed to be taken to the heavens, the National Aeronautics and Space Administration (NASA) was created the following year. While the stated purpose of the NASA legislation was peaceful and scientific, there was no question of the strategic implications.[46] Glenn, now with extensive experience testing planes such as the F7U Cutlass, F8U Crusader, and FJ-3 Fury, became interested in joining a new class of space explorers, the astronauts.

On the same day that the great architect Frank Lloyd Wright died, April 9, 1959, the country was abuzz with the announcement of the seven service pilots who would become the backbone of Project Mercury. Glenn, at thirty-seven, was the oldest, but all the men were in their thirties. Sporting a bow tie and grin, he joined his colleagues in a photo that appeared on the front page of the *New York Times*, as well as elsewhere throughout the nation.[47]

At the news conference, Glenn joked that Annie Glenn had suggested "that I have been out of this world for a long time and might as well go on out farther." Trite, of course, but Americans were mesmerized by all these men. They embodied a spirit of purpose that perhaps had lain dormant in the nation since the end of World War II. They wanted to push forward, as Colonel Glenn said at the time, and as a test pilot he was always challenging himself "to keep on going out."[48]

The honor of being the first American in space went to Alan Shepard, a navy commander and a test-pilot colleague of Glenn's. Shepard's flight in May 1961 lasted only fifteen minutes, but Americans had now entered space, matching a launch by Soviet cosmonaut Yuri Gagarin the previous month. In July

1961, Virgil "Gus" Grissom doubled Shepard's time aloft, and the stage was set for the first orbital flight.

Shortly after Thanksgiving in 1961, NASA announced that Glenn would take the program to its next level. Befitting a man with such extensive combat and test-pilot experience, he was ready—and fearless. "When you get educated you are no longer fearful," he said. "In this field, there are only a handful who understand—and they are not fearful."[49]

And now America's most famous astronaut, America's latest hero, was continuing to bask—albeit humbly—in the aftermath of that landmark flight of only two months before. It was appropriate that he would be here tonight with the nation's greatest achievers and enjoy the evening sitting at the table of America's reigning queen.

⌇

Among those starstruck with the green-eyed, five-foot-ten-inch astronaut was the elderly woman seated at his right, Pearl Buck. "I had very much wanted to meet" him, she said, "and I fear my dinner conversation was mainly with him."[50] Glenn was fortunate as well. Miss Buck was a great dinner companion, whose life was notable for achievements in many areas. Wearing an old-fashioned gown with lace patterns, a strand of pearls around her neck, and her white hair swept up in a bun, she was in her element.

In addition to being the only female Nobel laureate present, she had the distinction of being the first American woman to receive both a Nobel and a Pulitzer Prize in literature. While there were a number of distinguished writers in both dining rooms, she was the grande dame of American literature. In addition, she was familiar with the White House, being a friend, collaborator, and dinner guest of Eleanor Roosevelt.[51]

Born nearly seventy years earlier, Pearl Comfort Sydenstricker had taken an improbable route to tonight's event. The daughter of Presbyterian missionaries, she spent her childhood and most of the first half of her life in China. She came to be known by several names, including Pearl Buck for her first husband and Mrs. Richard Welsh, for her second, recently deceased husband; her invitation had been sent to her not as Pearl Buck, but rather as "Mrs. Richard

J. Welsh." She also was fittingly known by her Chinese name, Sai Zhenzhu, which is how she is identified on her gravestone.[52]

She was an expert on China and Asia, and many of her large number of books dealt with one or the other. Her masterpiece was *The Good Earth*, part of a trilogy of a fictional Chinese family written in the 1930s. It was largely for this work that she had been awarded the Nobel Prize in 1938 "for her rich and truly epic description of peasant life in China and for her biographical masterpieces." In her Nobel acceptance speech in Stockholm, she accepted not only for her achievement and the work she anticipated was to come, but for the United States and American writers and for the recognition of women.[53]

Among the books she wrote were novels such as *China Men*, about missionaries in China; nonfiction works such as *The Man Who Changed China: The Story of Sun Yat-sen;* separate biographies/memoirs of her parents; and many short stories. She would eventually write about *The Kennedy Women*, which included a discussion of tonight's dinner.

Buck also wrote about America and on the theme of democracy. In essays that comprise a 1943 book, *Asia and Democracy*—coming at the midpoint of the second world war—she discusses the prospects for enlightened self-rule in Asia, but also touches on race relations in the United States.[54] She was long engaged in the civil rights movement and various efforts for equality—sometimes working with Eleanor Roosevelt—so much so that by the mid-1940s she was being investigated by the House Un-American Activities Committee.[55]

There was another, more personal and painful side to Pearl Buck. He daughter, Carol, born in 1920, suffered from phenylketonuria and was mentally challenged. When Carol was thirty, her mother discussed her daughter's difficulties in a book, *The Child Who Never Grew*. She once wrote to a friend, "Sometimes I can scarcely bear to look at other children and see what she might have become."[56] In this tragic situation, she shared something with the president, whose sister, Rosemary, born fewer than two years before Carol, also was mentally challenged. According to one of Buck's biographers, her book "encouraged Rose Kennedy to talk publicly about" Rosemary's condition.[57]

But tonight was an opportunity to temporarily put some of these concerns away and enjoy a unique evening. While the guests were being served chef René Verdon's seafood mousse appetizer and she continued her conversation with Colonel Glenn, Pearl Buck surveyed the tableau of people assembled around her. She also was watching Mrs. Kennedy from across the table. "I observed her many changes of mood," she said. "Expressions of concern and merriment and chagrin drifted across her face as her conversation changed. She responded differently to each one who spoke to her."[58] But she also observed the shyness, even distance. As she put it: "In my brief exchanges with her, I found her withdrawn, as though she were not altogether among us, nor wanted to be: a quality natural to her, I was to discover, and easily understood when one knows her family history."[59]

⊂═⊶

If Pearl Buck added some international flair to the First Lady's table, the gentleman sitting to Mrs. Kennedy's left continued it. Lester Pearson, the Canadian political leader, was in between major achievements. For his work in helping to address the challenging Suez Crisis of 1956, Pearson had been awarded the Nobel Peace Prize. Currently the head of the Liberal Party, he would soon become his nation's fourteenth prime minister, taking over from John Diefenbaker, with whom President Kennedy had a strained relationship.

Known as "Mike" since his World War I aviator days, Pearson had studied at the University of Toronto and Oxford before entering the Canadian diplomatic service. He served at the Canadian embassy in London at the outset of World War II and then moved on to Washington, where he became the Canadian ambassador in the waning days of the war.

There was an affinity between Pearson and the Kennedy administration, at least in part as a result of the commonalities between the American Democratic Party and the Canadian Liberal Party. Also in play was the antipathy that the two men had toward Diefenbaker, who was an Eisenhower enthusiast. Eleven days before this dinner, a new Canadian election was announced for the early summer, and Pearson and the Liberals were ready to wage a campaign like that of Kennedy's in 1960. For political reasons as well as style, transporting Camelot to Ottawa was a goal of Pearson's party.[60]

Before tonight's dinner he and President Kennedy met. In his memoir, Pearson said Kennedy suggested the meeting. However, in a memo from his aide

Fred Holborn, Kennedy was informed that: "Lester Pearson is most anxious, if possible to have your ear for about five minutes this evening. He will not, however, insist that you campaign for him in Quebec or British Columbia."[61] It is not known what they discussed, but certainly the upcoming Canadian election was a main topic. Pearson's attendance at the White House tonight was enough to stir Conservative complaints about American "intervention in our election as a proof of their suspicion that Kennedy was hoping Diefenbaker would be defeated," Pearson recalled.[62]

Regardless of the politics of the evening, Pearson and his wife, Maryon, enjoyed themselves. Folksy, friendly, and informal, he was like most politicians who enjoy a quip. It was fitting that President Kennedy paid tribute to his wit when he said in the opening lines of his remarks tonight: "Mr. Lester Pearson informed me that a Canadian newspaper man said yesterday that this is the President's 'Easter egg-head roll on the White House lawn,'" referring to the intellectuals gathered here one week after Easter. "I want to deny that," he added. It received howls of laughter from the diners in both rooms.

Although easygoing, Pearson was also firmly committed to his principles. One former aide called him "a rumpled reformer."[63] He enjoyed the opportunity to promote his ideas of peace, and there was a sympathetic audience here tonight, including Ruth Harris Bunche, the wife of fellow Nobel Peace laureate Ralph Bunche, who was only a few seats away from him. Pearson and Bunche were former United Nations mediators.

Pearson strongly believed in international organizations for maintaining peace. He was actively engaged in creating the North Atlantic Treaty Organization (NATO) in the 1940s, which he called "a forward move in man's progress from the wasteland of his postwar world, to a better, safer ground."[64] For ten years he represented Canada at the United Nations, including a term as president of the General Assembly. He achieved his greatest acclaim for creating a United Nations Emergency Force to bring an end to the fighting in Egypt over the Suez Canal. He subsequently proposed that a group of middle powers in the United Nations, including Canada, establish a standby international police force.[65]

Awarded the Nobel Peace Prize in 1957, beating out United Nations Secretary-General Dag Hammarskjold, Pearson identified his "four faces of peace" in his Nobel lecture in Oslo. These were commercial prosperity, national self-defense, agile diplomacy, and the need to appreciate the role and importance of people.[66]

With his international stature high, the following year Pearson was invited to give the William L. Clayton Lectures at Tufts University's prestigious Fletcher School of Law and Diplomacy. The salient points delivered in his four lectures were the importance of coalition building and the need for negotiation. Perhaps these were obvious arguments at the height of the Cold War, but it was important for a political leader to stress them to a wider audience. He subsequently published the lectures as a book entitled *Diplomacy in the Nuclear Age*.

Of course, in addition to his strong interest in peace and forging international alliances to maintain it, Mike Pearson was also a politician. He became Liberal Party leader in 1958, but failed to lead his parliamentarians to victory in June 1962, despite what the Kennedy White House had hoped. He did, however, succeed in another national election one year later. Alas, the political alliance between John Kennedy and Mike Pearson would last only five months through the summer and fall of 1963.

⌐━⋯⊶

Just as with the entire dinner guest list, the people at the First Lady's table represented a "who's who" in many fields. At table seventeen was arguably America's most distinguished writer, a wildly popular astronaut, a rising Canadian public figure, and one of the nation's foremost actors, Fredric March. Born Frederick McIntyre Bickel, March was a versatile actor with a memorable voice, who had performed in dozens of plays and movies over three decades.

In 1932 he had received an Academy Award for best actor for his performance in *Dr. Jekyll and Mr. Hyde*. He was nominated again in 1937 for *A Star is Born* and then won again for a memorable performance as Al Stephenson in *The Best Years of Our Lives*—which poignantly dealt with servicemen and their difficult postwar adjustments—in 1946. Many at the dinner tonight would have seen and remembered him for his role as a fictionalized, but realistic, William Jennings Bryan character in *Inherit the Wind* in 1960. In that movie, he and Spencer Tracy, portraying a fictionalized Clarence Darrow, squared off in the famous Scopes evolution trial of 1925.

Now age sixty-four, he was playing fewer roles. He had just completed a successful, five-month run in *Gideon*, a play by Paddy Chayefsky at the Plymouth Theater on Broadway. In it he played the Agent of the Lord—in effect, God—and there was much humor about him playing that exalted role.[67] Next year he would play a US president in the political movie thriller *Seven Days in May*. Within a span of a year or so, he played both God and the president.

But tonight his talents would be employed in a different way, presenting excerpts from three Nobel laureates, most notably a new, longer piece by the late Ernest Hemingway. And it would be delivered to one of the greatest gatherings of scientists and writers ever assembled in the nation's capital.

From where March was sitting, he could catch a glimpse of the soaring Washington Monument, five hundred and fifty-five feet tall, through one of the windows across the room facing south. He might have wondered at least momentarily how this evening's performance would be received. Tish Baldrige said that the actor "told me later that he had played in palaces and before many distinguished audiences in his life, but never had anything meant so much to him as this night."[68] He would do well; he was a superb performer.

❦

One of the most interesting conversations at table seventeen was initiated by Sarah Gibson Blanding, the president of Vassar, who was seated on March's right. No doubt Tish Baldrige, a Vassar alumna, had a hand in this invitation. Oddly, when Blanding had assumed the presidency of the school in 1946, the year Baldrige graduated, she had become the first female to head the women's institution, which had been founded during the Civil War.[69]

Miss Blanding had flown to Washington that afternoon for what she called her "command" to attend the dinner and, as recounted in the college newspaper, "ordered herself a Cadillac so that she could drive to the White House in style." Once there, she was quickly met by friends such as Baldrige (who told her, "You're at a good table") and Robert Frost. She also saw Robert Oppenheimer, whom she had invited to deliver the Helen Kenyon Lecture at Vassar in October 1958.[70]

Wearing a blue sari trimmed in gold, she was enjoying the table discussion. John Glenn, she said, "was just charming" as they both talked about the prospect of women as astronauts. She pronounced Pearl Buck "a lovely person." As waiters refilled glasses, President Blanding also offered an assessment of Mrs. Kennedy's academic prowess to her fellow diners. "I always knew she was a good student," she said, "but to be sure I looked up her record before I left for Washington. Mostly A's and B's with a few C's."[71] Mrs. Kennedy was a member of the Vassar class of 1951, although she only completed her first two academic years there, 1947–1949.

<hr>

There were other notable people around the First Lady's table. Three of them were part of the small group that met with the president before dinner. Dr. Melvin Calvin, winner of the 1961 Nobel Prize in Chemistry "for his research on the carbon dioxide assimilation in plants" was on the faculty at the University of California at Berkeley. The son of Lithuanian and Russian immigrants, Calvin was there with his wife, Genevieve Jemtegaard Calvin, whose parents had emigrated from Norway. Presidential aide Arthur Schlesinger had suggested to Tish Baldrige that the 1961 laureates "should have the seats of honor," and that explains Dr. Calvin's position at the First Lady's table.

The Norwegian ambassador to the United States, Paul Gruda Koht, also was at the predinner meeting upstairs and now was seated next to Mrs. Kennedy. Koht was a career diplomat with tours that included Portugal, Denmark, and Romania; he had been the ambassador in Washington since 1958. The forty-eight-year-old ambassador was prominent tonight because the Nobel Peace Prize is awarded in Norway; the other prizes are awarded in Sweden. And Nancy Givan Hofstadter, the wife of Dr. Robert Hofstadter, the 1961 physics prize winner, was there too. Mrs. Hofstadter, a Democratic Party activist, was also involved with the developmental disability community, loved music, and was a fervent Stanford University baseball fan.[72] Everyone at this table had an intriguing story.

Mrs. Kennedy had to be pleased about the dinner that she helped develop. Looking around the room, watching these eminent people talking and laughing, she knew this was turning out to be a successful evening. She also would be making a mental note about what worked well and what did not; after each dinner she provided a critique to each White House staff member associated with the event.[73] Her staff knew that she was already looking ahead to the magnificent evening planned for French cultural leader and official André Malraux in only twelve days, but she was clearly enjoying what Tish Baldrige had called the "Brains' Dinner."

# CHAPTER FIVE ⟳⊷

# Redemption and Promise

THE MOST CONTROVERSIAL MAN at the dinner, physicist J. Robert Oppenheimer, was seated with convivial guests. The hostess at table eleven in the State Dining Room was the vivacious young wife of the attorney general, Ethel Kennedy. Among others there were his friend Nathan Pusey, the Harvard University president; Nobel laureate and United Nations negotiator Ralph Bunche; and the rising novelist William Styron.

Over Oppenheimer's right shoulder at the next table was the president. Looking in front of him, the tall, gray-haired scientist was only a few feet from an ornate eighteenth-century gilded mirror rising above a console table designed by A. H. Davenport, a noted Boston furniture maker.[1] The mirror reflected Healy's painting on the west wall with Lincoln and his pensive look.

Oppenheimer enjoyed gatherings like this—especially if strong martinis were available—and he helped set the mood as a good storyteller.[2] Although he could be opinionated, rude, and self-centered, he also exuded charisma and for years had many devoted followers. A number of those admirers were here tonight, including Dr. Rabi, Dr. Seaborg, and Arthur Schlesinger.

But like Lincoln, in the painting, he could not help but be pensive here in the White House. Oppenheimer, who had celebrated his fifty-eighth birthday the previous Sunday, had lived a life of exhilarating triumphs and painful losses. Tonight represented his official release from nearly a decade in political purgatory.

The first chairman of the Atomic Energy Commission, Dr. David Lilienthal, a friend and colleague of Oppenheimer, once said, "Robert is the only authentic genius I know."[3] Rabi, who met Oppie—a named used by his friends—in 1929 and was a Manhattan Project colleague, later eulogized him by saying, "Robert Oppenheimer was one of the most highly regarded personalities in the civilized world."[4] Although not a Nobel laureate, the "Father of the Atomic

Bomb" certainly was an intellectual equal of those who were being honored here tonight.

His career trajectory was one that an astronaut such as John Glenn could metaphorically understand. Born to wealthy parents in New York, his youth was one of privilege and sound intellectual training. His interests then and later on were broad, including art, music, literature, poetry, and even mineral collecting. A large collection of those minerals of all types eventually was given by Oppenheimer to Linus Pauling years earlier when they had been friends and colleagues at Caltech.[5]

Oppenheimer may have been a polymath, but his passion was for chemistry and, more especially, physics. He studied at Harvard, the University of Cambridge, and the University of Göttingen, where he met several important physicists whose work would coincide with his for decades.

As with many others at the dinner tonight, Oppenheimer's career included time at Caltech, where he befriended Pauling, and also at the University of California at Berkeley. At Berkeley, he worked with Dr. Ernest Lawrence, the inventor of the cyclotron and winner of the Nobel Prize in Physics in 1939. The scientific world in which Oppenheimer traveled was small; indeed, Lawrence's secretary, Helen Griggs, had married Seaborg, and she was here tonight, hosting a table in the Blue Room.

There were other prominent theoretical physicists in the 1930s and 1940s, but Oppenheimer rose to international prominence through his brilliance—and also because General Leslie Groves, military head of the Manhattan Project, needed someone to run the top-secret atomic bomb project, which eventually was housed at Los Alamos, New Mexico. The burly, demanding army engineer had surveyed the field of potential directors and chosen Oppenheimer as the best who was available. The physicist and the general initially met in October 1942, and for the next three years they forged a productive, if contentious, military-scientific partnership that produced the most awesome weapon in history.[6]

The high point of Oppenheimer's career, if not his life, took place on the early morning of July 16, 1945. There in the barren New Mexico desert, the ground shook, the sky exploded, the wind swirled, and the quiet was broken by a giant roar. The "gadget" was detonated for the first time. Trinity, long associated with religious connotations, was the code name for a new means of mass destruction. And the implications were immense: the six-year global war would be brought to an end in one month.

Rabi, who was there, recalls Oppenheimer's exhilaration: "I'll never forget the way he stepped out of the car. . . . his walk was like High Noon . . . this kind of strut. He had done it."[7] Oppie later said, "We knew the world would not be the same." And while his achievement was certainly satisfying, there was a sense of remorse, even fear. He recounted the scene and his immediate reaction: "A few people laughed, a few people cried. Most people were silent. I remembered the line from the Hindu scripture, the *Bhagavad Gita*: Vishnu is trying to persuade the prince that he should do his duty, and to impress him, takes on his multi-armed form and says: 'Now I am become death, the destroyer of worlds.' I suppose we all thought that one way or another."[8]

❦

The postwar years for Oppenheimer were challenging—sometimes because of his actions and sometimes because of vindictiveness. The difficulties could be characterized as personal, professional, and most especially, political. Oppenheimer, who had made a fumbled pass at Ava Helen Pauling in the 1920s, had been an unfaithful husband to his wife, Kitty, whom he married in 1940. There was an ill-fated affair with his longtime lover, Jean Tatlock, which continued during the war and ended with her suicide in 1944. After the war, his longtime friendship with Ruth Tolman, the wife of a Caltech associate, blossomed.[9] Unfortunately for Oppenheimer, both of these affairs would have a negative impact on his career.

The professional challenge was his increasing concern about the wide availability of nuclear weapons, something which was an issue to many scientists, including a number who had worked on the Manhattan Project. For Oppenheimer, there were two issues. One, as he saw it, was the need to internationalize the control of nuclear weapons, probably through the United Nations. This did not sit well with President Harry Truman, with whom he had a particularly unpleasant meeting in October 1945. Truman, who had little time for circumspection, especially for anything dealing with the decision to use the atomic bomb, was appalled by Oppenheimer's defensive arguments and the need to adopt multilateral controls. Truman was so angry that he said to Secretary of State Dean Acheson, "I don't want to see that son-of-a-bitch in this office ever again."[10]

The other issue was the prospect of the development of a hydrogen bomb, which was early on called the "Super." Dr. Edward Teller, a colleague at the Manhattan Project, was the primary proponent of this new weapon, which Oppenheimer opposed. His position was based on technical and moral issues. On the latter point, he wrote, "The use of this weapon will bring about the destruction of innumerable human lives." He added, "It is not a weapon which can be used exclusively for the destruction of material installations of military or semi-military purposes. Its use therefore carries much further than the atomic bomb itself the policy of exterminating civilian populations."[11] Teller had become a rival of Oppenheimer's, and the difference between the two men on a new, more powerful bomb that might boost American dominance over the Soviet Union became a major issue and played an important role in Oppie's most difficult trial.

Oppenheimer could be brusque. As two of his biographers noted, he was considerate with students, "But to those in authority, he was often impatient and candid to the point of rudeness."[12] This tendency, along with his affairs and surprising sense of naïveté, came to a head in 1954. Three men from the Atomic Energy Commission—Lewis Strauss, the chair and onetime friend and supporter of Oppenheimer, and staffers Gordon Gray and Roger Robb—were the driving force that revoked Oppenheimer's security clearance following a hearing before the Personnel Security Board.

Oppenheimer was tarnished by his association, primarily by innuendo, with communism and the Soviet Union. His affair with Jean Tatlock, an avowed communist, was observed by security forces. Frank Oppenheimer, his brother and also a scientist, had been a Communist Party member. It was also argued by some that Robert's opposition to the hydrogen bomb reflected a pro-Soviet perspective.

Especially damning was testimony given by Teller. While not questioning Oppenheimer's loyalty, Teller skewered him by saying, "If it is a question of wisdom and judgment, as demonstrated by actions since 1945, then I would say one would be wiser not to grant clearances."[13] Ernest Lawrence, angry over Oppenheimer's affair with the wife of a colleague, was also scheduled to testify, but in the end cancelled for health reasons. However, in an interview for the board, Lawrence argued that Oppenheimer "should never again have anything to do with the forming of policy."[14]

Over the past eight years, Oppenheimer had lived in exile from official Washington. He remained director at Princeton's prestigious Institute for Advanced Study, a position he had held since 1947 (ironically, with the support of Lewis Strauss). He was involved in scientific conferences and discussions and he published widely. One of his articles, "The Tree of Knowledge," appeared in the October 1958 issue of *Harper's* magazine directly before an article by another guest tonight, James Baldwin.[15]

While conservative Republican leaders saw Oppenheimer as a questionable character, if not worse, American intellectuals supported him and saw the security hearing as a witch hunt and whitewash. The Alsop brothers, for example, wrote an indictment of the proceedings, "We Accuse!"—harkening back to the Emile Zola's ringing defense of Alfred Dreyfus in 1898—for *Harper's*. They concluded by saying of the removal of Oppenheimer's clearance: "This act did not disgrace Robert Oppenheimer: it dishonored and disgraced the high traditions of American freedom."[16]

But all of this had taken its toll on the once swaggering hero and his wife. His friend the diplomat George F. Kennan tried to console him, citing the high regard in which he was held around the world. A hurt, teary-eyed Oppenheimer responded, "Damn it. I happen to love this country."[17] His patriotism had been challenged, and a question about his loyalty hung over him like a cloud.

The self-assured cockiness of the wunderkind scientist was now gone. Oppenheimer's shock of tousled dark hair was replaced by rapidly thinning gray. Always lanky, he now looked gaunt with his ears seeming much more prominent. The bon vivant photos of him from wartime with his trademark porkpie hat and dangling cigarette now seemed incongruous. He looked old and tired.

Worse, as Diana Trilling observed earlier this evening, you could sense the pain. She observed that his "appearance was like that of a spectre, a memento mori. He carried himself with great dignity, but that only made it worse." Speaking of Robert and Kitty, she added, "My heart ached for the two of them."[18]

And yet, an important form of redemption was at hand. Staring at his name in calligraphy at the place card here in the State Dining Room, seated at the table of the wife of the second most powerful political figure in America and only a few steps away from the president, Oppenheimer surely had to feel moved. With the help of White House insiders Arthur Schlesinger, McGeorge Bundy, and Glenn Seaborg, his ostracism was coming to an end. And of course, the person who allowed it to happen was President Kennedy, who would have more to say about his further rehabilitation.

⌖

Sitting two seats over from Oppenheimer and directly across the table from Ethel Kennedy was a rising, southern-born writer, William Styron. He had little in common with Oppenheimer—who was twenty-one years older—but would come to have much in common with Robert Kennedy's wife over the next five decades, as the entire Kennedy family and the Styrons, Bill and wife Rose, forged a close friendship.

There appeared to be two reasons that Styron was invited tonight. Most important, his friends Arthur Schlesinger and Dick Goodwin were both involved in the dinner planning.[19] As often happens in politics, as in other professions, social interactions are important: all three men were part of the Martha's Vineyard social set. In addition, Styron's most recent novel, *Set This House on Fire*, was being discussed in the Kennedy White House.

Styron said that Schlesinger told him that the novel, revolving around modern-day expatriates in Italy, was "the most 'controversial' book that the intellectuals at the White House have been reading. Some of them hate it, some of them love it passionately, but it causes constant and violent arguments, and they have just wanted to get a look at the instigator." So, he added, "Never underestimate the power of the written word."[20]

Styron, then thirty-six, was a native of Newport News, Virginia. After attending Davidson College and serving in the Marine Corps in World War II, he entered Duke University, where he immersed himself in literature. He was strongly influenced by Thomas Wolfe, of whom he told his father: "I think he's the greatest writer of our time."[21] He also enjoyed Dos Passos, tonight seated two tables over. Back in 1943 he wrote his father that Dos Passos's *U.S.A.* "is especially good" and it discusses Tidewater Virginia, including Newport News.[22] William Faulkner, who was invited to this dinner and declined, influenced him as well. Also important to Styron were two writers of an earlier era, Gustave Flaubert and James Joyce.[23]

Styron decided to become a writer, but struggled to finish his first novel, *Lie Down in Darkness*. According to his daughter, it "was a three-and-a-half year gamble, fraught with all the setbacks, occlusions, and long, dark nights of the soul that make up any great unmapped venture."[24] But the gamble paid off, and it was published in 1951. The story centered on the drama of a Virginia family, and it was a success; the good reviews were compounded by robust sales.[25] Styron's personal life was about to change too, when he spoke to a graduate class at Johns Hopkins University in Baltimore in January 1952. The talk, which he called his "first experience at speechifying," was disappointing. But there he met a student, Rose Burgunder.[26]

Rose finished her graduate work at Johns Hopkins and then embarked on a year in Europe. The professor of the class where Styron had spoken told her that the author been awarded the Prix de Rome for *Lie Down in Darkness*, and she connected with him in Paris.[27] A brief courtship ensued, during which Truman Capote said, "Bill, you ought to marry that girl."[28] In May 1953, he did, at Rome's city hall. The writer Irwin Shaw and his wife, Marian, held a reception. Among those attending were two other prominent writers, John Marquand Jr. and Peter Matthiessen.[29]

The early 1950s were an expatriate period for Bill and Rose Styron in Rome and Paris. Bill met or interacted with a number of writers, two of whom were present tonight: James Baldwin, who would become a close friend and who later lived with the Styrons, and James T. Farrell, who was largely noted for his three *Studs Lonigan* books written in the 1930s.[30] Styron also was active in the launching of *The Paris Review* with Matthiessen and another American expat, George Plimpton.

By 1954 Bill and Rose Styron were back in the United States, settling in to their home in Roxbury, Connecticut.[31] In 1960 Styron published his novel *Set This House on Fire*. He was watching the presidential race, with an obvious preference for the Massachusetts senator. He wrote to Marquand, "It looks as if your friend and mine, the Irishman from Palm Beach, is going to make it."[32] But Styron had never met Kennedy, and when the invitation arrived to attend the Nobel dinner, Styron was "somewhat baffled, if pleased, by the summons."[33] Rose said, "It was a magnificent surprise."[34] Bill added that "it was a giddy pleasure for my wife" to be invited.[35]

Styron had come from Paris to attend the dinner, while Rose and "Jimmy" Baldwin came from Roxbury, Connecticut, as did writer and critic Van Wyck Brooks and Fredric March. They were all neighbors. Styron's excitement for the dinner was high, as he later wrote, "I recall that it was the only time I ever shaved twice on the same day."[36]

Styron obviously was enjoying the dinner, but he was a little under the weather. He had been taking an antibiotic, achromycin, and that, combined with drinking, contributed to a state in which he later described: "I got prematurely plastered."[37]

As the Marine Band played, the servers continued their impeccable service, and the conversation flowed, Styron found his tablemates a mixed group. Oppenheimer, he said, "was utterly charming." But when Ralph Bunche, the peace negotiator, ignored him, Styron believed that he dismissed him because he was southern. Nathan Pusey, the Harvard president who was seated two places over from Styron, was judged by the writer as "one of the crashing knuckleheads of all time."[38]

Overall, the dinner was going well for Styron, who was savoring the experience. Still, having lived in Paris, he considered himself a gourmand, and he had some complaints: the Mouton-Rothschild, a sweet, smoky wine, was "lacking in maturity." And he dismissed the dessert, the Bombe Caribienne—a molded ice cream with vanilla, pineapple, cinnamon, and rum—as "much too sweet, a real bomb."[39]

Styron would be even less impressed with the after-dinner literary presentation, especially the newly unveiled Hemingway work, but the highlight of the evening lay ahead in the after-party, a private, intimate session upstairs in which he and Rose would launch a lifelong friendship with the entire Kennedy family.

⊙═⊷

Keeping the conversation alive at table eleven was the job of thirty-four-year-old Ethel Skakel Kennedy, who was sitting directly across from Styron. Since her marriage nearly twelve years ago to the president's brother Robert, she'd proven to be a perfect fit for the Kennedy family, an outgoing and fun-loving helpmate who was an asset to her husband's political career. She was athletic and relished the rough-and-tumble of a large family, including the raucous touch football games and the sailing, where she excelled.

Her large home at Hickory Hill, across the Potomac River in McLean, Virginia, had already become the center for informal administration parties. The property was once owned by Supreme Court Justice Robert Jackson and, briefly, by Senator and Jacqueline Kennedy. But it was brought alive by Ethel, Robert, and their brood of seven children as of April 1962. The nearly six acres of property included a menagerie of animals and a pool, which often became a focal point for hijinks of politicians and celebrities. Arthur Schlesinger, one of the organizers of tonight's event and a frequent guest at these events, said, "Hickory Hill was the most spirited social center in Washington. It was hard to resist the raffish, unpredictable, sometimes uncontrollable Kennedy parties."[40]

Ethel was comfortable with large families; she had six siblings who were raised as strict Catholics by wealthy Catholic parents, George Skakel, a Chicago industrialist, and his wife, Ann. They were both killed in an airplane crash in 1955. Although she handled the death of her parents well, Ethel had experienced a severe blow. As one Kennedy biographer noted, "She never spoke of her parents' death with friends."[41]

Ethel was an outgoing and sociable person—the extrovert counterpart of Robert Kennedy's introversion. She also was a free-spending person who had little interest in domestic chores.[42] But whatever deficiencies she had, she more than balanced that with a total devotion to her husband. Despite his reputation as the president's consigliere and enforcer, Robert Kennedy was a sensitive man who often seemed to stand apart within the Kennedy family. Ethel provided him with emotional ballast, and as Evan Thomas, an astute Kennedy observer, wrote, "She gave him the one thing he had never had before: unconditional love."[43]

Still a devout Catholic, she also had unwavering faith in him. One friend had said of her that "she looked at Bobby like she did at God. God did inexplicable things, but he was never wrong."[44] She also felt, as did Jacqueline Kennedy, that she should stay in the political background and make her husband's life enjoyable. "I don't think a politician's wife should get involved in politics. I think she should work at making her home a nice place for her husband to come home to, a place for him to forget politics, she said."[45]

And yet, she could be and was pressed into political service, as surely those events at Hickory Hill were part social, part political. She and Bobby befriended CIA director John McCone. When McCone's wife, Rosemary, died in 1961, Ethel was a source of great comfort to him, fulfilling both compassionate concern as well as cementing the relationship with McCone, who was the Kennedys' conduit to former President Eisenhower.[46]

She also accompanied him on political trips. In August 1961, they went to the Ivory Coast to commemorate that African nation's first anniversary. They took a much more extensive overseas trip in February, when the president sent his brother as an emissary and fact finder to Japan, Hong Kong, Singapore, Indonesia, Thailand, India, Pakistan, Italy, West Germany, and the Netherlands.[47] Ethel displayed flawless manners and sharp political instincts by giving the foreign service officer who shepherded them a personalized set of cuff links in appreciation.[48] With the memories from this round-the-world trip still fresh in her mind, Ethel Kennedy was reprising her role as a political wife again tonight, joined with her husband's ambition.

☙

As the diners talked, the waiters, all men dressed in white tie, carefully served the main course, which was *filet de boeuf* Wellington. The history of the dish is a bit unclear; it may have been associated with the legendary Duke of Wellington, Arthur Wellesley, the Napoleonic-era field marshal and later British prime minister. Or, it may be of later origin and refer to Wellington, New Zealand.[49] Regardless of its history, it is a special entrée—prime steak enveloped by puff pastry—and this one was prepared under the supervision of chef René Verdon.

As with all the components on the menu for this meal, the largest dinner of the Kennedy era, planning the meal was detailed. Verdon's food preparation for White House dinners began two days ahead of the dinner for a menu that Mrs. Kennedy needed to confirm.[50] A creative chef, Verdon had his own recipe for the main course, a crusted, flaked dish, and it was enhanced by cognac and Madeira wine.[51]

☙

At an event such as this, which draws from a specific stratum of people—the top American scientists and intellectuals—there are likely to be many people acquainted with one another. The seating plan was carefully implemented by Tish Baldrige, with guidance from others, most especially from the First Lady. Much thought went into the placement of guests, but sometimes a random serendipity developed. It is unclear whether the First Lady or Baldrige knew that Ethel Kennedy and Dr. Ralph Bunche, seated next to one another, had met more than a decade earlier when Ethel was a newlywed in her twenties.

At that time Robert Kennedy was a law student at the University of Virginia and president of the Student Legal Forum. He invited Bunche, who had been awarded the Nobel Peace Prize in 1950, to the Charlottesville campus. In March 1951 Bunche spoke on "The United Nations and Prospects for Peace."[52] But not before some challenges had to be overcome. Kennedy had to scream and demand that the audience be integrated, even yelling to his fellow student officials, "You're all gutless!"[53]

Bunche stayed overnight at the Kennedy home. But even that was marred; racist protesters trampled on the Kennedy lawn. Ethel later said, "We just thought, why would anybody get that exercised because of somebody's skin color?"[54] Surely Ethel and Bunche remembered that night eleven years earlier.

Bunche had taken an unlikely route to his lofty international status and to tonight's dinner. His maternal great-grandfather was a slave. He was born in 1904 and had a poor but happy childhood in Detroit. By the time he was thirteen, both of his parents had died, and he wound up with his grandmother in East Los Angeles. But the humble beginnings were balanced by his good upbringing, which instilled in him a competitive spirit about the future. He excelled at UCLA and then went on to Harvard for graduate work. Robert Weaver, an official in the Kennedy administration, knew him then, and said of his time at Harvard in the early 1930s, "What impressed me most about Ralph in those days was his optimism."[55]

That optimism led him to try college teaching and go on to work at a think tank. At the think tank, Carnegie Corporation, he met and assisted Gunnar Myrdal, the Swedish researcher who was studying race relations in the United States. The two men formed a bond and a collaboration that had important repercussions for American racial understanding. The resulting landmark book, *An American Dilemma: The Negro Problem and Modern Democracy*, according to one commentator, "helped to create a new racial liberalism that influenced political leaders, judges, civil rights activists, and thousands of educated white Americans."[56]

In 1945, the year after the book was published, Bunche's focus shifted to international affairs. After joining the State Department, he started working on the new United Nations Charter, which led to his distinguished career at that international body. By 1947 he was working on Middle East issues, specifically Palestine. The crowning achievement of his years at the United Nations was his role as a negotiator between the Israelis—Israel was founded in 1948—and the Arabs. Bunche's work resulted in his being named a Nobel Peace Prize winner. Echoing his friend Robert Weaver's observation, the Nobel committee referred to Bunche's "unfailing sense of optimism."[57]

With his selection as a Nobel Peace Prize recipient, Bunche joined a distinguished list of American statesmen, including presidents Theodore Roosevelt and Woodrow Wilson, Vice President Charles Dawes, and secretaries of state Elihu Root, Frank Kellogg, Cordell Hull, and George Marshall. He was the first African-American to be awarded the honor.[58]

Bunche had experienced racism throughout his life and career. He remembered his grandmother being told by a graveyard salesman that plots were reserved for white people.[59] He remembered that, while traveling on a train in 1941 and writing about democracy, "I could get the Pullman reservation only through deception."[60] Even when he reached the apex of international acclaim after being awarded the Nobel Prize, he experienced the ugly scene outside of the Kennedy house in Charlottesville.

Bunche was forming a bond with the Kennedys. In 1960 Robert Kennedy was dispatched by his brother to recruit him to join the presidential campaign and aid with international issues. He declined, preferring to remain at the United Nations.[61]

The Kennedy administration tried, unsuccessfully, to recruit Bunche in 1961. Later, while still at the United Nations, he was a back channel for the State Department to Secretary-General Dag Hammarskjold on issues regarding the Congo; the newly independent country was torn by civil war and was caught between support from the two rival superpowers. Bunche's role in being an intermediary and helping keep the peace during the tense Congo discussions drew him closer to the Kennedy camp.[62] Tonight, he and his wife of thirty-one years, Ruth Harris Bunche, were being feted at the White House; he was seated beside Ethel Kennedy, no longer a young law student's wife, but an influential figure in the administration, and Ruth was seated at the most prominent table in the Blue Room, two seats away from First Lady Jacqueline Kennedy. Bunche and James Baldwin, two very different men—one a conciliator and one a firebrand—were the most prominent African-Americans at the dinner.

Bunche, the elegant diplomat, received two graduate degrees from Harvard, the second being a PhD in 1934.[63] Seated almost across the table from him was the man who had been the president of Harvard since 1953. Far from being the "crashing knucklehead" that the acerbic Styron called him, Nathan Marsh Pusey was an understated scholar with a soft voice, who was widely respected and a national voice for liberal education. Although a Harvard graduate, Pusey was an anomaly—the first of Harvard's twenty-four presidents not to come from New England; he was an Iowa native.[64]

He had been president of tiny Lawrence College in Appleton, Wisconsin, the home of the late senator and communist hunter Joseph McCarthy. A contemporary account reported of his selection to Harvard: "He was an apparent nobody, plucked out of nowhere." McCarthy, who was then alive but had yet to be condemned by the Senate, said, "Harvard's loss is Wisconsin's gain." Pusey, who had written his dissertation on law in ancient Athens, had taken the measure of such men as McCarthy: "We are against fundamentalism of all kinds . . . and all kinds of mean-minded thinking that would make man less than he is."[65]

Oppenheimer, seated four chairs to the left of the handsome, trim, brown-haired Pusey, had known the Harvard president for years. As a member of the Harvard College Board of Overseers, he was privy to the discussions that brought Pusey back to Cambridge. The selection process, in hindsight, seems quaint, as the board looked at rather subjective assessments. One commentator said of Pusey, "He is as firm as iron. He always succeeds in getting what he wants done. He does not beat tom-toms and some say he gains his end without needing to resort to artificial means." And, he added, "His religion is top flight—100% all wool a yard wide Episcopalian." Even his wife, Anne Woodward Pusey, was sized up as being "charming, sincere, attentive, simple."[66]

As Oppenheimer conversed with his friend and continued eating tonight, he might have chuckled had he remembered one other preappointment assessment of Pusey: "No one is big enough for the Harvard presidency at the time he is selected. The question is whether the new president will have the capacity to grow into the job."[67]

Pusey, indeed, had grown into his position as head of the most prestigious university in America over the past nine years. Early on, he continued his sparring with McCarthy and the prevailing McCarthyism. McCarthy had called the university "a privileged sanctuary for Fifth Amendment Communists."[68] When McCarthy pushed to have several Harvard professors fired, Pusey responded: "Americanism does not mean enforced or circumscribed belief. . . . Our job is to educate free, independent, and vigorous minds capable of analyzing events, or exercising judgment, of distinguishing facts from propaganda, and truth from half-truths and lies."[69]

He was confident enough to go against the secular tide and instill some sense of religious tradition at Harvard. At the same time, he was working to modernize and upgrade the institution.[70] He also opened up admissions in the Ivy League and made it more meritocratic. In addition, he was a leader in the push for strengthening liberal education in the United States. Pusey was clearly in his element tonight.

❦

The other prominent and second Nobel laureate at the table was Dr. Owen Chamberlain, a forty-one-year-old bespectacled physicist from the University of California at Berkeley. He too had worked on the Manhattan Project at Los Alamos. A protégé of Enrico Fermi, Chamberlain had received the Nobel Prize in Physics in 1959. There also were three wives of Nobel laureates interspersed around the table: Jean Bailey Shockley, wife of physicist Dr. William Shockley; Beth Purcell, wife of physicist Dr. Edward Purcell; and Viola Tatum, wife of geneticist Dr. Edward Tatum.

This was a table full of people associated in one way or another with Oppenheimer, which certainly would make him feel comfortable on this night of redemption. The tenth diner at the table, Florence Laurence, was the wife of science writer William Laurence. Known as "Atomic Bill," he first met Oppenheimer in 1940 when he wrote a story on a talk that Oppie gave at the Massachusetts Institute of Technology. Laurence followed the development of the atomic bomb and was there at the Trinity blast. He was on board the B-29 Bockscar that dropped the atomic bomb on Nagasaki on August 9, 1945. His eyewitness account provided the story that landed him his second Pulitzer Prize.[71]

Whether Bill Styron felt awkward being at a table bereft of writers and literary people, we don't know. We do know that he was enjoying himself, despite his critiques, and that he and others at the table were being engaged by one of official Washington's most gregarious hostesses, Ethel Kennedy. Oppenheimer and Styron represented two very distinct arcs at the dinner—the scientist and the writer, as well as a declining, if partly rehabilitated, figure and a rising one with substantial success ahead of him. Although the dinner was identified as a tribute to Nobel laureates, it also was a broad celebration of American intellectuals—some early in their career and others later.

# CHAPTER SIX

# Is That Linus Pauling?

WHILE ROBERT OPPENHEIMER may have been the most controversial guest at tonight's dinner, many people were talking about Linus Pauling and his activism. Most were aware that the sixty-one-year-old, tall, balding man with the distinctive billowy gray hair and blue eyes had been protesting the president and his policies across the street only a few hours before.[1] He too had been questioned by Congress and conservative critics about his pacifist views, which included friendliness toward the Soviet Union. Many knew him—he was a Nobel laureate—and others were intrigued to have such brashness in their midst. And brash he was; one of his biographers said, "By the early 1960s Pauling had earned a reputation for being audacious, intuitive, charming, irreverent, self-promoting, self-reliant, self-involved to the point of arrogance—and correct about almost everything."[2]

Far from being self-conscious or defensive at the dinner, Pauling said, "I am enjoying myself tremendously."[3] Why not? In addition to dining with many friends at the most exclusive address in the United States, his odd juxtaposition with picketing against the president and being honored by him was helping his cause. In a letter to a friend he gloated that these nearly simultaneous actions "attracted much attention." In fact, he said, "I think that probably every newspaper in the United States made some mention of it, almost always favorable."[4]

He was seated one table away from the president and was facing only a few feet away from a portrait of Thomas Jefferson, modeled after Gilbert Stuart's rendering, and positioned between two closed wooden doors that open onto the grand Cross Hall. Pauling, if he paid any attention to the portrait, might have considered the view a fortuitous one. Like Jefferson, he was a brilliant, charming man committed to various intellectual pursuits and strongly assured of his own sense of moral integrity. Like Jefferson, his career moved him in some unusual directions.

Born in Portland, Oregon, as a small child Pauling and his family relocated to Condon, Oregon, a town of fewer than a thousand people, in 1905. Condon could claim two future Nobel Prize winners at tonight's dinner; William P. Murphy, whose work on anemia led to the award in medicine, was a teenager when the Paulings arrived. Missing one class, Pauling had not received his high school diploma, but he went on to study chemistry at Oregon Agricultural College, the land-grant school that is now Oregon State University.[5] It was here that Pauling would enter into the two most important professional and personal relationships of his life. He earned his undergraduate degree, began his teaching and research career, and met a student, Ava Helen Miller. Then a dashing young man with a full shock of dark hair, Pauling was her instructor in Chemistry 102, a course for home economics majors. Quickly, the teacher-student relationship expanded into a romance.[6] Ava Helen—as she was usually called—married Pauling in 1923, and they began a long partnership in which Pauling, the self-confident intellectual, would be supported, gently prodded, and at a crucial point, most likely saved from an early death.

Soon the Paulings moved nine hundred miles south to Caltech, a small but promising new institution. There they met and formed a fast friendship with Robert Oppenheimer, also in his twenties and who had recently attained his doctorate from the University of Göttingen in Germany. While the pass that Oppie made at Ava Helen chilled the relationship, equally unusual were the great attention and gifts that he showered on Linus, including rings, poems, and the giant mineral collection. Oppenheimer even began to emulate Pauling's classroom presentations. And of course, there was the slouch hat that seemed to indicate that Oppenheimer and Pauling were part of a special club.[7] But this all ended with Oppenheimer's clumsy suggestion that Ava Helen accompany him to Mexico. For decades, the two scientists' paths crossed—once again tonight—but the relationship was never fully repaired. It likely irritated Pauling that his wife, who could be flirtatious, enjoyed the attention: "I think she was somewhat pleased with herself as a femme fatale," he said.[8] Symbolizing the break with Oppenheimer, Pauling jettisoned his old hat and henceforth wore his new trademark black beret.[9]

As Pauling built his career in teaching and research in such widely disparate areas as quantum mechanics and hemoglobin studies in the 1930s, two developments occurred that affected his life. One was his growing concern about the rise of fascism in Europe. Increasingly he saw a coming conflict with the United States. In July 1940, still eighteen months before the United States entered World War II, Pauling spoke publicly for the first time on a nonscience issue. Speaking to the hometown Federal Unionist Club, he said, "The great decision which will be made before many years—surely during the present century, and possibly within the coming decade—is whether the world will be ruled by totalitarian masters or whether it will be a free democratic state."[10]

The other major development was the onset of a serious illness, glomerulo-nephritis, in 1941. Sometimes identified as Bright's disease, it is often fatal. It was only because of the careful regimen identified by a renowned specialist, Dr. Thomas Addis, and the diligent care from Ava Helen that he survived. Ava Helen took care of him and managed his very strict diet. Not only Dr. Addis, but Pauling's family believed that she was responsible for saving her husband's life.[11] Consequently, Pauling became more dependent on his wife. The significance of that was that she was the more politically active one, interested in a variety of social causes. Ava Helen's biographer said, "She was the one who persuaded Linus that it wasn't enough to do brilliant chemistry if the world was tumbling toward annihilation."[12] That put him on the road they traveled over the next twenty years—and beyond—to be engaged in advocating for democracy and peace.

Pauling had been involved in research on explosives at Caltech and would have been an asset to the Los Alamos project, but he turned down a job offer from Oppenheimer, probably on personal grounds. As with many other scientists, the unleashing of the atomic bomb in 1945 brought him a sense of profound concern. Pauling's new mission was disarmament. "We are truly forced into abandoning war as the method of solution of world problems," he wrote.[13]

His interest in social and political causes increased. Ava Helen was involved in a wide range of issues beyond war and peace, including civil rights, world government, and the treatment of Japanese-Americans. Linus was pulled along and became a partner. One interesting episode involved the blacklisted Hollywood writer Dalton Trumbo. Cleo Trumbo wrote to Pauling in 1950 asking him to be a parole advisor for her husband after his release for a politically motivated imprisonment. Pauling readily agreed: "I am happy to think that he would like to have me," he replied.[14]

In 1954 when Oppenheimer's security clearance was being investigated,

Pauling defended him. Although eight years earlier Pauling had questioned Oppie's "personal characteristics" in opposing him being named to the Atomic Energy Commission board—clearly those old wounds lingered—he now wrote an article in *The Nation* magazine in which he called Oppenheimer "a loyal and patriotic American" and labeled efforts to remove him "a disgraceful act."[15]

Pauling was involved with several petitions and declarations as an anti-bomb, antiwar movement gathered strength among scientists. In 1958 he spearheaded a worldwide petition of scientists to end atomic bomb testing and to internationalize control of nuclear weapons.[16] This petition was the subject of his questioning on "Meet the Press" and, more significantly, by the House Un-American Activities Committee. His activism was causing him to run into the same McCarthy-era quicksand that had hobbled his old friend Oppenheimer. In Pauling's case, the issue was not his security clearance, but he clearly was attracting publicity in a way that troubled the president and board at Caltech.

The petition, which had the endorsement of more than nine thousand scientists from forty-four countries, had become a political problem for Pauling. The Senate Judiciary Committee's subcommittee on internal security summoned Pauling for hearings in the summer and fall of 1960. He was grilled about how these signers came to be associated with the petition. Committee members and staff wanted to obtain the original copies of the original signatures, determine whether Pauling knew about the communist affiliations of certain members, understand why scientists from the Soviet Union and other countries were included, and ascertain whether certain people added themselves for nefarious reasons. Pauling steadfastly refused to provide the original copies of signatures—he referred the subcommittee to the names on file at the United Nations—and defended his methods and goals. He said that providing the names from his files would hamper his future ability to work for international peace.[17]

Interestingly, a number of people here at the dinner were signers, including Nobel laureates Harold Urey, Joseph Erlanger, Hermann Muller, Albert Szent-Gyorgyi, and Murphy, Pauling's onetime, youthful Oregon neighbor. Their presence—and Pauling's as well as Oppenheimer's—were a testament to how much had changed in the White House since January 1961. Pauling was hoping as much, as he had been a cautiously optimistic supporter of Kennedy in the presidential campaign.

Throughout 1961 the Paulings were perpetually engaged in antinuclear and antiwar efforts. Five days before Kennedy took office in January 1961, they wrote and circulated "An Appeal to Stop the Spread of Nuclear Weapons," stressing recent nuclear developments in Europe: France was expanding its nuclear capability, providing NATO with nuclear capability, and there was also the prospect of the Warsaw Pact nations joining the nuclear club.[18] Later in the year, the Paulings visited Norway, endorsing a disarmament statement, and Linus gave a talk on peace in Moscow. He also had telegraphed Nikita Khrushchev imploring him to scuttle a fifty-megaton nuclear test.[19] Pauling was not a critic of the Soviet Union, seeing little difference, perhaps naïvely, between capitalism and communism.[20]

Three months before the dinner, before the invitations were sent out, Pauling wrote to President Kennedy prodding him, as he had in the past, about nuclear weapons. He urged him not to resume nuclear testing, arguing that it was "not necessary" and that it would cause birth defects and various diseases.[21]

But Kennedy, frustrated by Khrushchev's unwillingness to agree to an arms deal, decided to move forward—which made the American peace movement, including the Paulings, angry. In a desperate effort, on March 1, Pauling wrote his most shrill letter to the president, a handwritten note sent while he was on the road in Durham, North Carolina. That's where he pointedly asked, "Are you going to give an order that will cause you to go down in history as one of the most immoral men of all time and one of the greatest enemies of the human race?" He sent a copy to Glenn Seaborg and Jerome Wiesner, both now present at the Nobel dinner.[22] The next day, Kennedy announced his plan to resume testing, explaining his reasons and placing the onus clearly on the Soviet leadership.

On April 9, however, Pauling sent a more measured letter to the president, urging him to reconsider his decision to resume atmospheric nuclear testing. Pauling argued that in addition to increasing worldwide radiation levels and harming "hundreds of thousands, even millions, of unborn children," the nation would not be any safer. Further, he said, "Controlled disarmament is not only possible, it is mandatory in the national self-interest of both sides."[23]

The decision to move ahead with renewed nuclear testing was what prompted demonstrations around the country, including the one in which Linus and Ava Pauling participated this last weekend in April outside the

White House. And yet, here they were, their first invitation to the president's home, and Linus was enjoying it. He understood how he was able to publicly leverage the outside drama with the inside calm. An extrovert and a raconteur who appreciated a good time, Linus was having a great time, apparently seeing no paradox in his behavior. Meanwhile, Ava Helen Pauling was having a challenging evening.

C===*-

Ava Helen, wearing a dark chiffon gown and mid-length white gloves, was seated several tables away from her husband in the State Dining Room with her back facing the windows looking out to the South Lawn. She had been excited about being invited to the dinner despite her jaundiced view of the Kennedy administration. Three weeks before the dinner, she wrote a friend, "A most exciting invitation has arrived!!"[24] If she thought the shift from protesting to dining was going to be seamless, that notion was dashed in the receiving line with the president and First Lady. Although Mrs. Kennedy's scolding of Linus was at least partly amusing, no doubt Ava Helen was on guard as to whether the First Lady might also mention the strongly worded letter that she had sent to her the previous July. She did not, but entering the State Dining Room, she was about to face a more seemingly unlikely critic.

Arthur M. Schlesinger Jr. was one of the most prominent members of the White House staff. The son of a distinguished Harvard history professor, Arthur was also a noted historian. He had two unusual professional characteristics: His biography of Andrew Jackson, published when he was twenty-eight, was awarded the Pulitzer Prize; and he was the rare academic whose sole degree was a bachelor's, albeit from Harvard. Other notable books were his 1949 argument for liberal democracy, *The Vital Center: The Politics of Freedom*—which influenced John Kennedy—and his trilogy on *The Age of Roosevelt*.[25] Easily spotted in lofty academic circles by his horn-rimmed glasses and ever-present bow tie, Schlesinger had been a professor and prolific writer as well as a liberal activist. He had been prominent with the Americans for Democratic Action (ADA) and was a close advisor to Adlai Stevenson and Eleanor Roosevelt, neither of whom had been fond of Kennedy.

But Schlesinger enjoyed the limelight and had hitched his star to the senator in the 1960 presidential campaign. It had paid off: he became the court historian, functioning as a policy dabbler, a liaison to liberals, and a speechwriter. He had written the original draft of tonight's speech, although it was greatly improved by Kennedy. He also had been involved in the planning for tonight's dinner. While his assistant, Toni Chayes, was identifying names and contact information for Nobel laureates, Schlesinger was prioritizing the "literary types," as he called them, and prominent scientists to be invited. He came up with multitiered lists, including alternates. And it was he who finally cleared Oppenheimer's attendance with the president.[26]

The Paulings needed to be invited because of Linus's Nobel status. Ultimately, Mrs. Kennedy and Tish Baldrige determined the seating arrangement, but it seems unlikely that Schlesinger did not have a hand in Ava Helen being seated next to him on her right physically, and thus ironically symbolically as well. Schlesinger was zealously loyal to the president and the court, clearly understanding the value of being so. Ava Helen was a critic of the administration and as Linus's wife an even more visible critic. Schlesinger knew of the Paulings' letters to the first couple and, of course, their picketing. The dinner was proving to be an opportunity for Schlesinger to berate Ava Helen and for her to parry his efforts.

The interaction between the two liberals resulted from differing agendas. Schlesinger, settling his chair on Ava's gown, inquired whether "I held the same opinions as my husband then asked if he could ask me a question." She said that they usually agreed, and then Schlesinger "asked how my husband could possibly accept the invitation to the White House after what he had said to the President" in his recent letter. She responded, "There was nothing personal in either [the] invitation [or] the acceptance," and that the whole evening was a Nobel event.

Unconvinced, the loyalist Schlesinger "repeated this [talk] about 'breaking bread' with [a] man who[m] he had accused of being more immoral than Hitler, Caligula, etc. I repeated nothing personal." Schlesinger then seemed to back off after Ava Helen, her blue eyes focused on him with her self-assured, high-pitched voice, attributed his rudeness to having been a Harvard professor.

What followed was small talk about their children; about Robert Frost, who was seated two tables over with the president and whose back was toward them; and about H. Stuart Hughes, a psychoanalyst, Harvard professor, and peace activist who was running as an independent against young Edward Kennedy for the Massachusetts senate seat that had been occupied by John Kennedy. Schlesinger said that Hughes "wants to coexist with Communists." He pushed this theme, asking Ava Helen whether she was acquainted with communists. As the grilling continued, Ava Helen caught him hoarding presidential matchbooks, which were placed on each table, and that reinforced her opinion of him: "He is a clout and a boor."[27]

Seated to Mrs. Pauling's left was Dr. Willard Libby, a chemist who had worked on the Manhattan Project, served on the Atomic Energy Commission during the Eisenhower administration, and was a Nobel laureate. He had long known Linus, and in fact, there was a serious disagreement between the two men on the dangers of nuclear radiation. Seven years earlier, Pauling took issue with a magazine article by Libby that stated, "The world is radioactive. It always has been and always will be. The natural radioactivities evidently are not dangerous"; and the same conclusion, he said, applied to atomic bombs.[28] Four months before the dinner, Pauling took issue again with Libby, this time for articles arguing that fallout shelters were effective and that, "A real shelter is a real life saver."[29] While Ava Helen's views were in concert with her husband's, the discussion with Bill Libby was not strained and included a conversation about scientists' children in general and theirs in particular.[30]

Among others at her table was Dr. George Kistiakowsky—known by friends, including Oppenheimer, as "Kisty"—another chemist associated with the Manhattan Project and a science advisor to President Eisenhower; Dr. Detlev Bronk, president of Rockefeller University; and Nobel laureate Dr. Edward Tatum, a chain-smoking geneticist at the Rockefeller Institute. Linus had known and worked with all three men. There also were three other spouses at the table: Gladys Brooks, Anne Pusey, and Doris DuBridge. Ava Helen would have much to tell her husband after dinner.

Meanwhile, Linus Pauling was amused by the attention that he was receiving. Many of the guests either knew him or knew of him. Some had even tangled with him. Peering from his table, he could spot Samuel I. Newhouse, the sixty-six-year-old newspaper mogul seated at Jean Kennedy Smith's table. Newhouse, a short, frenetic, old-school businessman, had been purchasing news-papers since the early 1930s; his empire had made him influential in largely second-tier markets. In 1955 he bought the St. Louis *Globe-Democrat*, the con-servative morning newspaper that competed with the liberal *Post-Dispatch* in the nation's tenth-largest city. And that was the connection with Pauling.[31]

In October 1960 as Pauling was about to appear again before the Senate In-ternal Security Subcommittee (SISS), the *Globe-Democrat* ran an editorial crit-icizing several people, including Pauling, for a previous hearing. It incorrectly stated that in not revealing those original signatures, Pauling "was cited for contempt of Congress." It went on to argue that his Nobel Prize in Chemistry "is no guarantee of either patriotism or correctness in foreign policy. It above all does not cloak him with an immunity to defy the Senate and to decide on his own prerogative what is best for America."[32]

Five days later an irate Pauling sent the publisher a letter, protesting and calling for "a retraction and apology" with the same prominence as the edi-torial. "I protest against your imputation that I am lacking in patriotism," he said. It was the same charge, though more implicit, that had been hanging over Oppenheimer's head for years. When the newspaper issued what Pauling considered an inadequate retraction, he sued. Subsequently, the newspaper published other articles and editorials against Pauling as the civil case worked its way through the system.[33] Newhouse, the owner but not the publisher of the *Globe-Democrat*, was surely aware of the legal challenge from Pauling. Observing Mitzi Newhouse, the mogul's chic wife, Pauling admired her ex-pensive necklace. He reportedly said to Ava Helen, "I'll get one of these for you, dear—as soon as I win my million-dollar libel suit against the St. Louis *Globe-Democrat*."[34]

❦

Since the dinner included so many Nobel laureates in science, it was not surprising that other scientists were also invited. Many of them were asso-ciated with the Manhattan Project or had some significant government role over the past decades. It was inevitable that many of these men would have known or had interactions—both pleasant and frustrating—with Pauling, who perhaps was the foremost American chemist at the time. These people were scattered across both rooms. Physicist Lee DuBridge, for example, knew Pauling at Caltech, where he was serving as president. DuBridge, seated in the Blue Room next to Dr. Glenn Seaborg, the chairman of the Atomic Energy Committee, was well aware of the views at Caltech regarding Pauling and his activism: trustees, largely negative; faculty, largely positive. One trustee had told DuBridge back in the 1950s that Pauling is "just a Communist, and we shouldn't have Communists on our faculty." DuBridge saw Pauling's picketing before the dinner as "not a very tactful thing to do" and chose not to talk to him about it.[35]

Pauling's table was hosted by Dr. James R. Killian Jr., who was a former president of Massachusetts Institute of Technology, another of President Eisenhower's science advisors, and a shaper of NASA. One astute observer called him "a brisk, incisive man with the manner and dispatch of a brilliant surgeon."[36] He also chaired a reconstituted Foreign Intelligence Advisory Board formed in response to the Bay of Pigs fiasco. When Killian was Eisenhower's science advisor, Pauling dismissed the work of his office as being "a puny effort." Pauling preferred that science, and the peaceful use of it, should be coordinated by a robust World Peace Research Organization, reflecting his and Ava Helen's consistent view on internationalizing security.[37] Pauling, who sat four seats over from Killian, surely would have had much to discuss with him.

That was also true with "Atomic Bill" Laurence, the journalist two seats away. Their perspectives on the atomic race since World War II were quite different. It wasn't that Laurence had devoted so many of those years to writing about the atomic bomb, but what set him apart from Pauling was his collaboration with the US government in reporting on the bomb. We would use the term "embedded" today to describe Laurence's work. General Leslie Groves requested that the *New York Times* cover the Manhattan Project, which accounts for why he was at the Trinity site in July 1945.[38]

At the time of the Trinity test, Oppenheimer, despite his angst about what had been unleashed, still believed in the value of what was being accomplished in the New Mexico desert. He told Laurence later on the day of the test, "Lots of boys not grown up yet will owe their life to it."[39] But Laurence was sold on the bomb and the use of nuclear power at least two months before. Showing his support for the Manhattan Project and in an unusual breach of journalistic ethics, he drafted a speech for Groves to present to President Truman back in May 1945. It was not used, and in fact, all copies but one were destroyed. But the comments made by Laurence were fascinating. First, he clearly knew much earlier than many of those associated with the bomb the strategy that was being considered. He wrote in the preface to his remarks that they were "to be delivered at the time of use of the atomic bomb over Japan, or, if Japan capitulates before such use, at a time to be determined shortly after announcement of capitulation."[40]

In the proposed speech, Laurence went on to praise American scientific achievement in producing the "greatest of all weapons" and its importance to the war effort. He continues on with an endorsement of atomic energy for everyday use. He also discusses the need to safeguard the proliferation of nuclear capability from "warlike nations." In the long, somewhat turgid, statistics-laden speech proposed for a radio address, Laurence praises Groves and several others—Oppenheimer's name is buried in a list of people on page fourteen—and emphasizes divine intervention: "One cannot fail to see the hand of Providence in the fact that it was our people that Almighty God saw fit to give this weapon to first."[41]

Not only was Laurence an atomic enthusiast in 1945, he also was identified as a consultant to Groves. He was being paid by both his newspaper and the us government; he had, in fact, become a propagandist for the government. That surely was the reason that he had a unique, birds-eye view of the mushroom cloud as he flew in a b-29 when it dropped the atomic bomb on Nagasaki. Overall, his reporting bolstered the government's position. In a front-page article in the *Times* in September 1945, shortly after the war ended, Laurence discounted the impact of the radiation from the atomic explosions in Japan. He quoted Groves, who was effectively his employer: "The Japanese claim that people died from radiations. If this is true, the number was very small." Laurence adds that Geiger counters used at the Trinity site "showed that less than two months after the explosion the radiations on the surface had dwindled to a minute quantity, safe for continuous human habitation."[42] Laurence received a Pulitzer Prize for his coverage of the Japanese bombings. He subsequently published a book on nuclear issues.

Clearly, Pauling and Laurence approached this most contentious issue from different perspectives. While it is not recorded what the two men discussed that night, their presence at table two highlighted the difference of opinion that existed on a matter of utmost importance to Pauling and millions of Americans—and surely was reflected at various tables this evening. The Kennedy White House was comfortable with serious debate.

❦

Seated on either side of Pauling were the wives of men prominent in different fields. On his right was Mary Waterman, whose husband was director of the National Science Foundation, and on his left was Pearl Ann Clement, whose husband, Rufus, was the president of Atlanta University. Rufus Clement had been the president of the school since 1937, and he had made important gains for the historically black university.[43] He also was engaged in civil rights issues, although his moderation put him at odds with W. E. B. Du Bois, also at Atlanta. Clement was the first African-American to become a member of the Atlanta school board since Reconstruction.

Another spouse at Pauling's table was Ellen Cousins, the wife of noted writer and peace activist Norman Cousins, who was seated in the Blue Room. He and Pauling were largely kindred spirits, but they also had their disagreements. Cousins was the longtime editor of *The Saturday Review*, which he used to promote a liberal agenda. The two men, who supported international oversight of atomic power as well as a world federalism movement, started to correspond in the 1950s.[44] In 1958 Pauling praised him "for the many fine actions that you have been taking about the great world's problem that must be solved [radiation]." And yet, in that same letter Pauling could not resist being his blunt and opinionated self. After questioning Cousins's wording on strontium radiation, he goes on to comment on an editorial: "I think that your discussion of radium dials of wristwatches is not very good." He continues to chide him and then says that Cousins needs "good advice about scientific questions. I should, of course, be pleased to have you call upon me at any time."[45]

The two men subsequently became friendly—both were active in the National Committee for a Sane Nuclear Policy (SANE)—but by 1961 there was tension between them. The tension was based on whether Cousins was suitably supportive of Pauling, who was under attack for his left-leaning views from some SANE members, concerned by negative media attention. Cousins told him, "It would seem strange indeed if two men with essentially the same basic commitments should be unable to get along, or even to communicate with one another with a fair degree of understanding."[46] But that was how personal interactions often were with Pauling, a man with strong views who could make common cause with those fundamentally in agreement with him, but not quite where he wanted them to be—as was his ambivalent relationship with President Kennedy.

⊂═◄►

Also seated at the table with Pauling were longtime Associated Press science writer Alton Blakeslee and Nobel laureate Dr. Edward Doisy, a biochemist. So, too, was Carolyn Keane Enders, the wife of Dr. John Enders, "The Father of Modern Vaccines" and another Nobel winner. Enders, Pauling, and Ernest Hemingway were connected in an important way: they were among the Nobel award winners in 1954. Also part of the Pauling conversation that evening at table two was Rosemarie du Vigneaud, wife of Vincent du Vigneaud, who followed Pauling with the Nobel Prize in Chemistry the following year. Dr. du Vigneaud, a practicing physician as well as a researcher, was a friend of Pauling's, and they shared an interest in peptide and amino acid studies. This was a small, distinguished circle of scientists with various connections, who were brought together and honored on this night by President Kennedy.

Linus Pauling was a complex man, and some of these relationships highlighted that. He was a controlled man, not very emotional. He was a serious scientist and political activist, but also had a softer side, if sometimes self-centered or intense. He and his wife were affectionate with each other: He called her "Mama" and she called him "Paddy," a combination of "papa" and "daddy."[47] He enjoyed the comics, including Peanuts, which featured the character Linus. His favorite movie was Lover Come Back, released the previous year and which starred Doris Day. It, too, had a Linus, whom Pauling called "the greatest chemist in the world." He enjoyed light reading, including detective novels. But, he "soured on Agatha Christie. She lost me when she mentioned 'the foul odor of carbon monoxide' which is an odorless gas."[48] There it was: Linus Pauling, ever critical and precise.

As the guests continued to enjoy their meal, savoring the beef Wellington and enjoying the side dishes that chef René Verdon and his staff had prepared, the conversations flowed. At Pauling's table, as well as others, eyes often glanced toward the president in the State Dining Room and the First Lady in the Blue Room. Most of these scientists and other honored guests were familiar with the limelight, but this was an evening to remember, to recount to their family and friends in the years to come. Soon Pauling, an aficionado of the tango and the Viennese waltz, would experience the most ethereal part of the evening as he and Ava Helen glided along the Cross Hall to the music of the Strolling Strings.

# CHAPTER SEVEN

# "The Fire Next Time"

AN IRISH-BORN IMMIGRANT had been selected in a competition to build a permanent home for the president in a swampy area of the newly created District of Columbia. James Hoban had gained experience as an architect in his home country before arriving in the United States in the 1780s. He lived in Philadelphia and Charleston, South Carolina, before permanently settling in the sparsely populated future capital city in 1792 to begin the work for which he would become most famous. It would take Hoban most of the decade to complete the building, and he would need many workers to haul stone from the quarry, make and lay bricks, and provide carpentry work. There were many notable characteristics related to the construction of the building, including its resemblance to the Duke of Leinster's house in Dublin, which Hoban knew well.[1] But in retrospect the most controversial issue was that Hoban used his own slaves—Ben, Harry, Daniel, and perhaps Pete—as carpenters. Other slaves also were used.[2] These slaves were not compensated, but rather their wages were given to their owners.

While appalling to Americans today, it is not surprising that slave labor was used to build the White House. Slavery was widespread in the coastal Carolinas and was common in Washington, DC, Maryland, and Virginia. In fact, slavery even existed in small numbers in Pennsylvania, New York, and other northern states in 1790. And it already had become a political, if not moral, issue by the time of the launching of the new federal government. Indeed, the founders hotly debated the counting of slaves in hypocritically determining representation in Congress, coming up with the Three-Fifths Compromise: a slave counted as three-fifths of a person, adding additional political influence to slaveholding states while not acknowledging the bonded person's humanity. So keen were the constitutional framers to gain southern support that it was two northerners, James Wilson of Pennsylvania and Roger Sherman of Connecticut, who crafted the compromise that brought it about.

Slavery had blighted American society since its first introduction in Virginia in 1619—ironically, the year of the first representative assembly in the North American colonies. Although the men who met in Philadelphia successfully brokered an agreement without which the Constitution might have been scuttled, the issue continued to haunt the nation through the Civil War, three-quarters of a century later. During that time, most of the occupants of the President's House—men who guided the nation, pledged to uphold the Constitution, and presumably, agreed with the soaring rhetoric of the Declaration of Independence—were either slave owners or passive on the issue of slavery.

The President's House or the Executive Mansion—it became known as the White House only in 1901—had been the scene of many events pivotal to the continuance of slavery and its legacy of racism. Thomas Jefferson, who wrote in the Declaration of Independence that "All men are created equal," was a slaveholder. More than a decade after he left the presidency, he finally understood the potential for harm that this "peculiar institution" held, saying that slavery "like a fire bell in the night, awakened and filled me with terror. I considered it at once as the knell of the Union."[3]

The cataclysm did come, of course, with the Civil War, largely caused by slavery and its impact on political power, economics, and—for many—morality. It was in this house that Abraham Lincoln signed the Emancipation Proclamation. Although the legal safeguards for slavery came to an end, racism and efforts to thwart full equality proved to be a vexing challenge that continues to this day. While Theodore Roosevelt withstood harsh criticism for inviting the black educator Booker T. Washington to dinner at the White House in 1901, other presidents were often less enlightened. Woodrow Wilson segregated federal government buildings. Franklin Roosevelt, whose social consciousness was enhanced by his wife, Eleanor, still was politically cautious: he refused to acknowledge Jesse Owens's outstanding achievement in the 1936 Olympics in Berlin. President Eisenhower, whose career was spent in the segregated army, was unenthusiastic about desegregating the schools in the1950s, but eventually capitulated and executed the law.

Despite his pursuit of liberals in the 1960 presidential campaign, President Kennedy was a political moderate and was ever conscious of the value of not alienating southern Democratic leaders, strongly segregationist. Although the civil rights movement had intensified over the past decade—and racial violence was becoming more serious—by April 1962 Kennedy might have been sympathetic to the plight of African-Americans, but he was still restrained in his engagement on race issues.

In July 1961 St. Louis-born mezzo-soprano Grace Bumbry, an African-American, ignited a small controversy when she was cast in a prominent role in a production of *Tannhaeuser*. The opera, written by the racist composer Richard Wagner, was produced by Wagner's nephew and performed at the noted Bayreuth Festival in Germany.[4] Mrs. Kennedy had heard of the rising twenty-five-year-old and invited her to the White House, where she had performed in the East Room two months before the Nobel dinner. It was Bumbry's initial engagement in the United States.[5] This invitation followed another symbolic invitation from the Kennedys. Marian Anderson, the great African-American contralto, who was blocked from singing at Constitution Hall in Washington, DC, by the Daughters of the American Revolution in 1939, sang the national anthem at President Kennedy's inauguration.

❦

This was the setting for James Baldwin, one of America's most fiery advocates for racial equality. His attendance at the Nobel dinner was a result of Arthur Schlesinger's meticulous planning. Schlesinger drew up various invitation lists, with Baldwin in the second tier of literary figures, behind the "musts." In the top-priority group were Dos Passos, Farrell, Styron, Lionel Trilling, and Robert Frost. Some other prominent writers, including John Steinbeck—who would win a Nobel Prize later in 1962—J. D. Salinger, and Carl Sandburg declined. Arthur Miller, Tennessee Williams, John Hersey, and Edmund Wilson—all "musts"—were held over to the next month's dinner for André Malraux. Baldwin was grouped with another of tonight's guests, Van Wyck Brooks. The lists indicate that the alternate for Baldwin was another, older and more famous African-American writer, Ralph Ellison.[6] Interestingly, Ellison had influenced Baldwin, who wrote: "Mr. Ellison, by the way, is the first Negro novelist I have ever read to utilize in language, and brilliantly, some of the ambiguity and irony of Negro life."[7]

The invitation might have gone to Ellison because at first the White House was having a difficult time tracking down Baldwin. The first invitation went to the offices of Alfred Knopf, which was not his publisher. It was then delivered to Dial Press, which was, and Baldwin accepted. In addition to not knowing the publisher, apparently the White House—or at least Schlesinger—did not know that Baldwin was gay; the White House social files for the evening have a notation: "Mr. Schlesinger thinks [Baldwin] is single."[8]

Baldwin, who was living on the property of Bill and Rose Styron on Rucum Road in Roxbury, Connecticut, accompanied Rose and their neighbor Van Wyck Brooks into the White House.[9] There was that brief awkwardness with Baldwin forgetting his invitation, but soon he was mingling with friends in the Cross Hall. Katherine Anne Porter was there and met Baldwin in a somewhat euphoric state. He "seized both my hands, put his face very close to mine and shouted, 'I LOVE YOU!' and leaped away, leaving me a little surprised to say the least," she recalls.[10] Bill Styron, who was a friend and writing colleague of Baldwin's, saw this all as a great adventure, saying that Baldwin and he were behaving "like Huck and Jim."[11]

Styron's comment was meant in a playful, innocuous way, but in later years such a statement would be considered racially insensitive. At the time, however, such a reference might have been seen as humorous. It was a time when racial stereotypes were common. However, more racially charged—and clearly more malevolent—was a comment made by another guest, the patrician historian Samuel Eliot Morison. Annoyed that Baldwin repeatedly approached him, Morison said with irritation, "Who *was* that ugly little dinge who pestered me all night?"[12] Perhaps equally disconcerting, attesting to the subtle—and not so subtle—racism even in this crowd of intellectuals was that others hearing it found it amusing.[13]

⚬══✧⚬

There were three prominent African-American guests at the dinner. Ralph Bunche clearly was the most distinguished, having achieved wide recognition for his peacekeeping efforts and the Nobel Peace Prize. Dr. Clement, the president of what was then called Atlanta College University, had had a distinguished career, but was not known nationally. And then there was Baldwin, a young writer who had already published important books, but his renown would come in later years and grow after his death.

Baldwin, a short, thin man with large, mournful eyes, was intense and articulate. Arthur Schlesinger said of him, "He drew into himself the agony he saw around him and charged it with the force of an electric and passionate personality."[14] Baldwin understood the racial hatred of his time, and offered insights on how America at midcentury was so much less than what it could be. He was often angry, but never bitter. Implicit in all of his writings, despite the bleak picture, was Baldwin's optimism that the country could improve. He took his role as a principled writer seriously, commenting, "I want to be an honest man and a good writer."[15]

James Arthur Baldwin had a poor, unhappy childhood in Harlem. In addition to the difficulties that young African-Americans faced on the streets, Baldwin struggled with a cruel stepfather. There were two bright spots in his teenage years. One was studying with a caring white school teacher named Orilla "Bill" Miller, who opened his world to reading and writing, and who became a pivotal nurturer. The other was also a teacher, but was more well-known: the Harlem Renaissance writer Countee Cullen, who became a mentor.[16] After graduating from high school, Baldwin began writing, mostly essays. As a young man, he was trying to cope with racism as well as his sexual identity. Believing that there was little future for him in New York, he left for Paris in 1948; he was twenty-four.[17]

Following in the footsteps of so many expatriate writers—including Hemingway, who also influenced him—Baldwin settled into Parisian life and wrote his early books there. By 1962 he had written six books, three of which were notable for different reasons. The first, *Go Tell It on the Mountain*, was published in 1953 and was largely an autobiography set in Harlem. John Grimes, the main character, struggles with two challenges—just like the young Baldwin—his family relationships, especially with his stern and abusive father, and with the Pentecostal religion that was practiced at home and attracted him at an early age. It was an important novel and a critical breakthrough for Baldwin, who surely viewed the writing of it as cathartic. And it was well received. Norman Cousins's *Saturday Review*, for one, compared the book favorably to works by William James and William Faulkner. Another newspaper reviewer pronounced it as "almost perfectly executed."[18]

*Notes of a Native Son* followed in 1955. Here Baldwin reprinted ten essays that he had published earlier. Most of these essays are memoirs that discuss his experiences with racism in the United States and elsewhere, including France, Switzerland, and Africa. Three of the pieces criticize literary people or their works: Harriet Beecher Stowe and *Uncle Tom's Cabin*, Richard Wright and his *Native Son*, and the 1954 black musical *Carmen Jones*. In "Everybody's Protest Novel," Baldwin calls *Uncle Tom's Cabin* "a very bad novel, having, in its self-righteous, virtuous sentimentality, much in common with *Little Women*."[19] To Baldwin, Stowe's novel falls into the trap of merely being a protest work.

While paying obeisance to Wright and his landmark work, which Baldwin calls "the most powerful and celebrated statement we have yet had of what it means to be a Negro in America," he nevertheless considers the presentation confining and as reinforcing a stereotype.[20] His critique of *Carmen Jones* focuses on the presentation of African-Americans as "ciphers."[21] In all three essays, which comprise the first part of the book, Baldwin argues for a more nuanced view of the African-American experience, one which presents the complexity of being black in a majority white America.

The second part of the book includes essays that discuss racism in Harlem and Atlanta, as well as a candid analysis of his stepfather. The third part—four essays—compares the black experience abroad with that at home in the United States. "A Question of Identity," which has been likened to Henry James and his *The Ambassadors*, takes up the issue of American expatriates in Paris and a newly found perspective on their native country from three thousand miles away.[22] This really represents an appreciation for the United States, despite its racism and flaws. He argues that these expats develop a respect for the culture and spirit of America, and a sense of the dynamism that helps create a forward-looking worldview. Here is Baldwin internalizing his own maturing perspective on America and perhaps the seeds of his own optimism.

These essays say much about James Baldwin. His perspective on race was not a superficial, easy response to the obvious sense of injustice. Rather, it was an understanding of the history and the complexity of humanity, both black and white, and a recognition that the United States was not alone in its mistreatment of minorities. And yet, the United States had the capability, if it wished to do so, to make itself a fair, more hospitable society. These themes would continue in his work, despite his frequent reliance on bluntness and outrage.

The issue of bisexuality and homosexuality was addressed by Baldwin in his 1956 novel *Giovanni's Room*, set in Paris and the South of France. Here Baldwin—obviously continuing in an autobiographical vein—deals with male relationships and social separation. While a shocking book for its time, it was successful and achieved some critical acclaim. "This novel," one reviewer said, "is more than another report on homosexuality. It is a story of a man who could not make up his mind, one who could not say yes to life."[23] This was Baldwin at the time—a tortured soul who sought relief in writing about it. Norman Mailer, with whom Baldwin had a largely strained relationship, called it "a bad book but mostly a brave one."[24]

While in Paris, Baldwin socialized—and drank—with other American expatriate writers, including Styron. But he headed back to a changing United States in 1957, and he began a new phase of his career, first as an observer on civil rights issues and then as an activist. Working on articles for two magazines, Baldwin toured the South beginning in September 1957, visiting Atlanta, Birmingham, Montgomery, Charlotte, Nashville, and other cities. He went to Little Rock, where the school integration battle was at a fever pitch. He met and was impressed by Dr. Martin Luther King Jr. and Coretta Scott King. While admiring the young clergyman-activist for his peaceful approach to racial conciliation, Baldwin was not convinced that King's prescription was sufficient.[25]

One of Baldwin's articles appeared in the October 1958 issue of *Harper's Monthly*—immediately following one by Oppenheimer. The five-page article, "The Hard Kind of Courage," is a well-written narrative with interviews from several people whom Baldwin encountered. An insightful piece, the article provides a snapshot of everyday life, particularly in the schools. "The South had always frightened me," he wrote, but his first visit to the region showed him the courage that African-Americans embodied. It educated him as to the challenges and turmoil in the South and then caused him to consider some broader implications, saying, "What is happening in the South today will be happening in the North tomorrow."[26]

Another article that was the result of Baldwin's southern tour was "Nobody Knows My Name: A Letter from the South," which was published in the winter 1959 issue of the *Partisan Review*. The article focuses partly on Charlotte, North Carolina, but more especially on Atlanta. Here he talks about the powerlessness of even well-to-do blacks, whose existence is always precarious. Baldwin argues that the race issue needs to be addressed directly, and it is the responsibility of everyone in the country to do so. Individuals—both black and white—need to examine the status of freedom in this country and, if not, "we may yet become one of the most distinguished and monumental failures in the history of nations."[27] Baldwin had a way of looking at the deeper, broader implications of the inequalities of racism in America, for the future good of all its citizens.

Entering the 1960s, Baldwin was searching for a way to channel his passion into the growing civil rights movement. By now he was a well-known writer with broad connections. He expanded his friendship with Styron and moved into his guesthouse. There they interacted. Baldwin acted as a tutor for the southern-born Styron, providing the liberal writer with a broader sense of the black experience. While Baldwin was there, Styron began his work on the controversial book *The Confessions of Nat Turner;* some even suggested that the character of Turner was based on Baldwin.[28] So it was rather serendipitous that both men were invited to the Nobel dinner.

Baldwin had been looking forward to the dinner. To be included in this distinguished group, along with the best American writers, was validation for his work. He also would have an opportunity to mingle with fellow wordsmiths whose work he knew and, in the case of writers such as Dos Passos, whom he admired. He found Hemingway, who would be honored at the dinner, an inspiration. He also respected the work of Faulkner, who had declined the invitation. Baldwin might have had an opportunity to patch up differences with Faulkner, who was near the end of his life. Faulkner had said some insensitive, if not inflammatory, things about blacks in a 1956 interview, and Baldwin felt compelled to respond.

Not only had Baldwin admired Faulkner's work, but he once placed him in the same lofty category as Ralph Ellison.[29] But when Faulkner said in his interview that desegregation efforts should "go slow" and aligned himself with whites in his home state of Mississippi regarding school integration "even if it meant going out into the streets and shooting Negroes," Baldwin had to react.[30] Taking to the *Partisan Review,* Baldwin wrote an essay entitled "Faulkner and Desegregation." Addressing various points raised by Faulkner, Baldwin criticizes his "middle of the road" position and argues that there is no time to waste in rectifying old wrongs. He says that Faulkner is hobbled by the common problem of "the Southerner [who] clings to two entirely antithetical doctrines, two legends, two histories." According to Baldwin, "The challenge is in the moment, the time is always now."[31]

Baldwin would not have the opportunity to debate Faulkner—or reconcile with him—but he would be able to represent his viewpoints to a crowd of white liberals, whom he looked at with suspicion. Among those would be the president and his brother, neither of whom had been particularly aggressive in pursuing civil rights objectives, largely in deference to southern politics and politicians. When they did meet for the first time tonight, Baldwin was drawn to the president, but had an instant distaste for his brother.[32] However, there would be another episode, more important and far reaching, that would occur as a result of this dinner concerning the two men. And that would be something of great importance.

Despite all the excitement and drama of being at the White House, James Baldwin could not help but ponder being received into this house. Any student of American history—and Baldwin was—would know that slaveholders held forth here for first part of the nineteenth century, that antiblack initiatives were either promoted or countenanced here, and that there were reminders all over the mansion. Indeed, a painting of president and slaveholder Thomas Jefferson was looking down upon him where he sat.

The host for Baldwin and the others dining at table ten, part of the last row of tables facing the wall leading into the Cross Hall, was Pierre Salinger. Salinger, a pudgy bon vivant, was the White House press secretary. At age thirty-six, one year younger than Baldwin, he was one of the most visible members of the New Frontier. Known as "Plucky," Salinger was a cigar-chomping former newspaperman. Like the president, he had served with the Navy in the Pacific during World War II. Like Baldwin, he had an appreciation for France and its culture—his mother was French. Salinger was in his element tonight, a gregarious raconteur holding forth on behalf of the administration.

Salinger's entrée into the Kennedy world began five years earlier. He had been working on a story for *Collier's* on the Teamsters, who were then being investigated by Senator John McClellan's Select Committee on Improper Activities in Labor and Management. Young Robert Kennedy was the aggressive chief counsel, and they became acquainted. In February 1957 Kennedy offered Salinger a position on the staff, and the two men with very different backgrounds worked well together for the next two years. "Inquisitive and indefatigable, he was of great help in getting the Committee started," according to Robert Kennedy.[33] This led to Salinger being named press secretary to John Kennedy in 1959 in preparation for the presidential campaign the following year.[34]

It came as no surprise that Salinger was named White House press secretary. Not only had he performed well in dealing with the press, but he and the Massachusetts senator had bonded, sometimes over their love of cigars. Salinger quickly became the prototype for the modern White House press secretary, at least partly because of the growing prominence of television news in the 1960s. Salinger would accompany the president on his well-received news conferences at the State Department and sit on his immediate left. And of course, he had constant interaction with an expanded news corps that had a voracious interest in the telegenic president. Kennedy had a spokes-of-a-wheel approach to White House management—there was no chief of staff—and Salinger was one of several men who had easy access to the president. Salinger was at the seat of power and engaged in all the major issues of the first fifteen months of the administration.

One of those major episodes was the Bay of Pigs, over which Kennedy was pummeled after the failed effort. In one of those rare instances in which his press recommendations fell short, Salinger encouraged the president to address the fiasco before the American Newspaper Publishers Association. Unfortunately, Kennedy's speech seemed to criticize the press, and the resultant coverage made the situation worse.[35] Still, Salinger was skilled at his job, and he showed it on various foreign trips. Among the easy selling trips were those in Paris, where the president and the First Lady captivated the French people. One of the most challenging was the disastrous summit with Nikita Khrushchev in Vienna.[36] He also had a backstage role in handling various issues with the press, such as the pique expressed by the two networks, ABC and NBC, that were passed over for the exclusive—and highly successful—White House tour by Mrs. Kennedy, broadcast by CBS two months earlier.[37]

Sitting next to Salinger was Diana Trilling, who was not impressed by her table host and seemed to be thwarted in making conversation with him. "I must have launched fifty topics of talk," she said, "all of which fizzled out. Nothing we said to each other involved more than two sentences: my remark, his answer. Then we'd have to start all over again. Eventually, I found it interesting that it was so dull with him."[38] Perhaps their different worlds, one from the realm of politics and the media, the other from the intellectual and literary realm, accounted for some stiffness. Or perhaps it was at least partly because of Diana's caustic manner.

Diana Trilling was a full member of an elite, sometimes self-important, set of writers and thinkers known as the New York Intellectuals. They were certainly liberal, but also staunchly anticommunist. The group included Lionel Trilling and people such as Norman Podhortez, Nathan Glazer, Irving Howe, Saul Bellow, Mary McCarthy, Alfred Kazin, and Susan Sontag. Many were Jewish and most argued about social, economic, and public issues among themselves—sometimes very strongly—and often in influential liberal publications such as *Commentary* and *Partisan Review*. Members of the group had strong opinions about politics, but were largely outside the hurly-burly political world that people such as Salinger inhabited.

Perhaps it is no surprise that Diana also did not enjoy her interaction with the person on her left at the table, Dr. Wendell Stanley. Stanley, a balding man with wire-rim glasses, was a biochemist, yet another researcher associated with the Rockefeller Institute and with the University of California at Berkeley, the cradle of American Nobel laureates. His work on sterols and stereochemistry led him to the Nobel Prize in Chemistry in 1946. Some of his research also involved tobacco, which turned out to be the major topic of discussion with Diana.

Diana introduced herself to Dr. Stanley in an odd way: "You haven't the vaguest idea who I am. You scientists don't read," she said, later reporting that he enjoyed her novel bluntness. Although smoking was prevalent in the room—indeed, there was a cup full of cigarettes placed on each table (eight cigarettes fit comfortably)—he singled her out: "He spent the entire dinner trying to persuade me to stop smoking, telling me in horrendous detail about the cancer I was heading into, and how I was going to rot inch by inch." And yet he acknowledged that his wife, Marian, also was a smoker. "What am I doing this for? I haven't been able to stop my own wife from smoking. Why am I trying to stop you? She's so nervous it's probably better for her to smoke than not to," he said.[39]

Others were enjoying themselves at the table, relishing the food and free-flowing wine. Well, maybe not Dorothy Milburn Russell Leger, the wife for the past four years of the French writer Alexis Leger (Saint-John Perse). The Legers lived part of the year in southeastern France, and presumably she and Salinger could talk about America's oldest ally. But according to Diana, Salinger was so dull that Mrs. Leger, sitting to his right, also was bored.[40]

Baldwin did not know the woman seated to his right, Catherine "Kay" Kerr. He asked Diana before sitting down, "Didn't she write a book, *Please Don't Eat the Daisies?*"[41] Baldwin, who apparently was keeping up with popular culture, had her confused with Jean Kerr, whose 1957 humorous book about a suburban family had been a best-seller. Three years later, the book was made into a movie starring Doris Day, David Niven, and several other stars. Kay Kerr had two roles. She was the wife of Clerk Kerr, who had been chancellor of the University of California at Berkeley and now was president of the entire University of California system. But she also was an early environmentalist. Working with a few faculty wives, she had recently launched Save the Bay, a nonprofit working to safeguard the sixty-mile by twelve-mile San Francisco Bay. Also, like the activist couple of Linus and Ava Helen Pauling, Clark and Kay Kerr had an interest in world peace; the Kerrs met and soon married twenty-eight years ago when she was a Stanford student and both attended a peace conference.[42]

There was another wife of a university president at the table, Catherine Stratton, whose husband, Julius Stratton, had been president of the Massachusetts Institute of Technology since 1959. A witty and intelligent woman, at home on both the farm and the campus, Mrs. Stratton made the arts a focus of her role as the wife of the MIT president. She held salons on campus, and as a neighboring university president said, "The conversation would be fascinating, and it would not only be about the topical issues of the day. Kay had an opinion about everything and everyone, and she was not afraid to share it. That's part of what made her so lively, so interesting, so young at heart."[43]

The other guest at the table was sixty-nine-year-old Alan Waterman, a physicist and the inaugural and current director of the National Science Foundation, having served since 1951. Dr. Waterman had greatly expanded the role and budget of the organization and was regarded as a determined professional at a time when American science was struggling to exceed the achievements of the Soviet Union in several fields. He also was respected for his demeanor. One colleague, Vannevar Bush, called him: "A quiet individual, a real scholar and decidedly effective in his quiet way, for everyone likes him and trusts him." Detlev Bronk, another scientist at the dinner, described him as "kind and gentle" while also being "firm and exacting."[44]

The conversation flowed and the food was served. Perhaps the dynamics at this table were not as lively as at others, but the guests were starting to think about the next part of the evening, the literary entertainment to be provided by actor Fredric March. As the desserts were delivered and coffee was poured, Diana Trilling finally saw signs of life from Pierre Salinger. He leaned over to Diana and said, "Cigars are moving slowly. If the President rises before they get to me, I won't have one. But I know all these waiters, and I'm not worried— they'll bring me a cigar."[45]

The guests were starting to ease away from their chairs and were about to be led by the social aides to the Red Room and Green Room for champagne and for what the president's briefing material called "powdering time."[46] Soon everyone would be headed for another historic room, the largest in the White House, the East Room.

## CHAPTER EIGHT ⟨⟨

# A Galaxy of Geniuses

THE DISTINGUISHED GUESTS honored tonight owed their presence to a Swedish dynamite manufacturer. Alfred Nobel was a chemist who found a safe way to use nitroglycerine and create an explosive that achieved widespread use in Europe in the second half of the nineteenth century. In addition to inventing dynamite, he created other explosives such as gelignite and ballistite, and he became rich. A brilliant and well-read man, Nobel was also aloof. "I am a misanthrope," he explained, "and yet, utterly benevolent, have more than one screw loose yet a super-idealist who digests philosophy more efficiently than food." He was a lifelong bachelor who wrote his will in 1895—one year before his death—and the bulk of the money in the brief document was relegated to establish financial "prizes to those who, during the preceding year, shall have conferred the greatest benefit on mankind."[1]

The Nobel Prizes commenced in 1901. In his will Nobel stipulated that five prizes would be awarded annually: physics, chemistry, physiology or medicine, literature, and peace. He also identified how the prizes would be awarded. Because Norway and Sweden were united under one king—it was a union that was established in 1814—each state had a role in the administration of the prizes. The Swedish government provided the head of a foundation board; the Norwegian parliament chose the committee members from prominent organizations and made the awards; and the annual awards were presented in both capitals: the Peace Prize in Oslo and the other prizes in Stockholm.[2]

Although this was a Scandinavian-based prize and administered by two separate but united Scandinavian states, it was understood from the outset that the prizes would be awarded to worthy recipients from throughout the world. For the first thirty years of the Nobel Prize, the United States was most successful in obtaining the Peace Prize, reflecting the growing international influence of the country. The first American Nobel laureate was President Theodore Roosevelt, who received the Peace Prize in 1906 for his role in bringing together the two sides in the Russo-Japanese War and signing a peace treaty. Roosevelt, looking to insert himself in the international arena and also keep watch on the regional power struggle in Asia, invited peace negotiators to Portsmouth, New Hampshire. In the fifth year of his presidency, Roosevelt added to his international stature with the Nobel selection. In remarks delivered on his behalf by the us ambassador to Norway at the award ceremony, he said, "There is no gift I could appreciate more and I wish it were in my power fully to express my gratitude."[3] Roosevelt's award was followed over the next quarter century by those of Secretary of State Elihu Root, President Woodrow Wilson, secretaries of state Charles B. Dawes and Frank B. Kellogg, peace activist Jane Addams, and educator Nicholas Murray Butler.[4]

The year after Roosevelt's award, the Prussian-born physicist Albert A. Michelson became the second American to win a Nobel Prize. Michelson's unique contribution was his experiments on the speed of light. His success was a harbinger of things to come: many Nobel Prizes in the sciences were made to Americans, and a number of them were awarded to immigrants fleeing Europe. In the early years of the award, up until 1914, the Germans and French dominated the science awards, representing about one-half. The United Kingdom and the Netherlands each represented 10 percent of the awardees. But in successive decades, Americans began to be recognized more and more. From 1925 to 1934, 20 percent of the science awards went to us researchers, and from 1935 to 1944, it was nearly 28 percent. Then, from 1945 to 1954, the Americans were dominant: nearly 42 percent of all science awards went to Americans in the period 1945–1954 and almost 45 percent in the next nine-year period.[5]

Overall, through the most recent year of the awards, 1961, seventy-six Americans were awarded Nobel Prizes, about one-third of these in medicine or physiology. Twenty-three percent of all Nobel recipients were Americans. In briefing material prepared for President Kennedy, a breakdown was given by decade. Over the past three decades, Americans were awarded between 34 percent and 43 percent of the prizes.[6] Clearly, the United States had become the leading country in producing Nobel-caliber scientists, writers, and peacemakers.

The president was proud of this. In a lengthy address at the University of California at Berkeley the previous month, he touted American success—and specifically those scientists at Berkeley. "Your faculty," he said, "includes more Nobel laureates than any other faculty in the world—more in this one community than our principal adversary [the Soviet Union] has received since the awards began in 1901. And we take pride in that, only from a national point of view, because it indicates, as the Chancellor pointed out, the great intellectual benefits of a free society." These laureates would see the president again at dinner tonight.[7]

⊂═✛⊱

Sinclair Lewis was the first American to receive the award in literature, in 1930, and he would be honored during tonight's after-dinner presentation. Dr. William Murphy, Dr. Harold Urey, Dr. Victor F. Hess, and Pearl Buck were the four Nobel laureates from the 1930s present at the dinner. The honorees would represent American achievement for the past thirty years, during which time the country was growing in stature in virtually every field as it rose to become a world superpower. Tonight it was at the height of its military strength, political influence, and intellectual attainment.

The forty-nine Nobel laureates being honored represented achievement in many ground-breaking areas. Pearl Buck was a literary giant, whose work on Asia, especially China, brought a greater appreciation of the Far East to many in the United States and elsewhere. The peacekeeping work of Ralph Bunche and the Canadian Lester Pearson represented important work done on a multilateral basis. The other Nobel laureate guests were scientists, and their accomplishments spanned virtually every aspect of the health field and the sciences. These men were instrumental in providing better and longer lives to Americans and people around the world with experiments, theories, and discoveries. The work of the chemists and physicists was critical in helping to win World War II—completing the rise of the United States—and in better understanding and improving our physical environment.

Dr. Glenn Seaborg was a sterling example of these people of achievement. His work was vital to the development of the atomic bomb at Los Alamos—as was that of a number of others at the dinner. But his research work went beyond that: he was instrumental in identifying ten chemical elements, the names of which were closely associated with his life—americium, berkelium, californium, curium, einsteinium, fermium, mendelevium, nobelium, and—certainly—seaborgium. There was even more luster to his career, since he had been a science advisor to President Eisenhower and for three years was the chancellor at the incubator of Nobel laureates, the University of California at Berkeley.[8]

Seaborg had voted for Kennedy, but the two men had never met or spoken before 1961.[9] Shortly before the inauguration, the president—in his effort to get the ablest people to join the administration—called Seaborg and asked him to head the Atomic Energy Commission.[10] When they had their first formal meeting in February 1961, Seaborg said that Kennedy, in addition to reviewing nuclear weapons, "brought out a number of other points that certainly gave me an early insight into his philosophy." These were scientific exchanges with the Soviet Union, identifying issues related to the upcoming talks on a nuclear test agreement in Geneva, the importance of an effective disarmament group, and his interest in attracting another scientist to the Atomic Energy Commission.[11]

The issues that the Atomic Energy Commission confronted in the early 1960s were in the forefront of the Cold War. Not surprising given Seaborg's expertise, he became an important member of the Kennedy administration. He and Dr. Jerome Wiesner, Kennedy's science advisor, met regularly with the president. Forty-eight years old when appointed as the fifth chairman of the Atomic Energy Commission, Seaborg was at the height of his professional career. The previous month he had been charged by President Kennedy to look at the peaceful uses of nuclear power. In a letter to Seaborg, he said that "we must extend our national energy resources base in order to promote our nation's economic growth." He also called for international cooperation in this field.[12] Shortly after, when Kennedy visited the University of California at Berkeley, he paid testament to the scientific work and the Nobel accomplishments of that institution. He also cited the presence of Berkeley people, including Seaborg, in his administration. In jest he said, "It is a disturbing fact to me, and it may be to some of you, that the New Frontier owes as much to Berkeley as it does to Harvard University."[13]

Seaborg also was an emissary for the administration. Before the dinner, he talked with his old friend and colleague Robert Oppenheimer. The two men had been friends since 1934; and Seaborg, because of his relationship and current role, was the right person to address what was perhaps an obvious question. Now he had the opportunity to quietly ask Oppie whether he would like to get his security clearance back. The caveat, however, was that once again he would need to have a hearing, presumably to answer questions about his loyalty before a friendlier committee. Oppenheimer's response: "Not on your life."[14] Oppenheimer had moved on, and he would soon be aided by a further development from the Kennedy administration.

⌐━◂▸

As guests mingled in the Red and Green Rooms, they smoked, drank champagne and liqueurs, and basked in the historic setting. There was much to admire. Guests who streamed out of the State Dining Room first came upon the Red Room as they enjoyed the music of the Strolling Strings ensemble. Next in a row facing the Cross Hall on the south side of the White House is the Blue Room—from which others exited from dinner—and then the Green Room. These rooms with their distinctive colors represent the three formal parlors in the White House.

The Red Room is a little more than one-third the size of the State Dining Room. Just in front of the entrance is an ornate French Empire pier table. Joseph Bonaparte, a brother of Napoleon Bonaparte, shipped the table to the United States in the early nineteenth century when he emigrated after his brother's defeat. As usual for a pier table, the back of it has a mirror, and some of the women tonight might have checked their gowns, which was the mirror's purpose. A floral basket rested on the table. Above the table is a painting of Joseph Stark, a Revolutionary War general from New Hampshire, painted by the multitalented Samuel F. B. Morse. Anyone who stopped and looked at the painting would have noticed the general's sharp blue eyes. Proceeding into the room, people would quickly take in the bright fuchsia-covered walls and the six doors.[15]

Moving around the room, guests would see a number of striking furnishings. There was a large, ornate gilded-wood chandelier, which illuminated the red silk upholstery of the chairs and sofas. One of the sofas, ornately embroidered, belonged to Dolley Madison, and the other—with dramatically rounded legs and armrests—belonged to Eleanor "Nelly" Parke Custis, the granddaughter of Martha Washington.[16] Mingling people, with coupe glass in hand, would have been drawn to the two most notable oil paintings in the room. Hanging above the fireplace is the vertical one: 94 ⅝ inches by 60 inches, a full-length portrait of Thomas Jefferson by Eliphalet Frazer Andrews, painted in 1884. He has a quill in his left hand, and a copy of the Declaration of Independence is on a desk[17] The other painting, a horizontal piece above the Madison sofa, is *Cannonading on the Potomac, October, 1861*. Painted by Alfred Wordsworth Thompson, this 33-¹⁄16-inch by 70-⁹⁄16-inch work commemorates the Battle of Balls Bluff in northern Virginia.[18]

The Red Room saw many roles over the past century and a half. At one time, a copy of the great Lansdowne portrait of George Washington by Gilbert Stuart, now in the East Room, was hung here. As was also the case with many other rooms in the White House, the Red Room was renovated in 1902 and 1952. Mrs. Kennedy, with her decorating team, did a major reworking of the room, and it was one of those she had shown to the public during the televised broadcast two months earlier. She was so proud of her efforts that the Red Room was featured on the Kennedys' Christmas card in 1962. As with her efforts in the Blue Room, she sought to reflect more of a look of the 1820s of roughly the Monroe era, which was considerably different from the Truman and Eisenhower eras as well as the Theodore Roosevelt renovation. In fact, in the early twentieth century the room was frequently referred to as the Washington Room, reflecting the prominence of the Gilbert Stuart portrait of Washington and the Andrews portrait of Martha Washington.[19]

If you were looking at the ornate girandole, a French-style or convex mirror topped by an eagle, you might see the image of some of the guests reflected. One of those milling about—and certainly avidly interested in the history of the rooms and the mansion—was Samuel Eliot Morison. Despite his distasteful comments about James Baldwin, Sam Morison was the foremost historian of his time. He was known as a consummate narrative historian, who brought life into his work through a compelling writing style and using meticulous research. A master sailor, Morison replicated Columbus's expeditions to the New World in order to better understand him as he wrote a biography of the explorer in 1942. Morison was a prolific writer, usually focusing on biographies and New England themes. His American history textbooks were classics that

went through multiple printings and educated several generations of colle-
gians. His great work, however, was a magisterial, fifteen-volume history of the
navy during World War II.[20]

Morison was a patrician. Born in Boston in 1887, he was a proper Bosto-
nian who could trace his lineage back to the seventeenth century. His views
represented an elite perspective on the world, perhaps explaining—but most
certainly not excusing—his crass remark about Baldwin and his once describ-
ing the Italian navy as the "dago navy." Of course, the Kennedys were not
Boston Brahmins, but Morison had a high regard for the president. In fact, he
considered John Kennedy in the same class as such presidents as Washington,
Jefferson, and Theodore and Franklin Roosevelt, saying they were all "gentle-
men born and bred—aristocrats in the proper meaning of that much-abused
word." And of this evening he said that it "was conducted with an elegance
that no European court could have surpassed."[21]

The other noted historian at the dinner was also a Harvard man, Arthur
Schlesinger. Both men had received Pulitzer Prizes—Morison was awarded
his second in 1960 for a biography of John Paul Jones. But there had not been
a great friendship between the men. When writing to the us ambassador to
Britain several years before about Schlesinger's bid for a prestigious post at
Oxford University, Morison said he was "rather smart-alecky and disagree-
able in personality. He is just the kind of person who would rub the English
the wrong way."[22] Schlesinger, in fact, later acknowledged his difficulties with
Morison, writing, "I can well see how as a brash young man (which I fear I was)
I could have got on Sam's nerves."[23] Surely Ava Helen Pauling would agree,
even though Schlesinger was no longer a "young man."

John Dos Passos was another towering but non-Nobel figure moving around
with his wife, Elizabeth ("Betty"), a witty and vibrant woman. Dos Passos,
at sixty-six, was now round with a chubby face, largely bald, and with wire-
rim glasses framing his brown eyes, one of which was a glass eye. Like John
Kennedy, his education was at Choate and Harvard. He had about two dozen
novels to his credit by this time, but much of his best work was written earlier
in his career. He was most noted for the novels *Manhattan Transfer*, published
in 1925, and the *U.S.A.* trilogy of *The Forty-Second Parallel, 1919,* and *The Big
Money,* all published in the 1930s. Most of his works were historical fiction,
often focusing on personalities such as Thomas Jefferson, William Jennings

Bryan, and Huey Long. He was currently working on a book entitled *Mr. Wilson's War*. Dos, as he was known by friends, wrote what he considered "contemporary chronicles. . . . They have a strong political bent because after all—although it isn't the only thing—politics in our time has pushed people around more than anything else."[24]

Politics, in fact, greatly influenced Dos Passos. He was affected by the Sacco and Vanzetti trial in 1927, against which he picketed and was arrested. The anger toward the injustice dealt to the radical immigrants being convicted of murder led him to a decade-long flirtation with Far Left ideology, even visiting the Soviet Union and supporting the Republicans in the Spanish Civil War. Acclaim followed Dos Passos in the 1920s and 1930s. Sinclair Lewis, who was shortly to be honored later this evening, had said, "I regard *Manhattan Transfer* as more significant in every way than anything by Gertrude Stein or Marcel Proust or even the great white boar, Mr. Joyce's *Ulysses*." Norman Mailer would eventually say, "Those three volumes of *U.S.A.* make up the idea of a great American novel." Jean-Paul Sartre pronounced him "the greatest writer of our time."[25]

Although Dos Passos continued his writing, he had reached the apex of his fame. Disillusioned with his experience in the Spanish Civil War, he began his long journey into more conservative politics. Such a move seemed to affect the critical reviews of his work, something that was anticipated by his onetime friend Ernest Hemingway.[26] A personal challenge followed. In 1947 Dos Passos and his first wife, Katy Smith, were involved in a freak automobile accident in which she was killed and he lost an eye. He married Elizabeth Hamlin Holdridge two years later.[27]

Ernest Hemingway was surely on Dos Passos's mind tonight. The two men, both from Chicago, met in Europe during World War I when they were in the ambulance service.[28] They became friends, fellow writers, drinking buddies, and traveling companions. Hemingway knew Katy Smith even earlier, meeting her when he was a boy. The Dos Passos–Hemingway friendship was such that Hem wrote Dos in 1925, "There's a girl named Hadley that's showing a lot of promise as a drinker and she wants to meet you."[29] Elizabeth Hadley Richardson became Hemingway's first wife. But Hemingway being Hemingway, the friendship with Dos Passos did not last. Hemingway was always envious of other writers' fame, and the rupture came over political disagreements regarding the Spanish Civil War.[30] It also was affected by Hemingway's belief that Dos Passos was responsible for his crumbling marriage to Hadley; "one-eyed bastard" is how Hem referred to him in his Paris memoir, *A Moveable Feast*.[31] In a final break with Dos Passos, Hemingway, upset over an article that Dos had written for *Redbook*, sent him a letter in 1938 in which he said, "So long, Dos" and added, "Honest Jack Passos'll knife you three times in the back for fifteen cents."[32]

Dos also knew Mary Welsh Hemingway, whom he met during World War II.[33] Mary respected his research and writing, but said later, "I found him disappointing as a companion."[34] One thing they did share, however, was their disagreement over their host's Bay of Pigs invasion. Mary's position was well stated directly to the president earlier tonight. Dos said, "When they pull something like the operation in the Bay of Pigs, I become extremely pessimistic, particularly when nobody seems to understand its significance."[35]

One of the other writers who had picketed with Dos Passos against the Sacco and Vanzetti trial was also at the dinner, and she was at the top of her career. Katherine Anne Porter, now white-haired and seventy-one, was enjoying the success of *A Ship of Fools*, a novel about a transatlantic cruise and the offbeat characters aboard the ship. This was Porter's first—and only—novel. Her previous works were short stories and essays, which were well received. In fact, her early success caused the ever-jealous Ernest Hemingway to treat her rudely the only time they ever met in the 1930s. Sylvia Beach, the proprietor of the legendary Shakespeare and Co. bookshop in Paris, introduced them. "I want the two best modern American writers to know each other," the expatriate bookseller said. Hemingway refused to acknowledge her and stomped out of the shop. Porter said that "it must have been galling to this most famous young man to have his name pronounced in the same breath as a writer with someone he had never heard of, and a woman at that. I nearly felt sorry for him."[36] Porter, interestingly, thought little of Dos Passos's writing, saying that he "has been lacking in almost every faculty required to make even a second rate writing man."[37] As fate would have it, the two writers, one at the top of her public acclaim and the other far from it, sat next to one another at a table hosted by Pierre Salinger's young, brown-haired second wife, Nancy Joy Salinger.

If Miss Porter looked toward the wall where Thompson's Civil War painting was hung in the Red Room, she would have seen Robert Frost sitting on the sofa below it, chatting with two young women wearing long white gloves, who were listening with rapt attention to the famous poet. Beside them were several wine glasses resting on a center table with an ornate top crafted by cabinet-maker Charles-Honoré Lannuier a century and half earlier. High above them on the wall, above the Thompson oil, was a portrait of Alexander Hamilton, painted by John Trumbull.[38]

Another prominent writer present was James T. Farrell, the person whom Diana Trilling was trying to dodge on the train down to Washington this morning. Perhaps the Trillings were reluctant to engage with him because of his background as a Far Left activist. Farrell was yet another prolific writer, gaining fame for his *Studs Lonigan* trilogy, set in Chicago's South Side and written in the 1930s at the height of the Great Depression. The work focused on the disillusioned life of an Irish-Catholic man from childhood through a crumbling adulthood. The book is an indictment of capitalism. Farrell also wrote short stories, often dealing with three themes: Irish ethnicity, Catholicism, and Chicago. Among his many short stories was "G.B.S. Interviews the Pope," an imagined satirical conversation between George Bernard Shaw and Pope Pius XI.[39] Farrell was ever the serious social activist. "Literature," he said, "is not, in itself, a means of solving problems: these can be solved only by action, by social and political action." One commentator said of him, "Like many others of his general persuasion, Farrell believes that freedom will only finally be won by man when the movement started in the French Revolution is 'completed.'"[40] Having met Robert Kennedy tonight, Farrell would become an enthusiastic political supporter in the future—perhaps he was the catalyst for change that Farrell sought.

❦

Despite the noted writers present, including the Nobel laureate Pearl Buck, the majority of people attending this dinner were scientists. In fact, this dinner represented the foremost gathering of scientists assembled at one time in American history. That was befitting the great success this country had in developing a first-rate scientific research community. Because of the importance that the Kennedy administration was placing on scientific achievement and the relationship that these scientists had with others in their fields, a number of other leaders in chemistry, physics, and health fields had been invited. Oppenheimer was one example, of course, but so were Dr. Jerome Wiesner, Dr. James Killian, and Dr. Lee DuBridge.

With dinner completed, these scientists and their wives also were refreshing themselves and chatting with others before moving into the East Room for the culmination of tonight's program. Some were in the Red Room, some in the Cross Hall, and others were in a second parlor, the Green Room. The Green Room is identical in size to the Red Room and has many of the same characteristics. It, too, has six doors and a dominating chandelier. Once used as a dining room, it also had undergone renovations during the Theodore Roosevelt and Truman administrations. It was significantly redone by the recent partnership of Jacqueline Kennedy, arts advisor Henry du Pont, and designer Stéphane Boudin. This room was a favorite of President Kennedy.[41]

The room's pale green trim, including the walls, some chairs, and the Great Seal Aubusson rug, is certainly very prominent. The room is accentuated by a number of paintings, most of which are either of important Americans or done by masters. Perhaps the most striking historical portrait is that of Benjamin Franklin, which hangs over one fireplace. Painted by David Martin, a Scotsman, in 1767, the portrait shows this quintessential American, bespectacled and well dressed, sitting at a desk and examining a document. In the left corner of the 50 1/16 by 39 5/16 inch oil is a bust of Isaac Newton. This famous painting is a testament to the Enlightenment.[42] The work certainly would have resonated with any scientists who examined it this evening.

As if to reinforce the tribute to Franklin, there is another eighteenth-century celebration of him here, "To the Genius of Franklin," a pencil and sepia drawing. This work, done by Jean-Honoré Fragonard, is an apotheosis of a prototype image of Franklin riding on the clouds and surrounded by protective gods warding off evil. The drawing is rich in symbolism for the new nation and, despite its light color, is quite striking. This work of art was the initial major gift received by Mrs. Kennedy's Fine Arts Committee in 1961.[43]

Above the mantel over another fireplace, this one on the east wall, is Henry Inman's 1842 portrait of President Martin Van Buren's daughter-in-law and White House hostess, Angelica Singleton Van Buren. She is attractive and the three-quarter-length portrait of her is impressive, but two things stand out: the bust of her father-in-law on a pedestal to her left and a heavy and ornate frame. There is a plate on the bottom-center of the frame that identifies her as "Mrs Major Van Buren."[44]

As people were mingling and talking in the Green Room, certainly some of them noticed some other masterpieces. In 1961 eight Cezanne paintings were returned to the White House from the National Gallery of Art. Two of them, *The Forest* and *House on the Marne,* were placed in the Green Room.[45] Both are approximately the same size, about twenty-eight inches by thirty-six inches. Both were done by the Postimpressionist painter around 1890.[46] Also catching the eye of visitors is Theobald Chartan's portrait of Edith Carow Roosevelt, Theodore Roosevelt's second wife and the nation's First Lady from 1901 to 1909.[47] This latter painting is centered above the sofa once owned by Daniel Webster and adds to the Federal furniture décor of the room.[48]

⊂≡≺∘⊷

Rose Styron and Bill Styron were reunited during this postdinner session. She had a pleasant dinner conversation seated beside her neighbor and friend Van Wyck Brooks, and Dr. Albert Szent-Gyorgyi, a physician and physiologist who received a Nobel Prize for his work on Vitamin C. A Hungarian émigré, Szent-Gyorgyi also did extensive work on human muscles, working at the Marine Biological Laboratory located at Woods Hole, Massachusetts.[49] Rose Styron's introduction to him was amusing. "I didn't know who he was. He said that he lived in Woods Hole so I thought that was the oceanographic society," she said. She asked him what he worked on, and he said, "Muscles." But she thought it was sea mussels and proceeded to quiz him on sea life until he corrected her.[50] It was all in good fun.

Another naturalized American citizen, also a Nobel laureate, was Austrian-born Victor F. Hess. Dr. Hess, seventy-eight, had produced his landmark work on radium from 1911 to 1913, before some of the guests—and certainly his hosts—were even born. Dr. Hess had received the Nobel Prize in Physics in 1936.[51] As with others here tonight, he also was involved with research on the atomic bomb, but his work was to look at the radiation levels from atomic tests, a topic very much on peoples' minds that week in Washington and around the world. Dr. Hess was in the Pauling camp: he was against further tests. "We know too little about radioactivity at this time to state definitely that testing underground or above the atmosphere will have no effect on the human body," he said.[52]

Oppenheimer was relaxed; he was among supporters. "Almost everyone there was an old friend," he said, "and that made it very nice." The American Nobel fraternity was a small, exclusive one in which many of the scientists had worked with one another and attended other dinners and gatherings, including the annual banquet in Stockholm. And their circle drew in people such as Oppenheimer who worked with them and, perhaps, were equally worthy of Nobel consideration. Tonight, however, was different. They were gathered together as a treasured group of American heroes, celebrated for their achievements by the president at the White House. This was a special night.

There was Dr. Harold C. Urey, who had received his Nobel prize in 1934—when John Kennedy was still a teenager attending Choate—for his work on heavy hydrogen. Dr. Urey was celebrating his sixty-ninth birthday today—quite a way to do it—but he was still active. Although he was a chemist, he had a keen interest in the moon, including its geology, and he was a supporter of the president's space initiative. Last year he said, "The space program is not only scientific in purpose but also is an expression of man's insistent determination to do the nearly impossible—to explore the unknown even at great risk. Therefore, the proper attitude of a scientist should be to try to participate in the program so that scientific objectives can be attained along with the thrills of exploration."[53] That sounds like something President Kennedy might say, and certainly something with which he would agree. Dr. Urey hoped to have an opportunity in this after-dinner session to talk with Colonel Glenn, tonight's representative of the new space era.

Glenn was squired around after dinner by the attorney general, being introduced and slowly attracting a crowd. Some asked for autographs.[54] It was an interesting sight to see heroes seeking to meet another hero, someone whose exploits were far more in the public arena than their work, often conducted within laboratories and away from newspapers and television coverage.

⊂═⋅⋗

One person whom Robert Kennedy would evade was Vice President Johnson. The relationship between the two of them, the only politicians among the guests, went back several years and was bitter and becoming increasingly acrimonious. Some of this was because of their conflicting roles. Robert Kennedy's sole interest was in protecting his brother and advancing his agenda. While Johnson was loyal to President Kennedy, he had been a political rival who now chafed at his underused, little appreciated role in the White House. Whether it was the contentious discussions related to the vice presidential nomination or later being shut out of important meetings and policymaking, the proud, vain, and insecure former Senate majority leader saw Robert Kennedy, seventeen years younger, as the culprit.

Johnson was constantly reminded of his lonely role in the administration, by specific actions as well as through the media. Three months earlier, for example, *Life* had a cover story on Robert Kennedy, which called him "Capital's No. 2 man," something that Johnson had hoped might have been him. In fact, as the article notes, "Nothing big goes on without Bobby being in on it." He is identified as being the most significant modern-day advisor to a president. "It is a rare day when he does not see the President or talk to him on the telephone."[55] John Kennedy's vice president certainly could not make that claim. This was galling to the former Senate master tactician, the legislator's legislator, who had given up his powerful position in exchange for being relegated to an insignificant, often largely ceremonial role. For a wily politician such as LBJ, who had won his first congressional election in 1937, to be stymied by someone never elected to anything was humiliating. Johnson's top aide, Bobby Baker, said that Johnson's criticisms of the attorney general "may have bordered on the paranoic."[56] Years later, Johnson said of his adversary, "I thought I was dealing with a child. I never did understand Bobby."[57]

For Robert Kennedy, there were episodes in their relationship that also angered him—and he had a long memory. He had taken insults from Johnson as far back as 1955 when the powerful senator addressed the young staffer as "Sonny Boy," and privately, a "snot-nose."[58] Senator Kennedy dispatched his brother to Texas to talk to Johnson about his presidential ambition in 1959. Johnson, in an effort to embarrass, took him hunting and gave him a shotgun that was difficult to handle. When Kennedy was knocked down by the gun's recoil, Johnson gloated: "Son, you've got to learn to handle a gun like a man."[59] The relationship became toxic after the vice presidential offer, which Robert Kennedy opposed, and had continued since then.

There also was a significant difference in upbringing and style between the two men. Robert Kennedy grew up with all the benefits that the wealth of Joseph P. Kennedy bought. He attended several elite prep schools before graduating from the prestigious Milton Academy. He went to Harvard College and the aristocratic University of Virginia School of Law. He had adopted the studied indifference of preppy clothing, including shirts with button-down collars and penny loafers. Johnson grew up in poverty, went to a small, rural public high school, and struggled to pay for his education at Southwest Texas State Teachers College. He often appeared garish, as he did tonight. Diana Trilling, ever the critic, said he "had on the most awful dinner jacket. I think it was gray, and I don't know what it was made of, but it seemed to shimmer, as if he were a master of ceremonies in some cheap night club."[60]

The Strolling Strings, an Air Force ensemble group formed eight years earlier, was entertaining in the Cross Hall. The group of nine tuxedo-clad men was playing the violin, cello, accordion, and harp. Suddenly, Linus Pauling, a tango and waltz enthusiast, asked the group to play a waltz; and Pauling and Ava Helen began dancing, seemingly oblivious to the other guests who looked on. One article later called side-by-side photos of Pauling picketing and the couple dancing as: "From picket to pirouette in one lesson."[61] Dancing had not been planned, and Jacqueline Kennedy, watching, was taken aback. She said, "Look, Jack, they're dancing." Dr. Szent-Gyorgyi, obviously enjoying meeting his new friend, asked Rose Styron to dance, and they joined the Paulings on the pink-and-white checkerboard-styled marble floor.[62] Three other couples joined them. This was all a brief, spur-of-the-moment episode, and soon the guests were being ushered into the East Room for tonight's literary presentation.

❦

Fredric March had played at many venues in his forty-year career, but tonight's was the pinnacle, a command performance at the White House. He was nervous. He had done an earlier run-through, accompanied by his friend Arthur Cantor, a Broadway producer with whom he had worked, and White House staff members. He would have checked the lighting, the size of the room, and the podium from which he would present tonight's readings. But he was still nervous. While the other guests were chatting after dining, Tish Baldrige brought him to the second floor to relax in the Lincoln bedroom. "I'll be back in twenty-five minutes," she said. "Here, lie down on the bed—there's a white bedspread. Don't worry about it. Just take-off your shoes. There's a blanket, too." March: "You mean, I'm to lie down on *that*, Lincoln's bed?" Baldrige: "Yes, special orders from Mrs. Kennedy. This is a sacred place—for Abraham Lincoln's ghost and you."[63]

Tish Baldrige said, "Tears came to his eyes. He told me later that he had played in palaces and before many distinguished audiences in his life, but never had anything meant so much to him as this night. Resting in Lincoln's bed, he said, was the crowning part of the evening for him."[64]

Fortified by his brief rest and also with the opportunity to talk beforehand with President and Mrs. Kennedy, March entered the East Room, the largest and perhaps most historic room in the White House. The size of the room— eighty by thirty-seven feet—made it an obvious choice for large-scale events. It was the site of many presidents and First Ladies lying in state, most notably Abraham Lincoln and Franklin D. Roosevelt—and would be once again the following year. Weddings were held here, including Alice Roosevelt's in 1906. It was the focus of many receptions. It was also where musicals and other performances, before and certainly during the Kennedy administration, took place. And according to legend, Abigail Adams hung laundry here.[65]

Unlike some of the other rooms, the East Room had not changed much in appearance since the Theodore Roosevelt administration. Mrs. Kennedy's work here was merely a refurbishment.[66] The room continued to be dominated by three huge Bohemian cut crystal chandeliers, acquired in 1902.[67] The two most prominent paintings in the room are of the Washingtons. The famous and imposing standing portrait of George Washington is 95 inches by 59 $13/16$ inches, instantly drawing one's eyes to it. Depicted with a large head, Washington is gesturing forward with his right hand and holding a sword with his left. The presidential chair is behind him, and the table on his right has important documents from America's founding era. This was the painting that Dolley Madison famously saved during the War of 1812.[68] The Martha Washington portrait is the one by Andrews and hangs along the same wall as her husband's.

Mrs. Kennedy had the windows refurbished, added under curtains, acquired tables and other furnishings, and returned four candelabra to the East

Room. An interesting addition was that ashtrays were now present in the East Room.[69] In a break with the past, the guests were allowed to smoke at the Kennedy dinners on this floor, and the ashtrays responded to that change.[70] Tonight these ashtrays were heavily used.

At approximately 9:45 pm, the guests began to arrive in the East Room. The social aides, who were shepherded by General Chester Clifton, the president's military aide, guided the guests. Mrs. Kennedy arrived, holding hands with and escorting the eighty-seven-year-old Robert Frost, who sat immediately to her left in the front row of a number of rows of stiff, round-back chairs temporarily assembled to face the podium. She was smiling, engaged in a conversation with Frost as the president sat with Pearl Buck, her three-stranded white necklace complementing her white hair. Lady Bird Johnson sat next to Miss Buck, looking somewhat lost. The guests filled the rows of chairs behind them.

Pearl Buck had just spoken with Katherine Marshall, no doubt eager for this part of the evening. Mrs. Marshall said, "I enjoyed your book *So Big*," confusing her with Edna Ferber, who wrote the Pulitzer Prize–winning book about a family and its farming community back in 1924. Buck was gracious and simply thanked her. The president arrived, sat down cross-legged, and placed his champagne glass on the floor beside his size 10 shoe. He immediately asked the foremost American novelist of Asia, "What do you think we should do about Korea?" "Why do you ask, Mr. President," she replied. "Because," he responded, "we can't go on as we are. Japan must help us to rebuild." While wanting to lecture the president on the historical background, she merely replied, "I am writing an historical novel about Korea now which explains the present situation in terms of the past. It is called *The Living Reed* I'll send you the first copy."[71] One of Buck's biographers said of the exchange: "Pearl was dumbstruck. Kennedy's proposal [to involve Korea's longtime rival] revealed an abysmal ignorance about Asian politics and history."[72]

By this time, the press pool had surfaced. They had arrived at the East Gate and were greeted by social aide Pamela Turnure. They would be writing stories for Monday's paper. The group of a dozen men and women included representatives from the two wire services; the *New York Times* and *Herald Tribune*; writers from three Washington papers (*Post*, *Evening Star*, and *News*); *Boston American*; and reporters for the Canadian and Swedish press. *Newsweek* magazine also was there, as was a Science Service writer.

The most well-known reporter from this group was United Press International's Helen Thomas, then forty-one, who was usually seen by television viewers as signaling the completion of Kennedy's new conferences by saying, "Thank you, Mr. President."[73] Frances Lewine from the Associated Press was there. Lewine, also forty-one, frequently covered White House dinners during the Kennedy era. The previous month she reported on Mrs. Kennedy's trip to India and Pakistan. Photographers also had been there earlier taking photos of the reception, dinner, and after-meal mingling.

With everyone settled in, the lights dimmed and Fredric March began the program. A circular spotlight focused on him, and the ample podium had small lights that helped him read. The first part of the program was going to be excerpts from Sinclair Lewis's 1920 classic, *Main Street*, which was awarded the Pulitzer Prize. Ten years later, Lewis became the first American Nobel laureate in literature. Lewis died in 1951, and there is no evidence that the White House staff had contacted any member of his family to be present. It took March less than two minutes to dramatize the excerpt, which was the introduction to the novel. He began: "This is America—a town of a few thousand, in a region of wheat and corn and dairies and little groves."[74]

After the Lewis reading, March moved on to General Marshall's commencement speech at Harvard in 1947, which outlined the European Recovery Program, generally known as the Marshall Plan. The speech was written by Charles E. "Chip" Bohlen, who became a pillar of the Washington foreign policy establishment, a member of the Georgetown salon crowd, and a Kennedy advisor.[75] But Marshall, of course, was being honored for his role in implementing the landmark plan of European reconstruction, not the speech. March read four paragraphs, adding, "I wish I had time to read it all."[76]

Finally, the actor came to the featured part of the evening's literary presentation, an unpublished work by Ernest Hemingway. This is what Mary Hemingway had been anticipating. She and March had worked on the nineteen-minute excerpt, with the actor adding substantial marks to assist in his dramatic reading. She was especially concerned about removing some profanity. The piece deals with Thomas Hudson, a painter living in the Bahamas. He and his associates pursue German U-boat survivors. This work eventually wound up as part of two chapters in the later part of *Islands in the Stream*, which literary executor Mary published in 1970.[77]

It was not well received. William Styron called it "a boring reading by Fredric March of a garbled and wretched piece of an unpublished Hemingway manuscript." He said that many of the elderly Nobel laureates had "nodded off to sleep."[78] Rose Styron was similarly critical.[79] Diana Trilling couldn't resist adding her critique. Sitting beside an anxious Katherine Anne Porter, she commended March but said "the chapter itself was so poor that one was pained for the man who had written it." She describes what happened when the reading ended: "When March finished, the President rose from his chair and walked over to Mrs. Hemingway; he virtually lifted her out of her seat and had her bow to the audience. She was having a tough time, poor woman, and I saw the President do something so nice. He squeezed her arm comfortingly. Then he went back to sit in his own place again."[80]

It was now 11 pm and the evening was winding down. As the guests got up and began to leave the room, President and Mrs. Kennedy mixed once again with the crowd. He had his left arm on her left shoulder.[81] Some asked the first couple, especially Mrs. Kennedy, for autographs.[82] Then guests began to say their good-byes. Arthur Schlesinger was hosting a party at his house, and James Baldwin and Joseph Rauh, the civil rights lawyer, would be leaving for his house at 3122 O Street in Georgetown.[83] Many would return to their homes in Washington or the suburbs, while some would find their way back to their hotel rooms. Katherine Marshall was, at seventy-nine, at first reluctant to attend. "But," she said, "I bought myself a dress so that I could come. This is my last time out and it's been a wonderful climax for me. Now I can go back to my briar patch."[84]

Bill Styron was ready to depart as well until he was approached by a social aide, who said, "The President would like you and Mrs. Styron to join him upstairs in his private quarters."[85] The same thing happened to Diana Trilling as she and Lionel were invited up to the Yellow Oval Room.[86] For them and a select few, the most memorable part of this unforgettable evening was still to take place.

# CHAPTER NINE

# An After-Party

THE MARINE BAND WAS PLAYING as Lionel and Diana Trilling were directed by a social aide to the nearby elevator off the Cross Hall. The elevator, one of three in the White House, is small and ornate. A carved, dark wooden frame outlined the outside of the elevator. Inside were mirrored walls with gold trim and a green patterned rug.[1] Unlike earlier in the evening, Caroline Kennedy was not at the controls. Presumably she was now in bed, tucked in by Maud Shaw, the Kennedys' strict but loving nanny. Now the elevator made its way to the second floor. When the door opened and the Trillings exited, they immediately stepped into the small Elevator Hall, a tastefully appointed vestibule. There are two chairs alongside a card table featuring an ornate gold-colored caryatid and paw feet, mostly likely also done by Charles-Honoré Lannuier. Atop the table are two candlesticks. On the wall is a Chippendale mirror balanced on each side by a nineteenth-century silhouette print.[2] The beautiful collection of perfectly matched antiques in this tiny, out-of-the-way room underscored Mrs. Kennedy's dedication to making the Executive Mansion a living museum.

The Trillings were directed to turn left and soon found themselves in the Center Hall, which is directly above the Cross Hall, where the string ensemble had been playing. Walking a few steps down the Center Hall, they approached the site of this informal and as yet undefined session, the Yellow Oval Room. Outside the room were four paintings by George Catlin: three of Native Americans and one of a teepee. On each side of the entrance was a tall table with flowers, and there was a settee at the left of the door and a chair on the right.[3]

They were ushered into the room, welcomed by another social aide, and soon offered champagne by a waiter. "Just make yourself at home. The President will be here as soon as he's free downstairs. Have a good time," he said. Diana and Lionel, seated alone in the private residence of the White House, were now flummoxed. Diana's thoughts: "What in the world are we doing here?"[4]

Bill Styron, drunk and perhaps equally puzzled, was also digesting this surprising invitation as he made his way up to the room. His initial reaction had been wariness. "Aha! It's just as I suspected," he said. "The son of a bitch is after my wife."[5] Soon Rose Styron and then Bill arrived in the room. Now the two prominent couples eyed each other. Diana thought that the Styrons were less anxious than she and her husband, but still confused about the invitation.[6] Bill Styron said, "Diana Trilling had the look of a woman who had just been struck a glancing but telling blow by a sledgehammer."[7]

Consequently, there was little conversation but much anticipation.[8] The waiting gave the literary couples an opportunity to take in the room. As with almost every room in the White House, this one had seen much history. President Zachary Taylor had died here in 1850.[9] The painter Francis Carpenter had done his early work on the famous *First Reading of the Emancipation Proclamation of Abraham Lincoln* in this room.[10] The Eisenhowers used the room informally, but Mrs. Kennedy chose to remake the room with a reflection of Louis XVI. President Kennedy used it for ceremonial meetings.[11] He also was comfortable in this room, which he called the "easy room," and he even added music speakers among its bookcases. It was thus a favorite room for both. As two art historians later noted, "Indeed, more than any other space, the Yellow Oval Room best represented their ideal backdrop for the Presidency—inviting yet somewhat formal, inspired by history while fashionable and chic."[12]

Scanning the room with the yellow walls and white trim throughout, the early arrivals could examine Mary Cassatt's French Impressionistic work *Cup of Tea,* featuring the painter's sister, Lydia, drinking tea and sitting on a chair in Paris in the late 1870s. Below that oil to the left of the fireplace was a nineteenth-century painting by Judith Lewis. What is interesting about this painting, *Elegant Figures Preparing for the Hunt,* is that the five horses receive attention equal to the people depicted. One woman is on a horse and another about to mount.[13] Mrs. Kennedy, an avid rider since her childhood, owned this painting.

In the center of the room was an attractive Louis XVI mahogany desk crafted by cabinetmaker Etienne Levasseur in 1766. Slightly longer than five feet, the desk had three drawers and was highlighted by gold all around. No one tonight could know this information, of course, but in August 1963 President Kennedy would sign the Nuclear Test Ban Agreement on its elegant polished surface.[14]

Set in front of the fireplace is the famous Kennedy rocking chair. While President Eisenhower was closely associated with golf and could often be seen on a course such as the Augusta National Golf Club, President Kennedy was perhaps most commonly seen in one of his rocking chairs, which he used especially to ease the pain from his persistent back problem. The history of the president and this chair could be traced back to his personal physician, Dr. Janet Travell, in whose New York City office he first saw the chair in the mid-1950s. Identified by the physician as a "Carolina Rocker," these chairs were made out of oak by the P and P Chair Company, in Asheboro since 1926. When Kennedy became president, the rockers became famous and were soon called the "Kennedy Rocker."[15] The chair had a relatively simple design. The seat and back were cane. It was covered by white seat, arm, and back cushions. It was 43 ½ inches high and 28 inches wide and was relatively short for a man of Kennedy's height.[16] But it was his favorite chair—he also had one placed in the Oval Office in the West Wing. The rocker appeared rather inviting, and Bill Styron, buzzed from his combination of drink and antibiotic, immediately sat down on it and got comfortable.[17] As Styron was rocking, his view included a double wooden door directly ahead of him on the far wall. Flanked by two large flag stands, one with the American flag and the other with the presidential, this door was the entrance into the president's bedroom.[18]

Mrs. Kennedy now entered the room and other guests joined her. Among them were Robert Frost, Fredric March, Dick Goodwin, Arthur Schlesinger, Pierre Salinger, Robert and Ethel Kennedy, Jean Kennedy Smith, and Sargent Shriver, the Peace Corps director whom Styron called "the simple-minded brother-in-law."[19] That was an unfortunate comment about Sarge Shriver because he was an able administrator, serving now as founding director of the Peace Corps, and would later lead the War on Poverty and be the US ambassador to France. As this now larger group moved about the room, in addition to taking in the historic and attractive furnishings, they also could see out three large, nearly floor-to-ceiling windows; the middle one, aligned with the chandelier in the center of the room, provided a breathtaking view of the 555-foot Washington Monument. Getting settled, the guests sat on one of two sofas or on various chairs.

Immediately, Mrs. Kennedy joked about the president's rocking chairs, calling them "eyesores," and then saying, "Do you know how much money is being made of this? Do you know how many thousands of these rockers have been sold?" Sitting down in another chair next to Lionel Trilling, Mrs. Kennedy then poked fun at the vice president. "Every time Lyndon Johnson sits on this chair, he breaks it. He's broken it three times so far. Now watch me. I'm going to sit on it, and, you'll see, it won't break under me. He doesn't know how to sit."[20]

The men had broken out the Havana cigars, and Styron was rocking away unaware that the president had entered. Schlesinger nudged Styron to move, and the embarrassed writer relinquished his seat. Kennedy sat down, continuing to smoke his Churchill cigar. Cigar aficionados know that the seven-inch Churchill should be savored, and the president did so. Styron retained an image in his mind: "The leader of the Free World wreathed in smoke, gently rocking."[21]

Frost, who seemed to be attracting admirers—including young women—all night, was cornered by Ethel Kennedy and Jean Kennedy Smith, who flirted with him. Ethel said, "Whom do you prefer, Jean or me?"[22] Styron was carefully observing the scene, while chatting with Lionel Trilling—who, he said in his biting fashion, had "a haggard, oxygen-deprived look"—about books; Styron and Trilling were the only cigarette-smoking men.[23] Styron then turned to Mrs. Kennedy, whom he said "has a great deal of charm," and they talked about sailing with the promise that the Styrons would join the Kennedys on the water in a few months.[24]

Mrs. Kennedy was clearly enjoying herself. This was her room—where she could unwind and smoke her L and M cigarettes—and on this night, a time to take center stage while still relaxing. Diana Trilling said, "I somehow had the impression that these little gatherings upstairs had become a kind of routine after large formal dinners, the price she demanded for having played her public part as conscientiously as she did."[25]

The conversation was relaxed and varied for the next hour or so. Mrs. Kennedy earnestly discussed literature with Lionel Trilling, each suggesting their choice of D. H. Lawrence's best book; she thought *The Rainbow* and he, *Women in Love*. They also picked up on the reception-line discussion of what Jackie Bouvier was like at Vassar; a diplomatic Trilling: "She was serious, devoted student, a good student, shy." The president was intrigued by this discussion. His response: "Shy, hmm," perhaps wondering what Trilling really meant. Kennedy did take this opportunity, now in private, to criticize Pauling for picketing and upsetting his daughter. Throughout the discussion, Mrs. Kennedy was clearly aware of her husband's presence. She was carefully watching her husband's reaction to her own conversation and mentioned him repeatedly as she spoke.[26]

Finally, the president stood up. At approximately 12:30 am the party was coming to an end. Final words were exchanged, the First Lady walked the group out, and Robert Kennedy jumped in the elevator with the guests.[27] After four and a half hours, the last dinner invitees were leaving. These men and women, many of whom were distinguished in their own right, would look back on the evening as a singular event in their lives. It was a special time at a special place. For them, this was Camelot.

Robert Kennedy's night continued. He went on to Arthur Schlesinger's three-story, white-brick townhouse, where a debate had been taking place, one the attorney general would engage in a year later with one of the participants, James Baldwin. Baldwin turned on Joseph Rauh, whose civil rights activism extended back at least fifteen years. Along with Schlesinger, Joe Rauh was a founder of Americans for Democratic Action; he was a liberal of long standing. But according to the fiery black author-activist, people such as Rauh were hypocrites. Schlesinger said, "It was evident that Baldwin could not abide white liberals." Baldwin's comments were only biting criticism, and he had no constructive suggestions on how to improve race relations; he seemed to be more interested in the theatrics of arguing with Rauh.[28] One of Baldwin's biographers reinforced this idea, saying, "His behavior was probably influenced by the setting, and he may have tried to create a debate to make an impression on the policymakers there. It was, after all, as close as he had come to the nation's center of power."[29] Among others at the Schlesinger party were Bill and Rose Styron, who were transported in Robert Kennedy's limousine, and Samuel and Priscilla Morison, who talked with Alexis Leger (Saint-John Perse).[30] No doubt Morison was surprised to see Baldwin there.

As the Schlesinger party in Georgetown was attempting to keep the last remnant of the Nobel night alive, Diana and Lionel Trilling were back on the train to New York. They were euphoric about the evening. "Lionel was unreservedly happy," Diana recalled, "and for once allowed his assessment of his personal situation to include the right to pleasure."[31] While they had not participated in the impromptu dancing at the White House, they literally danced through Washington's old Union Station, certainly a peculiar site as they waltzed in their evening clothes in the early morning hour.[32] Exhausted from the long day, they had stories to tell. Of all the people who had attended the Nobel dinner, it was Diana Trilling who later provided the most fulsome account of that special evening.

⊫⊶

The newspapers, of course, reported in the following day's editions. The *New York Times*, whose reporter Maggie Hunter filed her story after the dinner at 11pm, ran a front-page story. Headlined "49 Nobel Prize Winners Honored at White House," the lead read: "Much of the cream of scientific America gathered at the White House tonight for a dinner honoring Nobel Prize winners." The article mentioned some of the guests and the Lewis, Marshall, and especially, Hemingway readings, and highlighted the president's Thomas Jefferson quote. This remark, the most memorable of the evening, was already being raised to iconic status. The article also discussed the protest by Pauling and Clarence Pickett and the controversy regarding Oppenheimer. Senator Karl Mundt, a hardline conservative Republican from South Dakota, was quoted as saying that the overture to Oppie was "unfortunate but not surprising." A sidebar list of the Nobel laureates attending the dinner was included.[33]

The *Times* ran a short editorial the next day. It said, in part, "There was a twofold symbolism in this assemblage of intellectual elite. One aspect was public expression of the esteem in which our nation holds the most brilliant minds among us. The second was the deliberate underscoring of recognition that brilliance often goes hand in hand with nonconformity."[34] The last sentence surely applied to Pauling and the atomic scientists who now expressed their reservations about the power they had unleashed.

Dorothy Bartlett McCardle filed an article for the *Washington Post*, which was run on page B5 under the headline "Kennedy Salutes Nobel Winners." The lead: "President and Mrs. Kennedy dramatically saluted United States achievements in the sciences, literature and world peace last night." The article was largely similar to that of the *New York Times*, but made no mention of the Jefferson quote. The report did add some additional information on Mary Hemingway, including her attendance with Bill Walton at the Arena Stage in Washington, DC, of a performance of Anton Chekhov's *Uncle Vanya* on Saturday night. McCardle interjected a little flair with her sentence: "The dinner underscored the importance of the Thinking Man of the Western Hemisphere." A sidebar of the Nobel laureates also accompanied this article.[35]

McCardle's article was slightly recast and expanded for the following day's edition, May 1, notably with the lead, which now read: "Forty-nine Nobel Prize winners kicked formality to the winds Sunday night and had a wonderful time at one of the most stimulating parties ever given at the White House." This article gave more prominence to President Kennedy's quip about the eggheads and the Easter egg hunt over the Jefferson reference. There was considerable coverage of the Hemingway reading. The revised piece also noted the response to the president's toast by Nobel laureate Dr. William B. Shockley on behalf of his fellow honorees.[36]

The Associated Press wire service story run in local papers provided the basic information although it misidentified the number of guests as 173 rather than 175.[37] Frances Lewine's bylined AP story in the *Times* of Shreveport, Louisiana, was slightly different. It included a quote from Senator Mundt: "I hope, but not too confidently, that Alger Hiss won't be the next one invited." It goes on to explain: "Hiss, a former State Department official, was convicted of perjury for denying Communist connections."[38] The United Press International story was brief, at least as it was run in the *Logansport Pharos-Tribune* (Indiana). The lead said that "the Chief Executive described [it] as the greatest collection of intellectuals ever gathered in the White House." The Jefferson quote was mentioned as was the presence of Pauling and Oppenheimer.[39]

By far, the most extensive photographic coverage was done by *Life* magazine. In its May 11 issue, it devoted ten full pages to virtually every aspect of the dinner. The photographs were taken by Arthur Rickerby, who previously covered sports for United Press International and then went to *Life* to focus on the Kennedys. The title for the story, which included nine, mostly large photographs—including Linus and Ava Helen Pauling dancing—was "Cognoscenti Come to Call."[40] *Newsweek* also did a story, with no photo, giving a common description of the dinner, but also adding a paragraph on the Baldwin-Rauh after-dinner debate. Oddly, they titled the article "'Jean or Me?,'" referring to the Ethel Kennedy question posed to Robert Frost.[41]

⚬⇥⊶

In the decades to come, the Nobel dinner continued to receive attention, but Americans primarily remembered President Kennedy's quote about Thomas Jefferson. Indeed, it was one of the most memorable lines of the Kennedy years. But the dinner had a much greater importance. Certainly, it was a snapshot of a time that represented America at the height of its power, basking in achievement and eagerly anticipating a bright, perhaps unbounded future. It was noteworthy because it was a convocation of the nation's greatest minds, and it was an expression of gratitude and encouragement to them. The dinner reflected the glamour, grace, and civility of a time that seems so different from today. And it was historically important because of the interaction of these people, many for the first time, and for what that meant for history. The Nobel dinner represented the most important gathering of scientific and literary figures at the White House in history, and it may well have been the most significant American dinner hosted by a US president in the twentieth century.

# CHAPTER TEN

# Lives Connected

WHILE THE NOBEL DINNER WAS UNFOLDING, millions of Americans were at home watching television, the medium that was on the cusp of exploding from a novelty to a ubiquitous part of family life. At eight pm, the highly popular *Ed Sullivan Show* began its one-hour broadcast at Studio 50 in New York City. Still a black-and-white production, the long-running CBS show featured the young pop singer Johnny Mathis and the McGuire Sisters (Christine, Dorothy, and Phyllis), who were best known for their 1954 number-one hit, "Sincerely." Over at NBC, the madcap, half-hour comedy about two New York City policemen, "Car 54, Where Are You" was aired.[1]

Tonight ABC was running a special, *60 Hours to the Moon,* hosted by Jules Bergman, the network's science editor, who was already closely associated with the space program. The broadcast was being promoted in a newspaper advertisement that said: "Tonight we will place an Apollo space craft on the moon." The program featured John Glenn. For the night owls, WCBS in New York offered a late-night broadcast of the prestigious Tony Awards presentations, which had been held earlier that evening at the Waldorf-Astoria hotel.[2]

One of the big winners at the awards ceremony was *A Man for All Seasons,* a play about Sir Thomas More, the counselor to King Henry VIII, who chose principle over loyalty to the crown. Paul Scofield was given the award for best actor for his portrayal of More, and the drama was honored as best play.[3] Political observers searching for a modern-day parallel might have looked at Linus Pauling and his activities of that day. Unlike More, Pauling did not suffer martyrdom, but he was condemned by some in the government and the press. Still, he chose to hold to his principles and continue his protests against a president who would honor him in his house and on behalf of the American public. Perhaps this is too much of an extrapolation, but Pauling, convinced of his moral superiority, might have relished a comparison with the sixteenth-century scholar and Renaissance figure.

Pauling boldly pursued his antiwar and antinuclear activism. He seemed to be buoyed by the Nobel dinner, telling one friend, "I have formed the opinion that President Kennedy is in sympathy with my actions, and even wishes that the pressures from the people opposed to the cold war were greater than those from the cold-advocates." He went on to say of his encounter with the First Lady in the receiving line, "I think that this pleasantry by Mrs. Kennedy was in a sense an invitation of sympathy with our actions."[4] Or maybe not.

And so Linus Pauling continued to criticize the president; after all, despite the enjoyable event at the White House, the world was still threatened by nuclear fallout and, indeed, annihilation. His picketing and antiwar speeches continued. He also became paranoid about the government, or perhaps the suspicious Caltech administration. On July 9, for example, he wrote a statement in which he provided reasons why he thought his mail was being monitored.[5] But he was undaunted.

By the fall, Pauling had a new, related issue to crusade against: Cuba. The Cuban Missile Crisis, which gripped the nation and the world in October 1962, also aroused Pauling's pacifist instincts. On October 23, the day that the naval quarantine of the island was implemented, Linus and Ava Helen sent a telegram to President Kennedy. They wrote, "Your horrifying threat of military action on shipping on the high seas and possible massive retaliation by nuclear attack to any resistance places all the American people as well as many people in other countries in great danger of death thru nuclear war." Further, this "warlike act" could result in "the end of civilization."[6]

But the Paulings weren't finished. Four days later, Linus sent another telegram, this one while he was traveling in St. Louis. It was succinct: "I vehemently urge that for the sake of the reputation of the United States as a peaceful, moral, and law abiding nation you refrain from ordering the invasion of Cuba."[7] By this time, however, the two sides had made the quiet quid pro quo of removing missiles from Cuba and Turkey, and the greatest threat to post–World War II peace was resolved.

And yet, Pauling could not resist blaming the Kennedy administration for the hostile world situation. On November 1, he spoke to the Business and Professional Associates of the American Jewish Congress. Referring to the Cuba crisis, Pauling said, "I believe that the us has been greatly damaged by the President's action, which has caused us to be labelled as recklessly militaristic, relying on force rather than on negotiation, justice, and morality." Pauling added that the president's actions were hindering peace. "Khrushchev has assumed the stature of the *world leader who* is *rational*, who works for *peace*. The us is the warmonger, threatening the world with *nuclear* destruction."[8]

And in personal notes scribbled next to a newspaper column discussing the thirteen administration officials leading the government, Pauling noted: "This is a WAR CABINET, NOT a PEACE Cabinet." In his comments, he also rhetorically asked, Why aren't Glenn Seaborg and Jerome Wiesner and William C. Foster, the head of the us Arms Control and Disarmament Agency, included in the inner circle?[9]

Despite Pauling's strident comments, Kennedy did support the idea of a nuclear test ban agreement; but some thorny details, such as the inclusion of Britain's Polaris missile—Britain, of course, was a key us ally—and certainly inspections, thwarted progress. Also presenting a challenge were hawkish sentiments within the Kremlin. The president looked for ways to move ahead, and one person offering insights was Norman Cousins, who also was a guest at the Nobel dinner and had recently talked to Khrushchev. But the catalyst that opened a way forward was a speech Kennedy gave at American University on June 10, 1963. One Kennedy biographer called it "one of the great state papers of any twentieth-century American presidency."[10]

Kennedy laid out his premise: "As Americans, we find communism profoundly repugnant as a negotiation of personal freedom and dignity. But we can still hail the Russian people for their many achievements—in science and space, in economic and industrial growth, in culture and in acts of courage." It was interesting he toned down the bravado of American achievement that he had mentioned in the Berkeley speech and in the Nobel dinner remarks the previous year. Kennedy then offered to hold off on nuclear testing, resume bilateral meetings with the Soviet Union, and institute a superpower hotline.[11]

After further talks, a nuclear test ban agreement was signed on August 5, 1963. Pauling was pleased, writing to Kennedy "to express my gratitude," and encouraged by the Senate ratification. He closed his brief letter by referring to "the repeated expression of my support for your efforts."[12] That, of course, was a bit of an exaggeration, but clearly the outcome was the one that Pauling had been seeking for some time. Pauling's letter was given to national security advisor McGeorge Bundy, who sent back a very brief, most likely stock acknowledgment.[13]

Pauling's peace efforts did not go unnoticed. Coincidentally, on the effective date of the new treaty, October 10, the Nobel Peace Prize was awarded to Linus Pauling. His selection was a testament to his tireless speaking, organizing, and protesting against the use of nuclear weapons and on behalf of peace. It was awarded for the previous year because no award was given for 1962. Immediately, there was positive and negative reaction to the news. But Pauling, of course, was pleased: he became the first American to be awarded two Nobel Prizes. It was even more notable because the awards were in two diverse fields, chemistry and peace. The only previous double Nobel winner was Marie Curie, in chemistry and physics, in the early twentieth century.

Shortly before leaving for Oslo to receive Linus's honor, the Paulings were shocked by the assassination of President Kennedy on November 22. In a letter to Mrs. Kennedy, Linus wrote, "My wife and I send you our heartfelt sympathy. As are hundreds of millions of other people, all over the world, we are stricken with grief by the death of our great President, John F. Kennedy."[14] In December, Linus and Ava Helen traveled to Norway and then Sweden for the Nobel ceremonies and for Linus to deliver the traditional lecture. In addition to the obvious honor, Pauling received a gold medal with the inscription "Pro pace et fraternitate gentium" and a cash award that was equivalent to $49,465 (valued at slightly under $400,000 today).[15] In his remarks, he paid tribute to Ava Helen, saying, "In the fight for peace and against oppression she has been my constant and courageous companion and coworker."[16] But Pauling, being Pauling, was not entirely satisfied with the treatment he received from his government. In a letter to Jerome Wiesner, Pauling complained that the us ambassador to Norway, Clifton R. Wharton Jr., failed to meet him at the Oslo airport. He said that the Nobel event was "marred only by the boycott by the American Embassy." Although he acknowledged that "the public damage" was done, Pauling stressed that this was "a serious matter," and he hoped that Wiesner would bring the issue to Secretary of State Dean Rusk.[17]

Pauling later continued his political activism by opposing the Vietnam War. For those efforts, he was awarded the International Lenin Peace Prize by the Soviet Union. Among previous recipients were W. E. B. Du Bois, Nikita Khrushchev, Sukarno, Fidel Castro, and Pablo Picasso. In his later years Pauling became obsessed with vitamin C and its life-affirming potential. Ava Helen Pauling died in 1981, and Linus died twelve years later at the age of ninety-three. He left behind a rich legacy of scientific achievement and peace activism. He was a brilliant and controversial figure, who for a short period in the early 1960s had a well-known, ambivalent public relationship with President John F. Kennedy. Certainly, the focal point of that relationship was the Nobel dinner on April 29, 1962.

⊂═╾╼

Robert Oppenheimer wrote to Arthur Schlesinger after the Nobel dinner, "It was good to see you at the gay party Sunday. When we left you at midnight, still doing your duty, we had not the heart to come to your home and still further erode your time and life."[18] It might have been interesting if Oppenheimer and his wife, Kitty, a botanist with strong opinions of her own, would have contributed to the rousing conversation at Schlesinger's Georgetown home. In any case, the evening was a huge success for the Oppenheimers—Robert was able to take his first step toward official rehabilitation.

Over the next eleven months, Oppenheimer continued his writing, speeches, and administrative duties as director of the Institute for Advanced Studies at Princeton, now in his sixteenth year there. Then in April 1963, the next step in his public redemption occurred when he was chosen for the prestigious Enrico Fermi Award for contributions in the field of physics. The annual award, bestowed by the president, had been given to men such as Nobel laureates Ernest Lawrence and Oppenheimer's old friend Glenn Seaborg. The previous year it was awarded to his nemesis, Dr. Edward Teller. Unquestionably, Seaborg, still chairman of the Atomic Energy Commission, had a significant role in the selection of Oppenheimer.[19] But the award could not have been made without the support of President Kennedy, who certainly understood the potential for political criticism. By choosing Oppenheimer, Kennedy completed the rehabilitation that he had initiated by inviting him to the Nobel dinner. Oppie also understood what this meant and that there were people within the administration, including Schlesinger and McGeorge Bundy, who also supported his cause. He chose to be cautious in his response to the award. He told reporters,

"Look, this isn't a day for me to go shooting my mouth off. I don't want to hurt the guys who worked on this."[20]

Predictably, there was criticism and discomfort. Seaborg informed Lewis Strauss, Oppenheimer's primary foe from 1954, and the response was not good. "He looked as if I'd leaned over the table and punched him," Seaborg said.[21] And yet, Strauss sent a telegram to Oppenheimer congratulating him on his award. Strauss, who refused public comment, had supported Oppenheimer's selection and retention at Princeton. He had previously argued that Oppenheimer's scientific achievements were unrelated to his suitability for continued security clearance. "The areas are distinct," he said.[22]

There were conservative critics, but time and the trial balloon of the previous year's dinner attendance helped to smooth the general acceptance of the award, which came with a citation, gold medal, and $50,000 cash prize. Among the supportive editorials were those headlined in the *New York Herald Tribune*, "From Pariah to Hero," and the *Trenton Evening News*, "Vindication."[23] Seven months later, on Thursday, November 21, a date was finally set for the presidential ceremony to present the award. The next day, of course, tragedy struck and the president was dead. It was relegated to President Johnson to make the presentation ten days later.[24]

As President Kennedy did at the Nobel dinner, Oppenheimer referred to Thomas Jefferson at the ceremony.[25] He also said to President Johnson, "I think it just possible, Mr. President, that it has taken some charity and some courage for you to make this award today. That would seem to me a good augury for all our futures."[26] Teller, the most recent Fermi awardee, was present, and it was the first time that the two men had met since 1954 at the Atomic Energy Commission hearing. Showing that perhaps times soothes, they shook hands, with Oppie saying, "I am so very glad that you came."[27] Teller said in an interview, "I respect Robert Oppenheimer. There are many things that I admire in him." And Oppenheimer said, "For a long time I thought of Edward Teller as a friend. I do not think of him as an enemy."[28] While Kitty Oppenheimer was less forgiving, it did appear that the old wound had begun healing.[29]

Isidor Rabi, Oppenheimer's friend and a fellow guest at the Nobel dinner, said that the award "is a righting of a great wrong done to him and to the American people. We can rejoice, for the significance of this act is the restoration of sanity and understanding by people of importance."[30] The eight-year political ostracism of J. Robert Oppenheimer had come to an end. There were, of course, some who still questioned his loyalty and resented him—some strongly so—but the initiative that President Kennedy had launched, with help from Oppenheimer's friends in the administration, made the position in history of the "Father of the Atomic Bomb" less clouded and more reflective of his great contribution. A year before Oppenheimer died in 1967, Arthur Schlesinger wrote to him: "You have faced more terrible things than most men in this terrible age, and you have provided all of us with an example of moral courage, purpose and discipline—you probably are not aware of the meaning your life has had for my generation."[31]

⊙═⊷

Oppenheimer was the symbol of the great scientific quest of his generation. Many others who worked, either directly or indirectly, at Los Alamos were present at the Nobel dinner. Also in attendance was Colonel John Glenn, the symbol of a new great scientific adventure—that of the next generation—the Space Race. In some ways, the Nobel dinner was the passing of the baton from one great era to the next, the new one that the president was fully committed to promoting with a view to reaching the moon and outer space. In addition to scientific attainment, this move shifted the emphasis of the arms race from the earth to the heavens.

John Glenn, the All-American hero—the man of the hour—was at the midpoint of a long career serving his country. While he arrived at this celebrity status by courage and his own achievement, his association with the Kennedy family was instrumental in his continued rise. There was an immediate bond between President Kennedy and Glenn. The astronaut was influenced by the president, saying, "His vision set an inspiring example, and I saw that the Kennedy charisma could move millions to contribute to something that I thought was vital—a democracy of energized participation in which people shared their talents with the nation and kept it improving and evolving."[32]

Glenn also quickly developed a deeper connection with Robert Kennedy. A few months after the Nobel dinner, John and Annie Glenn visited Hickory Hill, Robert and Ethel Kennedy's bustling residence across the Potomac, where celebrities gathered and hijinks reigned. Soon he was water skiing with the First Lady and vacationing in Hyannis Port.[33] Glenn had become part of the Kennedy inner circle. A year later, Robert Kennedy proposed to Glenn that he consider running as a Democrat for a US Senate seat from Ohio and adding weight to the ticket for President Kennedy's reelection bid in 1964. Kennedy died, of course, in November 1963, but Glenn did become a candidate.[34]

Unfortunately for Glenn, a freak bathroom accident took place, and an episode of "traumatic vertigo" forced him to end his campaign in March 1964.[35] His friendship with Robert Kennedy, however, remained strong, and Glenn campaigned for him during his presidential run in 1968. He was with Kennedy the night that he was shot in Los Angeles on June 4, 1968. It was John Glenn who delivered the news to the Kennedy children and then accompanied them back home to Virginia. By that time, Robert Kennedy had died, and it was Glenn's duty to inform Robert's children. "It was one of the hardest things I've ever had to do," he said.[36]

Glenn was eventually elected to the US Senate in 1974 and reelected four times, ending his service in January 1999. During his long Senate career, he also ran an abortive campaign for president in 1984, losing to former vice president Walter Mondale. In 1998 he once again created history as a member of the *Discovery* Shuttle crew; he was seventy-seven, the oldest (civilian) astronaut. John Glenn's trailblazing in aeronautics had lasted a half century. When he died in 2016 at age ninety-five, he was given a justified hero's funeral in Columbus, Ohio. Four months later, he was buried at Arlington National Cemetery, about a quarter-mile from the burial site of President John and Jacqueline Kennedy.

⚬═⟡

At the time of the Nobel dinner, octogenarian Robert Frost had only nine more months to live. But he had one important mission to fulfill for President Kennedy. As a result of a dinner meeting between Secretary of the Interior Stewart Udall and Soviet Ambassador Anatoly Dobrynin in May 1962, it was agreed that the United States and the Soviet Union would initiate an exchange of poets. Certainly as a result of his close relationship with Udall, as well as the high regard in which the president held him, it was decided that Robert Frost would be the American poet sent to Russia.[37] Frost was elated, writing to the president in July: "I shall be reading poems chiefly over there but I shall be talking some where I read and you may be sure I won't be talking just literature. I'm the kind of Democrat that *will* reason. You must know my admiration for your *Profiles*. I am frightened by this big undertaking but I was more frightened at your Inauguration."[38]

Accompanied by Udall, a professor of Russian language who served as interpreter, and a librarian friend, Frost set off on his trip in late August. For ten days, Frost did what would be expected in a short cultural exchange—meeting and socializing with writers, reciting poetry such as his famous "Stopping by Woods on a Snowy Evening," and touring major cities. He visited Leningrad, Moscow, and the Crimea. The Crimean stop was the most important to Frost because that was where he met Khrushchev, which was the uppermost objective in his mind. At the meeting, Frost played diplomat, and the two men parried each other's arguments about the world and the superpowers' role in it, including culture. Frost was impressed, saying after the hour-and-a-half discussion, "He knows what power is and isn't afraid to take hold of it. He's a great man, all right."[39]

The trip was a success, but a brief news conference on Frost's arrival back in New York undid the goodwill, at least for his relationship with President Kennedy. One brief remark that Frost made created the problem. He told reporters, "Khrushchev said that we were too liberal to fight." That sentence, which implied that the United States was soft and liberalism was to blame, caused the cautious Kennedy to maintain his distance. Frost was not invited to debrief the president, and they never spoke again.[40]

In a letter to socialist Norman Thomas, Frost addressed the uproar that ensued about the "liberal" comment. Khrushchev, he said, "was just being good-natured and literary when he expressed concern for American liberalism." Complimenting Thomas and former vice president Henry A. Wallace for their liberalism, Frost said that if used properly the word "liberal" was not a bad thing.[41] Udall later drafted a twenty-page summary of the trip, which he shared with President Kennedy. He said that Frost "had plucked at the consciousness, and the conscience, of men in an alien land. True, he had nothing tangible to show for his ten-days of talk except some wilted summer flowers. But a poet plays for the long haul." Udall also addressed the "liberal" issue, suggesting it may have been an inadequate translation or poor hearing—or maybe, simply a description that Frost liked. Udall told the president in a cover memo with the summary, "Frost himself many times used the expression 'Too liberal to fight' prior to his Soviet trip. It was his gibe at professor-types who, he felt, had the Hamlet curse."[42]

Robert Frost died in January 1963. President Kennedy issued a statement that called him "the great American poet of our time. . . . His death impoverishes us all; but he has bequeathed his Nation a body of imperishable verse from which Americans will forever gain joy and understanding."[43] The following day, Kennedy sent a one-hundred-dollar contribution to the Robert Frost Fund as a memorial gift.[44] In October, less than one month before his own death, President Kennedy spoke at the groundbreaking ceremony for the Robert Frost Library at Amherst College. His speech included a line that could also have applied to others who attended the Nobel dinner: "In honoring Robert Frost, we pay homage to the deepest sources of our national strength."[45] It was John Kennedy's last speech in Massachusetts.

⚬⇥⋆

As Frost's career and life were coming to a close, the literary career of James Baldwin was advancing. Shortly after the dinner, Baldwin gave a speech in Spain to help secure the Prix Formentor book award for his friend Katherine Anne Porter, although she did not get the award.[46] Then it was back to his literary pursuits. In November 1962, he published a well-received essay entitled "Letters from a Region in My Mind" in *The New Yorker*. *Time* magazine, commenting on the essay, called him "the most bitterly eloquent voice of the American Negro." Baldwin further argued that his forte was to take his case to a white audience.[47] In early 1963 Baldwin came out with a book, *The Fire Next Time*, a thin, 128-page work that contained two previously published essays. The first, "My Dungeon Shook: Letter to My Nephew on the One Hundredth Anniversary of the Emancipation," was very brief and discussed black-white race relations. He ends his observations to his teenage nephew by saying, "You know, and I know, that the country is celebrating one hundred years of freedom one hundred years too soon. We cannot be free until they [whites] are free."[48] The second essay, "Down at the Cross: Letter from a Region in My

Mind," returns to his autobiographical writing, looking at Harlem, race, his early exposure to Pentecostalism, and his current views on religion, notably Islam. He returns to his theme of white people being naïve about blacks and not understanding the desires of blacks. Baldwin's editor at Dial Press, his publisher, said of the book: "It altered people's views of his literary talent. Jimmy had been practicing his whole life to write *The Fire Next Time*. It was a very sophisticated black man's warning to the white world."[49]

In May 1963, two events occurred that had an important impact on Baldwin's career and life. First, he was on the cover of the May 17 issue of *Time* magazine. The banner on it referred to the recent racial protests and police brutality in Birmingham, Alabama: "Birmingham and Beyond: The Negro's Push for Equality." His influence soared.[50] Simultaneously, Baldwin interacted anew with Attorney General Robert Kennedy, and the meeting—an outgrowth of the Nobel dinner—had important implications for the civil rights movement.

Baldwin dispatched a telegram to the attorney general in which he expressed his frustration with the status of race relations in general and the emergency in Birmingham, Alabama, where Commissioner of Public Safety Eugene "Bull" Connor was attacking peaceful protestors.[51] Baldwin was merely echoing what he had been writing about for some time. Kennedy administration aides Burke Marshall, Arthur Schlesinger, and Dick Goodwin all may have urged Kennedy to get together with Baldwin, whom he had met at the Nobel dinner.[52] For whatever the reason, Kennedy asked Baldwin to join him for breakfast at Hickory Hill, outside of Washington, DC, on May 23. It was a learning session for Kennedy, who asked, among other questions, "What do Negroes want?"[53] The meeting went well—it really was the first opportunity that the attorney general had to discuss issues at any length with Baldwin. According to Burke Marshall, "He and Bob Kennedy had a rather good conversation about the cities." Baldwin was pleased, saying, "I was really quite impressed by him." However, time limited the conversation, and Kennedy suggested on the spot that they meet the following day in New York and that Baldwin assemble a group of black leaders to join them.[54]

The meeting took place at Kennedy's high-rise apartment at Central Park South, across from Central Park and only steps away from the Plaza Hotel. Baldwin had gathered a dozen black leaders, including the noted psychologist

Kenneth Clark, performers Harry Belafonte and Lena Horne, and the writer Lorraine Hansberry, most noted for her play *A Raisin in the Sun*.[55] Years later, Kennedy biographer Larry Tye characterized it as "Harlem vs. Hickory Hill," and the meeting did not go well.[56] Kennedy, who was accompanied by several aides, was defensive, tone deaf, and even rude. He cited discrimination against his own Irish immigrant family, suggesting that someday the United States would have a black president. One participant, young activist Jerome Smith, only twenty-four-years old, was especially confrontational with Kennedy, arguing that violence might be the alternative for the civil rights struggle. Smith said that he would "Never! Never! Never!" fight in an American war, a sentiment that Baldwin had alluded to in *The Fire Next Time*: "There are some wars, for example . . . that the American Negro will not support, however many of his people may be coerced."[57] Kennedy recalled, "Lorraine Hansberry said that they were going to go down and get guns, and they were going to give the guns to people on the street, and they were going to start to kill white people."[58] Overall, Kennedy felt under siege, which he was, and was incensed. The three-hour meeting seemed to be a failure.

Kenneth Clark called the session "the most intense, traumatic meeting in which I've ever taken part . . . the most unrestrained interchange among adults, head-to-head, no holds barred . . . *the* most dramatic experience I have ever had."[59] Kennedy's own anger and disgust at the meeting soon dissipated as he began to consider what had been discussed. According to Larry Tye, "In Bobby's earlier years, the disastrous Baldwin meeting might have been the end of the story. But after a couple of days of fuming, Smith's tirade began to sink in for Kennedy."[60] Arthur Schlesinger said, "He began, I believe, to grasp as from the inside the nature of black anguish."[61] Kennedy was learning and, because of his crucial role in the administration, this was significant. Very quickly, he started to raise the issue of black equality in meetings.[62] Eighteen days after the Baldwin meeting, President Kennedy delivered his noted Civil Rights Address, covering many of the concerns discussed at the meeting and outlining the legislation that would become the Civil Rights Act of 1964. In this speech, the president placed civil rights in a new light; he said, "We are confronted primarily with a moral issue. It is as old as the scriptures and is as clear as the American Constitution."[63] Robert Kennedy was the only Kennedy advisor to support this televised, fourteen-minute speech.[64] Taylor Branch, the biographer of Dr. Martin Luther King Jr., later wrote, "As an authentic disaster, the Baldwin meeting made Robert Kennedy a pioneer in the raw, interracial encounters of the 1960s."[65] The attorney general was being educated. According to Tye, "By the end of his tenure, Bobby Kennedy had become the kind of attorney general that the Baldwin group had urged him to be, and that Martin Luther King had had faith he would become."[66] This all can be traced back to the Nobel dinner, where a line of communication between Robert Kennedy and James Baldwin was initiated and which eventually spurred progress on civil rights.

James Baldwin went on to write another dozen books—novels, plays, poems, and essays. While he was well known at the time of his death in 1987, in subsequent years his fame increased and he was reintroduced to another generation. In addition to the continued popularity of his work, Baldwin's recognition has been enhanced by two documentary films—*The Price of the Ticket,* directed by Karen Thorsen and released in 2013, and *I Am Not Your Negro,* directed by Raoul Peck and released in 2017. These films, as well as the rereading of his works, have shown that Baldwin's voice still speaks strongly on current race relations and its challenges in the twenty-first century. Perhaps a modern commentator best summarized his legacy: "Baldwin did not only write about what it means to be black in America. He also wrote, as fearlessly as any American writer, about what it means to be white."[67]

❧

Robert Kennedy became closely associated with the civil rights movement. In the years following his brother's assassination, he was increasingly engaged in issues related to African-Americans and other minorities, or marginalized people such as migrant farm workers. He was elected to the US Senate in 1964 and eventually used his platform there and his late entrance into the 1968 presidential race to oppose the Vietnam War. In one of the most memorable speeches of his career, Kennedy spoke impromptu to a group of African-Americans in Indianapolis informing them of Martin Luther King's assassination on April 4, 1968. This five-minute talk, in which he cited his brother's murder, provided empathy in what could have been a volatile situation. In fact, Indianapolis kept calm in the aftermath of the King assassination, an anomaly among large

American cities.[68] This incident alone showed how far Robert Kennedy had traveled in the five years since the acrimonious meeting with James Baldwin. Two months later, he too was murdered. At the age of forty-two, he was the fourth member of his family to die a violent death.

☞—⋆—

The other rising literary figure at the Nobel dinner was Baldwin's friend William Styron. While Bill Styron never achieved the intimacy that John Glenn formed with John Kennedy and Robert Kennedy, he and his wife began a more than fifty-year relationship with the broader Kennedy family beginning on April 29, 1962. True to the promise made by Jacqueline Kennedy in the Yellow Oval Room, the Kennedys and Styrons did go sailing that summer. On a Sunday morning the president's yacht, named the *Patrick J* for the president's paternal grandfather, sailed from Hyannis Port to Edgartown, on the eastern part of the island of Martha's Vineyard—a distance of about twenty miles. The Styrons and their mutual friends John Marquand Jr. and his wife, Sue, were ferried out to Vineyard Sound, where they boarded. Jean Smith, who had hosted one of the tables at the Nobel dinner, and her husband were already aboard as was the president, First Lady, and five-year-old Caroline Kennedy. On rough seas, they enjoyed Bloody Marys, hot dogs, cake, and venerable and popular—and banned—Partagas cigars from Cuba. The president and author discussed a range of issues, including books, politics, and race relations. The conversation turned to Styron's latest project, which would become *The Confessions of Nat Turner*. Kennedy was quite interested in the book, a fictionalized account of an actual slave rebellion that took place in southern Virginia in 1831. Styron later wrote, "At that time few Americans had heard of Nat Turner. I told Kennedy things about slavery he had obviously never known before."[69]

In November 1963, shortly before his death, the Styrons saw the president at a party in New York. "How is that book of yours coming along?" Kennedy asked. Styron was flabbergasted that the president remembered their discussion of sixteen months earlier. They discussed the slow writing progress as well as slavery.[70] The book was published in 1967 and received the Pulitzer Prize. But it was controversial, lambasted by many black leaders for the way Nat

Turner was portrayed. But Jimmy Baldwin, Styron's friend, defended him. Baldwin's biographer said, "In this support he demonstrated a commitment to art over politics or political correctness."[71]

Styron was devastated by Kennedy's assassination. But he was friends with Dick Goodwin, a neighbor on Martha's Vineyard and now an aide to Lyndon Johnson, and he collaborated with Goodwin on a speech discussing the Voting Rights Act of 1965.[72] And yet, Johnson was much different from his predecessor; as Styron said, "A far cry from J. F. Kennedy."[73]

William Styron's literary reputation was further enhanced by his publication of *Sophie's Choice* in 1979. Later made into a movie starring a young Meryl Streep, this was a story of an Auschwitz survivor and her lover in Brooklyn. Styron later suffered from depression and wrote about it as well as historical insights into the disease in *Darkness Visible: A Memoir of Madness*, which was widely read and discussed. It was the most significant work of his later years. He died in 2006 at the age of eighty-one. Before his death, the Styrons had developed a bond with Jacqueline Kennedy, Robert and Ethel Kennedy, and, especially, with Ted Kennedy. Kennedy children visited the Styron home at Vineyard Haven, and Ethel Kennedy even slept in a sleeping bag in their dining room.[74] That relationship continued after William Styron's death. Rose Styron, a writer, a widely respected poet, and an activist, served as the longtime chair of the Robert F. Kennedy Human Rights Award, which was established in 1984. Among the notable awardees have been the activists Wei Jingsheng and Winnie Mandela. For Rose Styron, this long family relationship would not have been possible without the night they enjoyed at the Nobel dinner.

The Trillings were the other literary couple present at the Nobel evening. Lionel Trilling died in 1975 at the age of seventy. Diana Trilling lived another twenty-one years. During that time, she continued to be seen as Mrs. Lionel Trilling, as she had feared, but her independent accomplishments became more evident. In addition to continuing to write articles in well-respected magazines, she waded into the sensational story of Jean Harris's murder of Dr. Herman Tarnower, the Scarsdale Diet doctor. Her book on the case, published in 1981, was a well-received best-seller.[75] *Kirkus Reviews,* the prominent book review magazine, called it a "tour-de-force account" and "a dynamite book."[76] In 1993 she published a memoir of her marriage to Lionel, which revealed some of the challenges she encountered during their forty-six years together.[77]

Diana Trilling outlived Mr. and Mrs. Kennedy, both younger than she, and was ninety-one when she died. Seven months later, her account of the Nobel dinner, "A Visit to Camelot," was published in *The New Yorker* in June 1997.

◉━✦

Jacqueline Kennedy, America's queen and social trendsetter of the early 1960s, continued to have elegant dinners after April 1962. The next one, twelve days later, was for French cultural leader André Malraux, and it was lavish and significant. Mrs. Kennedy was fascinated by Malraux. When asked about what made him special, she replied, "He happens to be a war hero, a brilliant, sensitive writer, and he happens to have a *great* mind." The dinner, like the Nobel event, was star-studded with many people from the literary world. Among them were Saul Bellow, Paddy Chayefsky, John Hersey, Archibald MacLeish, Robert Penn Warren, Thornton Wilder, and Tennessee Williams. Others included Charles Lindbergh, who sat at the president's table, and Anne Morrow Lindbergh—both of whom had met with the president at the White House earlier in the day—and Andrew Wyeth. Guests Alexis Leger (Saint-John Perse) and his wife, Arthur Schlesinger and his wife, and Mrs. Pierre Salinger had been at the Nobel dinner. Stéphane Boudin, who was so instrumental in the current refurbishment of the White House, also was there. Unlike the Nobel dinner, there were a number of political figures present. What was noteworthy about the Malraux dinner was that shortly afterward, the French government loaned Leonardo da Vinci's masterpiece, the *Mona Lisa*, to the United States, where it was shown at the National Gallery of Art and the Metropolitan Museum of Art.[78]

The Jacqueline Kennedy–Tish Baldrige relationship continued to fray. Baldrige said, "During our second year in the White House, I sensed the First Lady's resentment of my constant nudging."[79] She was correct. Not only was there a conflict about the workload and constant pushing from Baldrige, but they had different outlooks. "Tish is sort of a feminist, really," she said. "She used to tell me she loved to have lunch in the White House Mess so she could argue with men. She's great, but she was so different from me and just exhausted me so." In June 1963 she was replaced as social secretary by Nancy Tuckerman, a childhood friend of the First Lady and boarding school roommate.[80]

Linus Pauling picketing across the street from the White House.
*Source*: Associated Press. © 2018 The Associated Press.

Linus Pauling testifying before the Senate International Security Subcommittee. *Source:* Courtesy Ava Helen and Linus Pauling Papers, OSU Libraries Special Collections and Archives Research Center

Ava Helen Pauling also was an activist. Here she is speaking at a peace rally. *Source:* Courtesy Ava Helen and Linus Pauling Papers, osu Libraries Special Collections and Archives Research Center

J. Robert Oppenheimer at his desk at the Institute for Advanced Study, where he served as director from 1947 to 1966. *Source:* Alan Richards, photographer. From the Shelby White and Leon Levy Archives Center, Institute for Advanced Study, Princeton, New Jersey

Ethel Kennedy was a social presence in Washington, DC, during the Kennedy administration. Here she is at a children's party at the White House four months before the Nobel dinner. She hosted the table that included Oppenheimer and William Styron. *Source:* Abbie Rowe, White House Photographs, John F. Kennedy Presidential Library and Museum, Boston

John Glenn's historic
ticker-tape parade in New
York City, March 1, 1962.
At the time of the Nobel
dinner, Glenn was the hero
of the hour. *Source:* John
Glenn Archives, The Ohio
State University (NASA
photograph)

Parade for astronaut John
Glenn in Washington,
DC, after his orbital
flight. *Source:* John Glenn
Archives, The Ohio
State University (NASA
photograph)

Robert Kennedy and John Glenn formed a close friendship in 1962, which continued until Kennedy's death. Here they are at a presidential campaign stop in 1968. *Source:* John Glenn Archives, The Ohio State University

By 1962 James Baldwin was an important American writer. He also was becoming more engaged in the civil rights movement. At the time of the dinner, he was living on the property of his friend William Styron. Here he is several years later in London. *Source:* By Allan Warren (own work) [CC BY-SA 3.0 (http://creativecommons.org/licenses/by-sa/3.0) or GFDL (http://www.gnu.org/copyleft/fdl.html)], via Wikimedia Commons

William Styron was on the cusp of writing important novels when he met President Kennedy at the Nobel dinner. Here he is in 1989 after the success of *The Confessions of Nat Turner* and *Sophie's Choice*. *Source:* By William Waterway (own work) [CC BY-SA 3.0 (http://creativecommons.org/licenses/by-sa/3.0)], via Wikimedia Commons

*above* Attorney General Robert Kennedy chats with several guests in the center of the Entrance Hall in front of a portrait of Andrew Jackson. *Source:* Robert Knudsen, White House Photographs, John F. Kennedy Presidential Library and Museum, Boston

Preceding dinner the guests mingle in the Cross Hall, entertained by the Strolling Strings. *Source:* Cecil Stoughton, White House Photographs, John F. Kennedy Presidential Library and Museum, Boston

At the White House dinner on 28 Ap. 1962, as Ava Helen & I went through the receiving line, Pres. Kennedy said to me "Dr Pauling, how do you do— [You've] been around the White House a couple of days already, haven't you?" May I introduce you to Mrs Kennedy?" Mrs Kennedy then said "Dr Pauling, do you think it is right to walk back & forth out there where Caroline can see you, so that she asks "What has Daddy done wrong now?" — You shouldn't do it."

Boris Arwandtes says that 1/3 of all Paraguayans are exiles. 27 concentration camps in Paraguay.

— I hope that you will continue to express your opinions.

Linus Pauling's hand-written account of his conversation with President and Mrs. Kennedy in the receiving line before dinner. *Source:* Courtesy Ava Helen and Linus Pauling Papers, osu Libraries Special Collections and Archives Research Center

Before dinner a group photograph was taken of the Nobel Prize winners in the East Room. Mary Welsh Hemingway, on President Kennedy's right, represented her late husband, Ernest Hemingway, and Katherine Tupper Marshall, on the President's left, represented her late husband, George C. Marshall. *Source:* Abbie Rowe, White House Photographs, John F. Kennedy Presidential Library and Museum, Boston

Seating plan for the State Dining Room (*top*) and the Blue Room (*bottom*).
*Source:* Papers of John F. Kennedy, Presidential Papers, White House Staff
Files of Sanford L. Fox, Social Events, 1961–1964, Events: April 29, 1962,
Dinner, Nobel Prize Winners: Seating plan, John F. Kennedy Presidential
Library and Museum, Boston

The four-page remarks that President Kennedy delivered at the dinner with handwritten notes added. *Source:* John F. Kennedy Presidential Library and Museum, Boston

The President
Remarks
Nobel Prize Dinner
April 29, 1962

I am proud to welcome to the White House the winners of the Nobel Prize in the Western Hemisphere. I doubt whether in the long history of this house we have ever had on a single occasion such a concentration of genius and achievement as we have tonight.

The Nobel Prize, of course, is intended for humanity in general. It knows no geographical or political frontiers. With brisk disregard for his fellow countrymen Alfred Nobel even took care to specify in his will, "I declare it to be my express desire that, in the awarding of prizes, no consideration whatever be paid to the nationality of the candidates, that is to say, that the most desrving be awarded the prize, whether he or she be a Scandanavian or not...".

Nobel's passion was to honor men and women who served mankind in the fields of science and in literature and in the cause of peace. His faith was that the spirit of inquiry and the extension of knowledge would best guarantee the freedom and welfare of humanity. "Knowledge", said Plato, "is the food of the soul". We must all agree with Nobel that the free and disinterested pursuit of knowledge has always been-- and always will be-- the mainspring of human Progress.

While respecting Alfred Nobel's wish that no consideration should be paid to nationality, I hope you will forgive me if I express particular pride over the fact that during the past thirty years nearly 40 percent of the Nobel Prizes have been awarded to citizens of the Western Hemisphere. The atmosphere which permits and encourages the unfettered pursuit of knowledge surely holds the greatest promise for the advance of science and the benefit of mankind. It is in the long run the foundation of the Alliance for Progress-- and of the hope we all nourish for a better life for all.

I would note alo that many of the prize winners in this room were born in other lands and have come to live in the Americas-- another fact in which citizens of our hemisphere may take great pride. I hope you will forgive me too if I express satisfaction over the fact that more Nobel peace prizes have been awarded to citizens of the United States than of any other nation. The record of thirteen American winners of the Peace Prize suggests, I think, how deep-rooted the quest for peace is in the American tradition and the American ethos.

Nobel wished the Peace Prize awarded, in his own words, "to the person who shall have most or best promoted the fraternity of nations and the abolition or diminution of standing armies and the formation and increase of Peace Congresses". It is only superficially a paradox that the inventor of dynamite

should also have been the prophet of peace.  Those who understand
the ultimate horror of annihilation have the best reason to hate
the weapons of destruction.  Nobel himslef once remarked to a
pacifist friend, "Perhaps my factories will put an end to war
even sooner than your congresses.  On the day when two armed
camps may mutually annihilate each other in a second, all
*civilized*
citizens nations will probably recoil with horror and disband their
troops."

We have now reached that day of mutual capacity for
annihilation-- and I deeply believe that the response which Nobel
predicted will come, if not with the speed he anticipated.  Our
effort now must be to keep his goal constantly before us and
labor responsibly and unceasingly for peace-- in *the* hope that the
genius of humanity may then dedicate itself, not to the destruction
of man's hopes, but to the fulfillment of man's vision of a good
and decent and just life.

I would like to propose a toast to the 1961 Nobel Prize
winners and, through them, to all the Nobel Prize Winners
now resident in our hemisphere--- and I would propose the
toast in the spirit expressed nearly two centuries ago by the
man who above all Americans should have been with us here
tonight, Benjamin Franklin:

"The rapid progress true science now makes, occasions my

regretting sometimes that I was born so soon. It is impossible
to imagine the height to which may be carried, in a thousand
years, the power of man over matter.

We may perhaps learn to deprive large masses of their
gravity, and give them absolute levity for the sake of easy
transport. Agriculture may diminish its labor and double its
produce; all diseases may by sure means be prevented or cured,
not excepting even that of old age, and our lives lengthened at
pleasure even beyond the antediluvian standard.

"O that moral science were in as fair a way of improvement,
that men would cease to be wolves to one another, and that human
beings would at length learn what they now improperly call
humanity!"

The Strolling Strings performed throughout the evening. *Source:* Robert Knudsen, White House Photographs, John F. Kennedy Presidential Library and Museum, Boston

President Kennedy speaking with Pearl Buck, and Mrs. Kennedy speaking with Robert Frost. Lady Bird Johnson is on the left and Agnes Charlier Jarring, the wife of Gunnar Jarring, Sweden's ambassador to the United States, is on the right. *Source:* Robert Knudsen, White House Photographs, John F. Kennedy Presidential Library and Museum, Boston

President Kennedy speaking with Pearl Buck, and Mrs. Kennedy speaking with Robert Frost. *Source:* Cecil Stoughton, White House Photographs, John F. Kennedy Presidential Library and Museum, Boston

President Kennedy speaking with future Canadian prime minister Lester Pearson, Mary Welsh Hemingway, and Pearl Buck. *Source:* Cecil Stoughton, White House Photographs, John F. Kennedy Presidential Library and Museum, Boston

President Kennedy and guests mingling. *Source:* Cecil Stoughton, White House Photographs, John F. Kennedy Presidential Library and Museum, Boston

Mrs. Kennedy with Nobel laureate Alexis Leger (Saint-John Perse) and others. President Kennedy is also present in the East Room. The painting in the background is a copy of Gilbert Stuart's full-length portrait of George Washington. *Source:* Robert Knudsen, White House Photographs, John F. Kennedy Presidential Library and Museum, Boston

President and Mrs. Kennedy signing autographs after the dinner. *Source:* Cecil Stoughton, White House Photographs, John F. Kennedy Presidential Library and Museum, Boston

Entertaining in the White House continued, with René Verdon serving as executive chef throughout the administration. On November 22, 1963, that all came to a tragic end and Mrs. Kennedy began a new life. Over the next thirty years, she continued to be a person of great interest and an obsession with some photographers, journalists, and a large part of the general public. Her marriage to Greek tycoon Aristotle Onassis in 1968 received considerable attention. But after his death seven years later, she entered the book publishing world in Manhattan as an editor at Viking Press and then Doubleday. The activist and writer Gloria Steinem, an admirer of Mrs. Kennedy, said, "As for why she chose to be an editor as opposed to some other profession, I think it's quite simple: She loved books. They were windows into hearts, minds, ideas, and the world. Books were powerful."[81]

For nearly twenty years, Mrs. Kennedy edited works from a diverse group of writers, including Princess Grace of Monaco, fashion writer Diana Vreeland, George Plimpton, Joseph Campbell, dancer Martha Graham, musician André Previn, Carly Simon, Bill Moyers, and Stewart Udall, who had served as secretary of the interior in her husband's cabinet.[82] Given her high regard for Thomas Jefferson and President Kennedy's famous reference to him at the Nobel dinner, it may seem surprising that she also worked with Barbara Chase-Riboud on her controversial novel *Sally Hemmings*. The story of Hemmings, a slave and mistress of Jefferson, was very popular but criticized by historians seeking to protect Jefferson's image. Mrs. Kennedy stood by the author, who went on to have a long career in writing and sculpture.[83]

Mrs. Kennedy also was active in historic preservation in New York City, including helping to save Grand Central Station from the wrecking ball in 1975. When she died on May 19, 1994, at age sixty-four, she was mourned throughout the nation and the world. Sargent Shriver, her brother-in-law, said of her: "Beauty, brains, courage, passion, artistic sensibility. One of the most unusual personages of these times."[84] John Glenn, whose thirty-two-year friendship with her began in 1962 and was cemented with occasions such as the Nobel dinner, eulogized her: "For her grace, for her courage, and, above all, for her unfailing dignity, Jacqueline Kennedy Onassis will be remembered as a woman not just for her time but for all time, and we shall miss her greatly."[85]

There were others associated with the Nobel dinner who continued to have a relationship with the memory of President Kennedy after his death. Fredric March hosted *A Tribute to John F. Kennedy from the Arts* on the ABC television network immediately after the assassination. Arthur Schlesinger, who became an advisor to Robert Kennedy, published the first and most authoritative—if highly sympathetic account—of the Kennedy administration in his book *A Thousand Days: John F. Kennedy in the White House*. He received a Pulitzer Prize for it in 1966, nine years after Kennedy's *Profiles in Courage* had won the award. And Mary Welsh Hemingway continued to manage her husband's literary estate until her death in 1986. She published *Islands in the Stream*, which was excerpted at the Nobel dinner, in 1970. With the intercession of Bill Walton and working with Mrs. Kennedy, she also deposited the papers of Papa Hemingway at the new Kennedy Library in Boston, where 90 percent of his manuscripts and papers now reside and where the Kennedy and Hemingway researchers continue their work under one roof. Mary Hemingway's papers are also there.

For more than fifty years John Fitzgerald Kennedy has remained a largely revered, if sometimes enigmatic figure. The shortness of his presidency seems to prevent his being included among the greatest American presidents, but public approval of his tenure remains high. He is remembered for staring down Nikita Khrushchev and avoiding a nuclear holocaust during the Cuban Missile Crisis. But there was more. The space program, true to Kennedy's prediction, landed a man on the moon by the end of the 1960s. He is remembered for his initiatives on civil rights, many of them implemented by his successor, Lyndon Johnson. His creation of the Peace Corps, which has attracted nearly a quarter-million Americans to service and affected the lives of millions throughout the world, has been a singular, ongoing achievement. He launched initiatives that resulted in the creation of the National Endowment for the Arts and the National Endowment for the Humanities. Periodically stories still surface about the nuclear test ban agreement in the international arena or economic successes such as tax cuts at home. But for many, it was the promise of a better, more hopeful America that he articulated. The frequent refrain is: "What if."

We will never know, of course, but the Nobel dinner provides some insights into what the young leader valued and how he hoped to honor the past and inspire others for the future.

Among the Americans awarded the Nobel Prize since this dinner have been John Steinbeck (1962), Dr. Martin Luther King Jr. (1965), Saul Bellow (1976), Elie Wiesel (1986), Jimmy Carter (2002), Barack Obama (2009), and Bob Dylan (2016). Some of the selections have been controversial, but every one of the awardees made contributions that underscore the important role that the United States has played in the sciences, literature, economics, and peace. Alfred Nobel could not have imagined many of the achievements of the men and women chosen for his awards, but he certainly would have been impressed by the gathering that President Kennedy assembled on that warm spring night in April 1962. And President John F. Kennedy would be impressed and pleased to see that, despite all the challenges we have faced in the past half century, the United States continues to be the envy of the world in scholarship and research in many fields. The beacon still shines bright.

# Nothing Like It Since

IN AN INTERVIEW for this book, Rose Styron spoke with unbridled enthusiasm about the dinner Bill Styron and she attended at the White House in April 1962. "Because it was Camelot," she said, "we were all excited, impressed, moved by the promise of his presidency, which we thought was the peak of American accomplishment and hope." For her, and surely for many others at the dinner that night, the experience was etched in their minds. She recalls, "We all had a common cause which was America in those days." And for her, it was a dividing line: "We never again thought of our country the way we had that night."[1]

The Styrons were invited to White House dinners in the Carter and Reagan administrations, but it was not the same.[2] Perhaps it was nostalgia. Or perhaps it was that Rose and Bill Styron had formed a broad friendship with the Kennedy family.

For many others there that night, despite lofty reputations in their fields, this event was a singular honor, one that no doubt lasted a lifetime. Ava Helen Pauling, despite her skepticism about President Kennedy and the uncomfortable grilling that she received from Arthur Schlesinger, kept a soiled menu card from her table. And of course, she and Linus danced and enjoyed themselves as part of a unique evening for all those present.

So many of the events of the Kennedy years—the brief, 1,036 days—are now clouded by the Camelot story that sometimes it is difficult to extract achievement from myth, substance from legend. Surely, the tragic circumstances of the death of the forty-six-year-old charismatic leader added significantly to the mystique. Then the aura was enhanced by the brief presidential campaign of Robert Kennedy, who suffered a similar, untimely death. The centennial celebration of John Kennedy's birthday in 2017 has only added more to the story.

Often from a perspective of more than two generations, people look back on the events of their youth or that of their parents' and see all the good and wonderful things that have come and gone. Longing for the past has a powerful pull on the emotions. That's why the 1950s, a seemingly carefree time when all was well with the world, appear so wonderful. The same applies to the early 1960s. When nostalgia is combined with myth, an image is created that frequently distorts reality even more.

The period of the Eisenhower and the Kennedy years was one of turmoil, some of it visible and some bubbling below the surface. Certainly, that was true in relation to racial equality and harmony. It was true regarding women's rights. President Kennedy had only begun the push toward a national environmental movement. And in many other areas, the nation had not fully lived up to its promise. And yet, more careful analysis suggests that the Kennedy years, with the Nobel dinner at its midpoint, represented much that was great in America. Rose Styron's exuberance is understandable; it cannot be denied that the country was on the cusp of great change, much of it traumatic.

⚬═✦⠂

It is not uncommon for writers and pundits to chronicle the various crises that the United States has suffered from 1963 onward. There was, of course, the violent death of President Kennedy, the first president to be assassinated since 1901 and the only such murder of a national leader that virtually any American then alive had witnessed. It was a huge jolt: the idea that a president was fair game for a sniper, and that it was all witnessed in horrific immediacy through television, which was just becoming a national unifier. The events of that sad weekend in November became scarred in the minds of millions. While perhaps those who had experienced World War II might challenge the assumption, it has been widely argued that the United States lost its innocence on that crisp autumn weekend.

And yet, much more was to come. The war in Southeast Asia, while it had engaged the Kennedy administration in a modest way, soon began to escalate. By 1968, the country was in turmoil, so much so that Lyndon Johnson was forced to eschew the presidential nomination. For those who lived through that year, the murders of Dr. Martin Luther King Jr. and Robert Kennedy chillingly revived the nightmare of five years before. Violent riots in many of the nation's largest cities and the great upheaval at the Democratic National Convention in Chicago raised questions about whether the fabric of society was in jeopardy.

The sixties ended and the seventies began with the Vietnam War rising to the level of our principal preoccupation, as night after night television viewers watched the gruesome reporting on the news. And then, with the war slowly winding down, the nation had to grapple with the most significant constitutional crisis in a century, as the misdeeds of the Nixon administration ended in the first resignation of a president.

In retrospect, we saw that the apogee of the United States' imposing postwar power and influence was reached during the Kennedy administration. Following the painful dilemma of the Vietnam War and Watergate, the American ability to solve problems at home and resolve tensions abroad seemed more limited. The energy crisis and inflation roiled the economy and challenged the lifestyles of many. The inability to swiftly end the Iranian hostage episode and the Soviet incursion into Afghanistan showed the difficulty of imposing our will around the world despite having a vast military arsenal.

Over the course of recent decades, there have been successes in different fields, including the amazing proliferation of technology into every aspect of life. But during the past quarter century, despite being arguably the world's only superpower during that time, the United States has been mired in challenges related to a host of issues, none more imminent than the security of the homeland. The tragic events of September 11, 2001, have become the modern-day equivalent of the attack on Pearl Harbor or the assassination of John Kennedy for a previous generation—a defining moment. Seventeen years ago, we were made painfully aware that even a great, powerful nation is vulnerable.

Other major problems have emerged to vex today's America, some of which return us to a darker, uglier period in our history. Unquestionably, one of those areas is in race relations and the failure to ensure that all citizens are afforded the same opportunities and respect. Vile racism, which has long been associated with an earlier era—presumed to be gone or at least below the surface—has become far too widespread, blatant, and in some cases, even mainstream. The 2016 presidential election, following an increasing trend from the 1990s, became the most bitter of modern times. The political battle lines have become so rigid that any hint of compromise is condemned as traitorous by one side or the other. The word that best characterizes the United States in 2018 is polarization.

⊂≡·-

The Kennedy years, viewed through the prism of the Nobel dinner, present an opportunity to see how the American government responded to major national issues and to provide a blueprint to address these issues again. No one would argue that the United States in April 1962 was anything approaching a utopia, but it was a time when optimism was widespread and the future looked promising—that this country could achieve great things and live up to its potential if all of us worked together. That is in marked contrast to the gloomy and sometimes even apocalyptic outlook that is seen today, fostered by many people identified as our national stewards.

What can we learn from this dinner that attracted what President Kennedy said was "the most extraordinary collection of talent, of human knowledge, that has ever been gathered at the White House—with the possible exception of when Thomas Jefferson dined alone"? There is the obvious lesson that our greatest minds, our most productive men and women of science and letters, were honored and collectively valued for their achievement. The idea of bringing these distinguished people together—some of whom were immigrants—to the president's house to say thank you for their amazing accomplishments, was unprecedented. No such event has ever been attempted by subsequent presidents.

Those at the dinner helped win World War II, establish American hegemony, and push us into space. They wrote about issues that profoundly described the human condition and tried to provide insights into the national character. They sought to wage peace and create a safe world for the nation's children and grandchildren. This was a remarkable galaxy of people whose work represented some of the seminal achievements of the twentieth century and whose impact continues.

It was the desire of President Kennedy and the remarkable staff that he assembled to pay tribute to these scientists, writers, and statesmen. It was consistent with a goal that was launched at the very beginning of his administration to uplift people of achievement and highlight their stories. On other occasions, invitees to the White House represented the richness of American art and music. Overall, the Kennedy White House believed that intellectual and creative attainment was something to be cherished and promoted, not envied or held in suspicion. There was a commitment to the ideal of "the best and brightest."

The Nobel dinner represented a sense of elegance befitting a great nation and a city slowly emerging as a peer to great capitals such as London and Paris. In previous decades Washington, DC, despite its growing importance in world affairs, had been struggling to break the shackles of being a sleepy, southern town or, as Kennedy himself called it, "a city of southern efficiency and northern charm." Largely under the leadership of First Lady Jacqueline Kennedy, that was changing as the White House became the grandest salon in America. Suddenly, fashion, style, art, and music seemed to focus on the activities at 1600 Pennsylvania Avenue.

The symbols represented by the Nobel dinner—an appreciation for intellectual and scholarly achievement and a desire to promote events that showcased the new spirit in the capital—were perhaps obvious. This dinner reflects themes that were synonymous with the times and which could be used to help America regain its footing today. As such, the Nobel dinner, independent of the important and historic connections made, can be legitimately hailed as one of the most important social events of the twentieth century.

⊂═⊷

American political history is replete with episodes in which partisanship was strong, pervasive, and even vile. The founders warned against factions, but very quickly conflicting ideologies developed in Washington's cabinet and the country. The Hamiltonians and Jeffersonians had very different views on the role of government, and increasingly their skirmishes turned bitter. John Adams and Thomas Jefferson, once allies, became estranged. Laws such as the Alien and Sedition Acts were passed to quell dissent. Newspapers, financially supported by either the Federalist or the Republican party, spewed vitriol. Political opponents were demonized. This is precisely what the framers in Philadelphia had hoped to prevent.

Politics became a rough-and-tumble profession, and low points were reached during the feuds between the Jacksonians and Republicans and, later, the Whigs. The gradual and then headlong rush toward civil war made the country's politics especially toxic in the 1850s, and then came the Armageddon of the 1860s. The politics of the following century went through patches of bitterness, sometimes reflecting personal pique, such as the quixotic campaign of third-party candidate Theodore Roosevelt, or personal disdain as evidenced by some wealthy opponents of his cousin, Franklin D. Roosevelt. And of course, the stridency of discourse in the McCarthy era of the early 1950s was notable for its lack of decency and for playing on fears and paranoia.

No one would suggest that American politics in 1962 was a benign sport. But despite the Kennedys' well-known embrace of bare-knuckle electioneering, President Kennedy understood the importance of civility and the value of treating disagreements in a broader perspective. His widow recalled his admonition: "In politics you don't have friends or enemies, you have colleagues."[3] Kennedy understood that in the engagement on public policy questions, there are shifting alliances and different points of view. There is no better example of this than his friendly and even encouraging greeting of Linus Pauling at the dinner. Pauling had been lambasting the president in letters that were overwrought, and he had the audacity to picket him outside the White House only hours before joining the focus of his protest for a grand dinner. Kennedy's response was pure pragmatism. And it was civility, a quality that is lacking in the political "dialogue" that characterizes public policy debates today.

Kennedy had good relationships with Republicans; we need look no further than his prepresidential friendship with his political opponent Richard Nixon. Kennedy appointed C. Douglas Dillon, a Republican, as treasury secretary, a key post in any administration. Henry Cabot Lodge, whom Kennedy unseated as senator from Massachusetts and beat as the vice presidential candidate in 1960, was appointed by his old adversary as us ambassador to South Vietnam, another critical position. John Kennedy was a partisan and did his best to promote the Democratic agenda. Republicans were sometimes criticized, sometimes lampooned, but not demonized. Policymakers from both parties can learn from that example.

Kennedy also appreciated the value of conciliation. It was a bold act to release Robert Oppenheimer from his political purgatory. Oppenheimer had served the nation and the scientific community with great distinction, but he was rebuked and ostracized by official Washington, largely because of vindictiveness and partly because of the physicist's naïveté. Inviting Oppenheimer to such a highly visible dinner honored his achievements and made a statement that he still held a place among the nation's greatest scientists. Kennedy took this effort at conciliation and redemption a step further when he selected Oppenheimer for the prestigious Fermi Award, which was presented at the White House a week after Kennedy's death.

The importance of having open communication, even with people who disagree with the administration, is also exhibited by the relationship between James Baldwin and Robert Kennedy. Baldwin was skeptical of the Kennedys and had a strong initial distaste for the attorney general. But one year after the dinner, Baldwin felt comfortable meeting Robert Kennedy to help with the tense racial situation in Birmingham, Alabama, and with race relations in general. The brief breakfast meeting and the resultant, contentious meeting with African-American leaders the next day was the outcome. The meeting represented two sides that had little appreciation for the other's point of view—most especially on Kennedy's side—but the impact of the meeting was significant. Robert Kennedy was slowly becoming sensitized to black issues, and three weeks later President Kennedy broadcast his civil rights address, containing the outlines of what became the Civil Rights Act of 1964. Over the next five years, Robert Kennedy developed a profoundly different understanding of race relations in America. While there were certainly other factors that educated him, the impact of the May 1963 meeting in New York—really initiated by the Nobel dinner a year earlier—was instrumental. You can draw a line from the Nobel dinner to the us government's key achievements on civil rights in the 1960s.

John Kennedy valued briefings and the input of the best minds in the country. He did his homework and sought out experts. He surrounded himself with people who were well educated and experienced in government. Kennedy demonstrated his understanding of the issues through the unprecedented live, informative, and witty news conferences—sixty-four in all. Hosting this dinner symbolized how he appreciated the collective wisdom of American leaders in many areas of endeavor and learned from them.

Another characteristic that was reflected in an indirect way at the Nobel dinner, but was widely practiced by Kennedy, was the willingness to compromise. Kennedy had sought a nuclear test ban agreement, the reason for Pauling's protest that Sunday afternoon. The president was reluctant to resume United States testing, but felt he was forced to do so. Still, he kept the channels of communication open with the Soviet Union. The Cuban Missile Crisis, which occurred later in 1962, is often seen as a determined show of force by the United States—or by some as reckless brinksmanship—but it also reflected compromise. In effect, the resolution of this dangerous confrontation was accompanied by the Soviet Union removing missiles from Cuba and, as an implicit quo pro quo, the United States removing missiles from Turkey. In 1963, with give-and-take on both sides, a Limited Nuclear Test Ban agreement was signed by the two superpowers. Compromise, in public policy decisions at home and working with adversaries abroad, has become rare to such an extent that gridlock has resulted and major problems are exacerbated or remain unresolved.

He also appreciated the value of public involvement and even encouraged healthy dialogue within the government. His inaugural address famously called all Americans to service: "Ask not what your country can do for you—ask what you can do for your country." In his first State of the Union address, only ten days after his inauguration, he said, "Let the public service be a proud and lively career. And let every man and woman who works in any area of our national government, in any branch, at any level, be able to say with pride and with honor in future years: 'I served the United States government in that hour of our nation's need.'" And he said, "Let it be clear that this Administration recognizes the value of dissent and daring—that we greet healthy controversy as the hallmark of healthy change."[4]

⊂⇒⤙

As Rose Styron noted, the people assembled at the Nobel dinner represented a group that loved their country and did what they could to see it succeed. The idea of American unity has waxed and waned over the years, but in 1962 there was an appreciation and understanding of what held us together as a people. It was a time of consensus building. And John Kennedy was a master at doing that. Such an effort began at the very outset of the administration with an inaugural address that called on Americans to work together to achieve a peaceful world and to live up to our responsibilities and fight "the common enemies of man: tyranny, poverty, disease, and war itself." The speech, certainly one of the greatest inaugural addresses, was a call for every citizen to do their part.

Kennedy's memorable remarks at the Nobel dinner continued in that vein. Highlighting achievement and encouraging Americans was the theme of this dinner. In his speech, Kennedy said, "I think the pursuit of knowledge, the pursuit of peace, are very basic drives and pressures in this life of ours—and this dinner is an attempt, in a sense, to recognize those great efforts, to encourage young Americans and young people in this Hemisphere to develop the same drive and deep desire for knowledge and peace."

President Kennedy appealed to our nobler instincts, using eloquent, finely crafted language to help inspire confidence in ourselves and confidence in our ability to accomplish great feats by working together. Especially for those who did not live through it, it is easy to ignore the deep concerns that overlay the early 1960s, including the threat of nuclear annihilation, and yet Americans were optimistic. The sense of pessimism, foreboding, and failure—abetted by calls for divisiveness—that is often encouraged by our national leaders today was rare, if not absent.

President Kennedy was a voracious reader and student of history. He understood the value of applying the lessons of the past to solve current problems. On the issue of immigration, a topic that has spawned such a vexing national debate, he appreciated the role that myriad groups of different ethnicities and religions played in American life. Granted, immigration was not the acute issue that it has become today, but Kennedy approached it in a spirit of respect, not paranoia. Kennedy was proud of his immigrant heritage, and eschewed any appeal to nativism. In his book *A Nation of Immigrants*, expanded and republished in 1964, he quoted from historian Oscar Handlin: "Once I thought to write a history of the immigrants in America. Then I discovered that the immigrants were American history."[5] A number of the distinguished guests at the Nobel dinner were immigrants, people who brought their unique expertise to this country and made it richer, greater. There was important symbolism in doing that, and it is something which seems to elude many governing in Washington today.

The central foreign policy issue of 1962 and throughout the Kennedy administration and subsequent administrations was the relationship with Russia. At the height of the Cold War, Kennedy understood the threat that the Soviet Union posed, and he was neither cowed nor mesmerized by the leadership skills of Khrushchev or the Politburo. He had a steely-eyed view of his adversary, but also understood how to negotiate with them from a position of strength. And through an effort to get bipartisan support, he followed the foreign policy concept that partisanship stops at the water's edge. He helped place the nation on the road to establishing a relationship with the leading communist nation, a country whose interests were diametrically opposed to those of the United States, and that eventually led to greatly eased tensions.

The approach to national security threats in the early 1950s was a fevered paranoia, led by Senator Joseph McCarthy. The approach of the Kennedy administration, as seen by his overture to Oppenheimer, was measured. The great internal security issue of the time was understood and addressed, but without the hatred and demonization that has come to embody the nativist approach of 2018.

When the Nobel dinner took place, many of the momentous events that would help define our contemporary world were yet to come. And the presidents of the next six decades, all affected in different ways by the Kennedy presidency, were emerging in different parts of the country.

Lyndon Johnson, of course, would become president in nineteenth months. At the time of the dinner, Richard Nixon was campaigning for the Republican gubernatorial nomination in California; Gerald Ford was serving his seventh term in Congress, representing the Grand Rapids, Michigan, area; Jimmy Carter had already served on the county school board and would run for the Georgia state senate that fall; Ronald Reagan was ending his affiliation with *General Electric Theater* and would switch from the Democratic to the Republican party in August 1962; and George H. W. Bush was president of Zapata Petroleum Company in Texas.

The next generation of presidents was still quite young. Bill Clinton was a student at Hot Springs High School in Arkansas; George W. Bush was at Philips Academy in Andover, Massachusetts; and Barack Obama was one and one-half years old and living in Hawaii. Donald Trump, age fifteen, was at New York Military Academy in Cornwall, New York. Trump's vice president, Mike Pence, was a two-year-old living in Columbus, Indiana; he later said that John F. Kennedy was a boyhood hero.

Although the dinner can be seen now as part of an increasingly lengthening past, that does not diminish its significance. And indeed, it was the dying days of an old order, one in which experienced, well-educated citizens were indispensable to governance. But we have lost much in our retreat from excellence. The relevance of these men and women to the United States in 2018 is high, and their contribution and the themes that the dinner reflects provide insights on how to grapple with our current polarization and challenging national issues.

Other comparisons can also be made to President Kennedy's reference to his long-ago predecessor Thomas Jefferson, and perhaps even stretch back to the intellectuals who gathered at the fabled library at Alexandria, Egypt, during the Hellenistic era. What is quite clear, however, is that these men and women who came together in two rooms underscored that the United States can be an equal opportunity incubator for great ideas in the sciences, humanities, and public policy, and that nothing like that night has been seen since. And yet, the spirit of the Nobel dinner can be resurrected and provide a guidepost for the twenty-first century.

## ACKNOWLEDGMENTS

MANY PEOPLE AND INSTITUTIONS assisted me in the three years that I worked on this book. The initial stages were crafted during summers at the Yale Writers' Conference under the direction of M. G. Lord. Kai Bird and Evan Thomas also were very helpful at the outset. As the project progressed, I profited from suggestions made by Leslie Rubinkowski.

This book could not have been written without the extensive resources and assistance of staff at the John F. Kennedy Presidential Library and Museum. Also extremely helpful was Chris Petersen at the Ava Helen and Linus Pauling Papers, Oregon State University Libraries. Thomas Jeffrey at the Ohio Congressional Libraries of the Ohio State University Libraries answered various questions related to John Glenn. Living in the Washington, DC, area, I was able to easily use the unparalleled resources of the Library of Congress. Overall, I was greatly aided by the vast amount of rich secondary material on the Kennedy family as well as many of the distinguished people associated with this special dinner.

Rose Styron was very generous in providing her recollections of that evening. I am deeply honored that she wrote the foreword to this book. I also benefited from a lengthy interview with Linus Pauling, Jr., who provided insights into his parents.

My agent, Roger S. Williams, was valuable throughout the process, and I appreciate his efforts in getting the manuscript in the right hands. I am grateful for the opportunity given to me by Steve Hull, my editor at ForeEdge, and for the diligence of his colleagues at the University Press of New England.

Throughout the process many other people provided timely and helpful responses to my inquiries. To all of them, I extend my appreciation.

Finally, I want to thank my wife, Hope, for her tireless support in this and other pursuits; her role, as usual, was pivotal. My sons, Joseph and Nicholas, also were a source of encouragement.

PROLOGUE | HEADING TO DINNER

1. The various accounts of the picketing usually identify the group, which included a Quaker contingent, as being "outside the White House" or "in front of the White House." The Associated Press reported: "The picketing had to be conducted on H St., across Lafayette Park from the White House, instead of on the sidewalk in front of the White House on Pennsylvania Ave." See "Dr. Pauling Joins Pickets at Capital," *Independent Star-News* (Pasadena), April 29, 1962, 1. Also see the short video at "Dinner—and Picketing—at the White House," Linus Pauling Papers, Oregon State University Libraries (hereafter, LPP–OSUL), accessed May 17, 2017, http://scarc.library .oregonstate.edu/coll/pauling/peace/narrative/page43.html.

2. Dennis Hevesi, "Dagmar Wilson, Anti-Nuclear Leader, Dies at 94," *New York Times*, January 23, 2011, http://www.nytimes.com/2011/01/24/us/24wilson.html.

3. Ibid. The article notes that "Washington police barred picketing within 500 feet of the White House."

4. "Caroline's Pony Has a Guest—A Pony," *Los Angeles Times*, April 30, 1962, 22.

5. See the photo at "Cognoscenti Come to Call," *Life*, May 11, 1962, 38.

6. Linus Pauling to John F. Kennedy, March 1, 1926, LPP–OSUL, accessed March 2, 2017, http://scarc.library.oregonstate.edu/coll/pauling/peace/corr/corr198.3-lp-kennedy -19620301-transcript.html.

7. See the photo at "Cognoscenti Come to Call," *Life*, May 11, 1962, 38.

8. Ted Goetzel and Ben Goetzel, *Linus Pauling: A Life in Science and Politics* (New York: Basic Books, 1997), 175.

9. "Cognoscenti Come to Call," *Life*, May 11, 1962, 36.

10. Priscilla Morison, wearing a bright floral gown, was escorted in to the dinner by Robert Frost; she and her husband had arrived with him. Samuel Eliot Morison, *Vita Nuova: A Memoir of Priscilla Barton Morison* (Northeast Harbor, ME: privately printed, 1975), 190–91.

11. Rose Styron, interview with author, November 20, 2014, Cambridge, Massachusetts.

12. Letitia Baldrige, *In the Kennedy Style: Magical Evenings in the Kennedy White House* (New York: Madison Press Books, 1998), 88.

13. Diana Trilling, "A Visit to Camelot," *New Yorker*, June 2, 1997, 58.

14. "City Turns Out for Glenn; Parade in Paper Blizzard 'Overwhelms' Astronaut," *New York Times*, March 2, 1962, 1.

15. Mary Welsh Hemingway, *As It Was* (New York: Knopf, 1976), 514.

16. Quoted in Peter Goodchild, *Edward Teller: The Real Dr. Strangelove* (Cambridge, MA: Harvard University Press, 2004), 239. The adversary was Roger Robb, special counsel for the Atomic Energy Commission and an interrogator of Oppenheimer.

17. Shirley Streshinsky and Patricia Klaus, *An Atomic Love Story: The Extraordinary Women in Robert Oppenheimer's Life* (Nashville, TN: Turner, 2013), 58–59; Ray Monk, *Robert Oppenheimer: A Life Inside the Center* (New York: Anchor Books, 2014), 150–51; "A Lost Ally," LPP–OSUL, accessed May 17, 2017, http://scarc.library.oregonstate.edu /coll/pauling/bond/narrative/page20.html.

18. Linus Pauling Jr., phone interview with author, June 2, 2015.

19. John F. Kennedy Presidential Papers, White House Staff Files of Sanford L. Fox, Social Events, 1961–1964, April 29, 1962, Dinner, Nobel Prize Winners (1 of 3 folders), John F. Kennedy Presidential Library, Boston (hereafter, JFKPL).

20. Diana Trilling, "A Visit to Camelot," 58.

21. "Best Seller List," *New York Times Book Review*, April 29, 1962, sect. 7, 8.

22. Diana Trilling, "A Visit to Camelot," 58.

23. Quoted in Ann Hulbert, "'It's Complicated . . . It's Very Complicated,'" *New York Times*, October 24, 1993, http://www.nytimes.com/1993/10/24/books/it-s-complicated -it-s-very-complicated.html?pagewanted=all.

24. See Diana Trilling, "The Oppenheimer Case: A Reading of the Testimony," *Partisan Review* 21 (1954): 604–35.

25. Diana Trilling, "A Visit to Camelot," 60.

26. Jay Parini, *Robert Frost: A Life* (New York: Henry Holt, 1999), 408–9.

27. Ibid., 410.

28. William Styron to William Blackburn, May 2, 1962, in Rose Styron, ed., *Selected Letters of William Styron* (New York: Random House, 2012), 325.

29. Hamish Bowles, *Jacqueline Kennedy: The White House Years; Selections from the John F. Kennedy Library and Museum* (New York: Metropolitan Museum of Art, 2001), 94–95; Diana Trilling, "A Visit to Camelot," 59.

30. William Styron, *Havanas in Camelot: Personal Essays* (New York: Random House, 2008), 6.

31. Diana Trilling, "A Visit to Camelot," 59.

32. Pearl Buck, *The Kennedy Women: A Personal Appraisal* (New York: Cowles), 52.

33. Linus Pauling to Gunnar Jahn, May 8, 1962, LPP–OSUL, accessed May 17, 2017, http://scarc.library.oregonstate.edu/coll/pauling/calendar/1962/05/8.html#sci14.043 .1-lp-jahn-19620508.tei.xml.

34. Linus Pauling Interview, "The Test Ban Treaty," Institute of International Studies, University of California at Berkeley, accessed May 17, 2017, http://globetrotter.berkeley .edu/conversations/Pauling/pauling4.html. There are conflicting accounts of whether Mrs. Kennedy or President Kennedy introduced Pauling to the other; it seems likely that it was President Kennedy.

35. Linus Pauling to Hermann Arthur Jahn, May 8, 1962, LPP–OSUL, accessed May 17, 2017, http://scarc.library.oregonstate.edu/coll/pauling/calendar/1962/05/8.html #sci14.043.1-lp-jahn-19620508.tei.xml.

36. Ava Helen Pauling to Mrs. John F. Kennedy, July 15, 1961, LPP–OSUL, accessed May 17, 2017, http://scarc.library.oregonstate.edu/coll/pauling/peace/corr/ahp1.006 .2-ahp-jakennedy-19610715.html.

37. "Scientists Entertained at the White House," *Courier-Journal* (Louisville, KY), April 30, 1962, 17.

38. Kennedy gave Rauh's name to social staff member Mary Boylan; see John F. Kennedy Presidential Papers, White House Staff Files of Sanford L. Fox, Social Events, 1961–1964, April 29, 1962, Dinner, Nobel Prize Winners (1 of 3 folders), JFKPL.

39. Styron to Blackburn, May 2, 1962, in Rose Styron, *Selected Letters of William Styron*, 325.

40. Diana Trilling, "A Visit to Camelot," 59.

41. Clint Hill, interview with the author, May 7, 2016, Washington, DC.

42. Pierre Salinger, *With Kennedy* (Garden City, NY: Doubleday), 318.

CHAPTER ONE | AMERICA IN TRANSITION

1. Martin Amis, "Diana Trilling at Claremont Avenue," in *The Moronic Inferno and Other Visits to America* (New York: Viking, 1987), 53, 56.

2. Louis Menand, introduction to *The Liberal Imagination: Essays on Literature and Society*, by Lionel Trilling (New York: New York Review of Books, 2008), vii.

3. Amis, "Diana Trilling at Claremont Avenue," 53.

4. William Seale, *The President's House: A History*, vol. 2 (Washington, DC: White House Historical Association, 1986), 667–73.

5. Diana Trilling, "A Visit to Camelot," 56.

6. E. W. Kenworthy, "Kennedy Agrees with Macmillan on Summit Delay," *New York Times*, April 29, 1962, 1.

7. Ibid., 3.

8. "Pauling Opposes Nuclear Tests" and "Pauling Pickets White House," *New York Times*, April 29, 1962, 29.

9. Peter Braestrup, "No Time for Bingo on A-Test Island," *New York Times*, April 29, 1962, 29.

10. "A-Test Accuracy Is Reported High," *New York Times*, April 29, 1962, 29.

11. Quoted in Kai Bird and Martin J. Sherwin, *American Prometheus: The Triumph and Tragedy of J. Robert Oppenheimer* (New York: Knopf, 2005), 309.

12. "Tokyo Reds Lead Protest on Tests," *New York Times*, April 29, 1962, 29.

13. "British Demonstrators Fined" and "Indian Papers Assail Tests," *New York Times*, April 29, 1962.

14. "Curb on Aid Opposed," *New York Times*, April 29, 1962, 29.

15. *TV Guide*, April 28–May 4, 1962, April 29, 1962, A-15. The interview was with William C. Foster.

16. "Tests by U.S.," *New York Times*, April 29, 1962, sect. 4, 1.

17. Ibid.

18. Ibid.

19. Max Frankel, "PROPAGANDA: Washington Argues It Tried Hard for Accord

and Now Must Keep Pace with Moscow," *New York Times*, April 29, 1962, sect. 4, 3.

20. John W. Finney, "FALL-OUT: Public Fear and Uncertainty Grow as the Extent of the Danger Is Still Unknown," *New York Times*, April 29, 1962, sect. 4, 3.

21. "The Nuclear Tests," *New York Times*, April 29, 1962, sect. 4, 10.

22. Diana Trilling, "A Visit to Camelot," 56. The Tip Toe Inn was a family favorite; Lionel's mother was a frequent visitor. See Diana Trilling, *The Beginning of the Journey: The Marriage of Diana and Lionel Trilling* (New York: Harcourt Brace, 1993), 17.

23. Peter Glassman, "In Memoriam: Lionel and Diana Trilling at Columbia University—with Guest Appearances by Quentin Andersono and Edward W. Said," accessed May 18, 2017, http://peterglassman.net/literature/in-memoriam-lionel-diana -trilling-at-columbia-university-with-guest-appearances-by-quentin-anderson-edward-w -said/.

24. Louis Menand, "Regrets Only: Lionel Trilling and His Discontents," *New Yorker*, September 29, 2008, http://www.newyorker.com/magazine/2008/09/29/regrets-only -louis-menand.

25. Diana Trilling, *Beginning of the Journey*, 11–21.

26. Ibid., 147.

27. Menand, "Regrets Only."

28. Diana Trilling, *Beginning of the Journey*, 9.

29. Ibid., 420.

30. Richard N. Goodwin to Mrs. Kennedy, memorandum, November 28, 1961, White Social Files, box 946, folder 19, JFKPL.

31. Tad Szulc, "U.S. Closes Rift on Latin Policy," *New York Times,* April 29, 1962, sect. 1, 39. Szulc had broken the Bay of Pigs story for the *Times* the previous year.

32. "Castro Foes Stage Havana Outbreak; Arrests Reported," *New York Times*, April 29, 1962, sect. 1, 40.

33. "Cuba Exiles Fear U.S. Shifts Views," *New York Times*, April 29, 1962, sect. 1, 40.

34. Richard J. H. Johnston, "Loyalty Day Paraders Compete with Lure of Day at the Beach," *New York Times*, April 29, 1962, sect. 1, 64.

35. Richard Rutter, "Defense Is the Biggest Business; Pattern Shifts on West Coast: 49.7 Billion Is Sought," *New York Times*, April 29, 1962, sect. 3, 1, 14.

36. Gladwin Hill, "Defense Is the Biggest Business; Pattern Shifts on West Coast: No Rosie the Riveter," *New York Times,* April 29, 1962, sect. 3, 1.

37. "Work Under Way on Space Center," *New York Times*, April 29, 1962, sect. 3, 15.

38. Foster Hailey, "Negro Bus Trip Here Is Delayed, But White Council Sends Couple," *New York Times*, April 28, 1962, sect. 1, 13.

39. Claude Sitton, "The Negro Migration," *New York Times*, April 29, 1962, sect. 4, 8.

40. Ibid.

41. "Opinion of the Week: At Home and Abroad," *New York Times*, April 29, 1962, sect. 4, 11.

42. "'Travel agents'" (cartoon), *New York Times*, April 29, 1962, sect. 4, 8.

43. "Traffic in Human Misery," *New York Times,* April 29, 1962, sect. 4, 10.

44. Howard Taubman, "In His Own Voice," *New York Times*, April 29, 1962, sect. 2, 1.

45. "A Wide Gap in Excellence," *New York Times*, April 29, 1962, sect. 4, 9.

46. Homer Bigart, "U.S. Making Army of Vietnam Tribe," *New York Times*, April 29, 1962, 1.

47. Gay Talese, "Fair Takes Shape on Office Charts," *New York Times*, April 29, 1962, sect. 1, 81.

48. Ada Louise Huxtable, "Controversy Widens on Design of Development in Washington, *New York Times*, April 29, 1962, sect. 1, 62.

49. Bill Becker, "Tactic of Brown Used against Him," *New York Times*, April 29, 1972, sect. 1, 52.

50. Richard P. Hunt, "Mayor Rules Out Governor Race; Decision 'Final,'" *New York Times*, April 29, 1972, 1.

51. Diana Trilling, "A Visit to Camelot," 56.

52. Theatre Directory, *New York Times*, April 29, 1962, sect. 2, 4.

53. Ibid.

54. Ibid.

55. Ibid., 6.

56. Diana Trilling, "A Visit to Camelot," 54.

57. Ibid., 55–56.

58. Ibid., 56.

59. Ibid., 56–57.


CHAPTER TWO | CAMELOT AT MIDPOINT

1. Theodore H. White Personal Papers, Box 40, Camelot Documents, item III-A, JFKPL.

2. The typewritten notes are in the Theodore H. White Personal Papers, Box 40, Camelot Documents, item III-A, JFKPL; the handwritten notes, taken from November 29 to 30, are in the same file, same location, but are item I.

3. To show how White's article forever recast Camelot, a review of the play *Camelot* on December 3, 1963, the publication date of the *Life* article, never critiques a performance, but does not allude to the Kennedys; see Claudia Cassidy, "'Camelot,' a Long, Dull Musical in Much Too Large a House," *Chicago Tribune*, December 3, 1963, sect. 2, 3.

4. Theodore H. White, *In Search of History: A Personal Adventure* (New York: Warner Books, 1981), 524.

5. Quoted in Bill Adler, ed., *The Eloquent Jacqueline Kennedy Onassis: A Portrait in Her Own Words* (New York: William Morrow, 2004), 13.

6. Hamish Bowles, "Defining Style: Jacqueline Kennedy's White House Years," in *Jacqueline Kennedy: The White House Years; Selections from the John F. Kennedy Library and Museum* (New York: Metropolitan Museum of Art, 2001), 17.

7. Joseph Short to Mrs. Phillip D. Soliday, April 23, 1952, Truman Papers, Official file,

50-Misc. Reconstruction folder, Harry S. Truman Library and Museum, Independence, Missouri, https://www.trumanlibrary.org/whistlestop/qq/april23.htm.

8. J. B. West, *Upstairs at the White House: My Life with the First Ladies* (New York: Open Road Integrated Media, 2016), 224–25.

9. William Seale, "President Kennedy's Garden: Rachel Lambert Mellon's Redesign of the White House Rose Garden," *White House History*, no. 38 (Summer 2015), 36–77.

10. For more on Lorraine Waxman Pearce, see J. B. West, *Upstairs at the White House: My Life with the First Ladies* (New York: Open Road Integrated Media, 2016), 225–27.

11. "The First Lady Brings History and Beauty to the White House," *Life*, September 1, 1961, 63.

12. Jacqueline Bouvier Kennedy Onassis Personal Papers, Textual Materials, Pamela Turnure Files, Subject files: White House: Fine Arts Committee: (General) (1 of 2 folders), JBKOPP-SF034–006, JFKPL.

13. James A. Abbott and Elaine M. Rice, *Designing Camelot: The Kennedy White House Restoration* (New York: Van Nostrand Reinhold, 1998), 29.

14. "The First Lady Brings History and Beauty to the White House," 54–65.

15. See, for example, Arthur M. Schlesinger Jr., "Jacqueline Kennedy in the White House," in Bowles, *Jacqueline Kennedy,* 3–7; Abbott and Rice, *Designing Camelot.*

16. Untitled document, Jacqueline Bouvier Kennedy Onassis Personal Papers, Mary Gallagher Files, Box 131, JFKPL.

17. Jacqueline Kennedy, *Historic Conversations on Life with John F. Kennedy: Interviews with Arthur M. Schlesinger, Jr., 1964,* foreword by Caroline Kennedy, introduction by Michael Beschloss (New York: Hyperion, 2011), 143n.

18. Jack Gould, "Mrs. Kennedy TV Hostess to Nation," *New York Times*, February 15, 1962, 1, 18.

19. Cynthia Lowry, "Tour of the White House TV at Best," *Biddeford-Saco Journal* (Biddeford, Maine), February 15, 1962, 4.

20. Three scrimshaw teeth were prominently displayed on his desk (from the *Resolute*) in the Oval Office. Three Oval Office maritime paintings were *Bonhomme Richard, Constitution-Guerriere,* and *United States versus the Macedonia.*

21. Peter Grier, "John F. Kennedy: Why Books Were a Big Part of His Life (+ Video)," *Christian Science Monitor,* November 23, 2013, http://www.csmonitor.com/USA /Politics/Decoder/2013/1123/John-F.-Kennedy-Why-books-were-a-big-part-of-his-life -video; Hugh Sidey, *John F. Kennedy, President: A Reporter's Inside Story* (New York: Atheneum, 1963), 65; see also Arthur M. Schlesinger Jr., *A Thousand Days: John F. Kennedy in the White House* (Boston: Houghton Mifflin, 1965), 105.

22. Saville Bookshop on P Street, a few steps from Wisconsin Avenue, was a wonderful bookshop that closed in 1979.

23. The title of the thesis was "Appeasement at Munich: (The Inevitable Result of the Slowness of Conversion of the British Democracy from a Disarmament to a Rearmament Policy)." In his inscription to a copy of the book given to Krock, Kennedy wrote: "To Mr. Krock Who Baptized, Christened and was Best Man for this book—with my sincere

thanks Jack Kennedy." (Offered for sale on May 25, 2017, by James Cummins Bookseller, abebooks.com.)

24. See, for example, John T. Shaw, *JFK in the Senate: Pathway to the Presidency* (New York: Palgrave Macmillan, 2013), 172–73; John F. Kennedy, "New England and the South," *Atlantic*, January 1954, https://www.theatlantic.com/magazine/archive/1954/01/new-england-and-the-south/376244/.

25. "Remarks of Senator John F. Kennedy, Mississippi Valley Historical Association," Minneapolis, Minnesota, April 25, 1958, JFKPL, https://www.jfklibrary.org/Research/Research-Aids/JFK-Speeches/Minneapolis-MN_19580425.aspx.

26. Theodore C. Sorensen, *Kennedy* (New York: Harper and Row, 1965), 384.

27. Kay Halle Personal Papers, no. 92, series 2.2, box 54, JFKPL.

28. Kay (Katherine Murphy) Halle Oral History Interview, JFK no. 1, February 7, 1967, JFKOH-KMH-01, JFKPL.

29. Kevin M. Bailey to author, e-mail, March 17, 2015. He cites the Mary Jane McCaffree Papers, box 4, Dwight D. Eisenhower Library, Abilene, Kansas.

30. Joseph W. Alsop Oral History Interview, JFK no. 2, June 26, 1964, JFKOH-JWA-02, JFKPL. Alsop, a noted columnist and opinion leader, was last in the White House when Franklin Roosevelt was president.

31. Pamela Turnure Files, John Kennedy Office Papers, box 131, JFKPL.

32. Jacqueline Kennedy, *Historic Conversations*, 168.

33. Ibid., 174–75.

34. Craig Claiborne, "White House Hires French Chef," *New York Times*, April 7, 1961, 15; Pamela Turnure Files, John Kennedy Office Papers, Box 131, JFKPL.

35. West, *Upstairs at the White House*, 196–97. Louvat, however, did not become an American citizen until 1967; see "News Briefs," *Chicago Tribune*, August 9, 1967, sect. 1, 3.

36. Claiborne, "White House Hires French Chef," 1, 15.

37. Craig Claiborne, "Johnson Food Disagrees with Chef," *New York Times*, December 17, 1965, 1.

38. Quoted in "René Verdon, White House Chef for the Kennedys, Dies at 86," *Washington Post*, February 3, 2011, https://www.washingtonpost.com/local/obituaries/rene-verdon-chef-at-the-kennedy-white-house-dies-at-86/2011/02/03/ABzm8mP_story.html?utm_term=.bf8090e66b55.

39. Letitia Baldrige, *A Lady, First: My Life in the Kennedy White House and the American Embassies of Paris and Rome* (New York: Viking, 2001), 191–92. Baldrige's assessment may have been inaccurate; Mrs. Kennedy and Princess Grace were and remained good friends.

40. Letitia Baldrige, *In the Kennedy Style: Magical Evenings in the Kennedy White House* (New York: Doubleday, 1998), 48–65.

41. Harold C. Schonberg, "Casals Plays at White House; Last Appeared There in 1904," *New York Times*, November 14, 1961, 1, 33.

42. Baldrige, *In the Kennedy Style*, 67–68.

43. Ibid.

44. Ibid., 33.

45. Ibid., 33; "List of White House Guests for Concert by Casals," *New York Times*, November 14, 1961, 33; Baldrige, *In the Kennedy Style*, 66–71.

46. Baldrige, *In the Kennedy Style*, 66–79.

47. Ibid., 82–85.

48. White House Social Files, box 946, folder 19, JFKPL.

49. Ibid.

50. Seymour Lawrence to Arthur Schlesinger Jr., November 27, 1961, John F. Kennedy Presidential Papers, White House Staff Files of Sanford L. Fox, Social Events, 1961–1964, April 29, 1962, Dinner, Nobel Prize Winners (1 of 3 folders), JFKPL.

51. William H. Shriver Jr. to R. Sargent Shriver, February 14, 1962, John F. Kennedy Presidential Papers, White House Staff Files of Sanford L. Fox, Social Events, 1961–1964, April 29, 1962, Dinner, Nobel Prize Winners (1 of 3 folders), JFKPL.

52. Arthur M. Schlesinger Jr. to Richard Goodwin, March 6, 1962, Papers of Arthur M. Schlesinger Jr., White House Files, WH-17, JFKPL.

53. John F. Kennedy Presidential Papers, White House Staff Files of Sanford L. Fox, Social Events, 1961–1964, April 29, 1962, Dinner, Nobel Prize Winners (1 of 3 folders), JFKPL.

54. Steinbeck's agent, who declined for him, sent a letter to Baldrige on April 5 saying that he was "abroad for some months and will not return until June." Steinbeck received the Nobel Prize for Literature later that year. John F. Kennedy Presidential Papers, White House Staff Files of Sanford L. Fox, Social Events, 1961–1964, April 29, 1962, Dinner, Nobel Prize Winners (3 of 3 folders), JFKPL. Hersey, MacLeish, Wilder, Miller, Williams, Warren, and Bellow were at the May 11, 1962, White House dinner for André Malraux.

55. John F. Kennedy Presidential Papers, White House Staff Files of Sanford L. Fox, Social Events, 1961–1964, April 29, 1962, Dinner, Nobel Prize Winners (3 of 3 folders), JFKPL.

56. Ludwig Bemelmans to Letitia Baldrige, April 9, 1962, John F. Kennedy Presidential Papers, White House Staff Files of Sanford L. Fox, Social Events, 1961–1964, April 29, 1962, Dinner, Nobel Prize Winners (3 of 3 folders), JFKPL.

57. André Bleikasten, *William Faulkner: A Life through Novels* (Bloomington: Indiana University Press, 2017), 469. It may have been because of his uneasiness with Kennedy as a white southerner, Bleikasten suggests.

58. John F. Kennedy, "Address in Berkeley at the University of California," March 23, 1962, in *Public Papers of the Presidents of the United States: John F. Kennedy: Containing the Public Messages, Speeches, and Statements of the President, January 1 to December 31, 1962* (Washington, DC: United States Government Printing Office, 1963), 263–66.

59. Dr. Selman A. Waksman, telegram, John F. Kennedy Presidential Papers, White House Staff Files of Sanford L. Fox, Social Events, 1961–1964, April 29, 1962, Dinner, Nobel Prize Winners (3 of 3 folders), JFKPL.

60. John F. Kennedy Presidential Papers, White House Staff Files of Sanford L. Fox, Social Events, 1961–1964, April 29, 1962, Dinner, Nobel Prize Winners (3 of 3 folders), JFKPL.

61. Baldrige, *In the Kennedy Style*, 88.

62. "Rusty" Young to Miss Rowley, April 28, 1962, John F. Kennedy Presidential Papers, White House Staff Files of Sanford L. Fox, Social Events, 1961–1964, April 29, 1962, Dinner, Nobel Prize Winners (1 of 3 folders), JFKPL.

63. Carl Sandburg, telegram, April 24, 1962, John F. Kennedy Presidential Papers, White House Staff Files of Sanford L. Fox, Social Events, 1961–1964, April 29, 1962, Dinner, Nobel Prize Winners (3 of 3 folders), JFKPL.

CHAPTER THREE | POETRY, PROSE, AND POLITICS

1. See John F. Kennedy Presidential Papers, White House Staff Files of Sanford L. Fox, Social Events, 1961–1964, April 29, 1962, Dinner, Nobel Prize Winners: Seating Plan, JFKPL.

2. William B. Seale, *The President's House: A History*, vol. 1 (Washington, DC: White House Historical Association, 1986), 123–34.

3. Perry Wolff, *A Tour of the White House with Mrs. John F. Kennedy* (Garden City, NY: Doubleday, 1962), 101.

4. See John F. Kennedy Presidential Papers, White House Staff Files of Sanford L. Fox, Social Events, 1961–1964, April 29, 1962, Dinner, Nobel Prize Winners: Seating Plan, JFKPL.

5. "Cognoscenti Come to Call," *Life*, May 11, 1962, 36–37.

6. Katherine Tupper Marshall, *Together: Annals of an Army Wife* (New York: Tupper and Love, 1946).

7. Ed Cray, *General of the Army: George C. Marshall, Soldier and Statesman* (New York: Cooper Square Press, 2000), 674.

8. Mary Welsh Hemingway, *How It Was* (New York: Knopf, 1976), 95.

9. Ibid., 29.

10. Mary Hemingway Personal Papers, no. 105, series 2.2, box 23, JFKPL.

11. Hemingway, *How It Was*, passport photo between pp. 88 and 89.

12. Ibid., 107.

13. Ibid., 513.

14. John F. Kennedy, *Profiles in Courage* (New York: Harper and Brothers, 1956), 1.

15. Carlos Baker, *Ernest Hemingway: A Life Story* (New York: Charles Scribner's Sons, 1969), 557.

16. Ibid., 558.

17. John F. Kennedy, "Statement by the President on the Death of Ernest Hemingway," no. 268, July 2, 1961, American Presidency Project, http://www.presidency.ucsb.edu/ws/?pid=8220.

18. Walton knew Ernest Hemingway from World War II and the Kennedys from Georgetown. For more, see Megan Floyd Desnoyers, "The Journey to the John F. Kennedy Library," accessed May 15, 2017, https://www.jfklibrary.org/Research/The-Ernest-Hemingway-Collection/Journey-to-the-John-F-Kennedy-Library.aspx.

19. "Carl D. Anderson—Biographical," Nobelprize.org, accessed April 23, 2016, https://www.nobelprize.org/nobel_prizes/physics/laureates/1936/anderson-bio.html.

20. "Carl D. Anderson—Banquet Speech," Nobelprize.org, accessed April 23, 2016, https://www.nobelprize.org/nobel_prizes/physics/laureates/1936/anderson-speech.html.

21. Hammarskjold had received the Nobel Peace Prize in 1961.

22. "Maryon Pearson Spoke Her Mind," *Toronto Star*, December 28, 1989, A4.

23. Jay Parini, *Robert Frost: A Life* (New York: Henry Holt, 1999), 408–11.

24. John F. Kennedy to Robert Frost, April 11, 1959, in Lawrance Thompson, ed., *Selected Letters of Robert Frost* (New York: Holt, Rinehart and Winston), 580–81.

25. Robert Frost to John F. Kennedy, telegram, circa December 1, 1960, in Thompson, *Selected Letters of Robert Frost*, 585.

26. John F. Kennedy to Robert Frost, telegram, December 13, 1960, in Thompson, *Selected Letters of Robert Frost*, 585.

27. Robert Frost to John F. Kennedy, telegram, December 14, 1960, in Thompson, *Selected Letters of Robert Frost*, 586.

28. Perini, *Robert Frost*, 335, 413.

29. Ibid., 414–15.

30. Ibid., 415.

31. Martin W. Sandler, ed., *The Letters of John F. Kennedy* (New York: Bloomsbury Press, 2013), 130–33.

32. John F. Kennedy, "Remarks upon Presenting a Congressional Award to Robert Frost," March 26, 1962, in *Public Papers of the Presidents of the United States: John F. Kennedy, 1962*, 266–67.

33. "Muriel Beadle; Author and Former L.A. Journalist," *Los Angeles Times*, February 17, 1994.

34. "Muriel Beadle, Free-lance Writer, Author," *Chicago Tribune*, February 22, 1994.

35. *Encyclopaedia Brittanica*, 15th ed., s.v. "George Wells Beadle," accessed April 26, 2016, https://www.britannica.com/biography/George-Wells-Beadle.

36. "Cognoscenti Come to Call," *Life*, May 11, 1962, 36.

37. Richard N. Goodwin, *Remembering America: A Voice from the Sixties* (Boston: Little, Brown), 3.

38. John F. Kennedy, "Annual Message to the Congress on the State of the Union," January 30, 1961, in *The American Presidency Project*, ed. Gerhard Peters and John T. Woolley, http://www.presidency.ucsb.edu/ws/?pid=8045.

39. John F. Kennedy, "The President's News Conference," April 21, 1961, in Peters and Woolley, *American Presidency Project*, http://www.presidency.ucsb.edu/ws/?pid=8077.

40. William V. Shannon, "The Kennedy Administration: The Early Months," *American Scholar* (Fall 1961): 481.

41. John F. Kennedy, "The President's News Conference," April 11, 1962, in *Public Papers of the Presidents of the United States: John F. Kennedy, 1962*, 316.

42. Ibid.

43. Schlesinger, *A Thousand Days*, 635.

44. Interestingly, the Law School Association awarded Roger Blough, chairman and chief executive of U.S. Steel, a Citation of Merit on April 28, and Kennedy sent a congratulatory message. See "Yale Honors U.S. Steel's Blough," *Independent Star-News* (Pasadena, California), April 29, 1962, 1.

45. "April 1962—President Kennedy's Schedule," April 27, 1962, History Central, http://www.historycentral.com/JFK/Calendar/April1962.html.

46. John F. Kennedy, "Remarks at the White House Correspondents and News Photographers Association Dinner," April 27, 1962, in *Public Papers of the Presidents of the United States: John F. Kennedy, 1962*, 158–59.

47. Clay Blair Collection, William Walton Folder, box 56, folder 4, 1974, American Heritage Center, University of Wyoming, Laramie.

48. Hemingway, *As It Was*, 514.

49. Ibid.

50. Baker, *Ernest Hemingway*, 551.

51. Ibid., 543.

52. Hemingway, *As It Was*, 514.

53. Clay Blair Collection, William Walton Folder, William Walton Oral History Interview, March 30, 1993, JFK no. 1, JFKPL. The two oral histories from Walton, taken nineteen years apart, are substantially the same, but vary in the details.

54. Clay Blair Collection, William Walton Folder, box 56, folder 4, 1974, American Heritage Center, University of Wyoming, Laramie.

55. Peter Conn, *Pearl S. Buck: A Cultural Biography* (Cambridge: Cambridge University Press, 1996), 346.

56. Hemingway, *As It Was*, 514.

57. Ibid.

58. William Walton Oral History Interview, March 30, 1993.

59. Charles T. Cullen, "Jefferson's White House Dinner Guests," in *White House History*, collection 3, nos. 13–18, ed. William Seale (Washington, DC: White House Historical Association, 2008), 309–27.

60. The draft and final speeches are available at the Kennedy Library. John F. Kennedy Presidential Papers, President's Office Files, Speech Files, Remarks at Nobel Prize Winners Dinner, April 29, 1962.

CHAPTER FOUR | AMERICA'S QUEEN AND AMERICA'S HERO

1. Clint Hill, *Five Presidents: My Extraordinary Journey with Eisenhower, Kennedy, Johnson, Nixon, and Ford* (New York: Gallery Books, 2016), 87.

2. Ibid., 89.

3. Clint Hill, *Mrs. Kennedy and Me* (New York: Gallery Books, 2012), 151.

4. Hill, *Five Presidents*, 95.

5. *Life*, July 20, 1953, 96–99.

6. "Notables Attend Senator's Wedding," *New York Times*, September 13, 1953, 25.

7. "Text of Speech by Kennedy and Transcript of His News Conference in Paris," *New York Times*, June 3, 1961, 6.

8. Gallup Poll, "Most Admired Man and Woman," accessed October 12, 2016, http://www.gallup.com/poll/1678/most-admired-man-woman.aspx.

9. Carl Sferrazza Anthony, *As We Remember Her: Jacqueline Kennedy Onassis in the Words of Her Friends and Family* (New York: HarperCollins, 1997), 37.

10. Letitia Baldrige, *A Lady, First: My Life in the Kennedy White House and the American Embassies of Paris and Rome* (New York: Viking, 2001), 174.

11. Theodore Roosevelt had young children, but only two of the six, Archibald (seven) and Quentin (three), were under ten years old when he became president.

12. Jacqueline Kennedy, *Historic Conversations,* 259–60.

13. Ibid., 132–34.

14. Ibid., 168, 170, 174–75.

15. Pearl S. Buck, *The Kennedy Women: A Personal Appraisal* (New York: Cowles, 1970), 53.

16. J. B. West, *Upstairs at the White House: My Life with the First Ladies* (New York: Open Road, 2016), 179.

17. See, for example, Barbara Leaming, *Jacqueline Bouvier Kennedy Onassis: The Untold Story* (New York: Thomas Dunne Books/St. Martin's Press, 2014), 6–13.

18. Buck, *The Kennedy Women,* 73.

19. Anthony, *As We Remember Her,* 155.

20. West, *Upstairs at the White House,* 209.

21. Ibid., 179.

22. Hill, *Mrs. Kennedy and Me,* 59–60.

23. *Life,* September 1, 1961, 63.

24. Wolff, *Tour of the White House,* 142.

25. Ibid., 144.

26. Isabelle Shelton, *The White House: Today and Yesterday* (Greenwich, CT: Fawcett Publications, 1962), 69.

27. "The First Lady Brings History and Beauty to the White House," *Life,* September 1, 1962, 62.

28. Shelton, *The White House,* 64.

29. "The First Lady Brings History and Beauty to the White House," 62.

30. Jacqueline Kennedy, *Historic Conversations,* 143n.

31. Shelton, *The White House,* 62.

32. Ibid., 63.

33. Wolff, *Tour of the White House,* 144.

34. Jacqueline Kennedy, *Historic Conversations,* 143, 143n.

35. Baldrige, *A Lady, First,* 182.

36. The term "the Establishment" was first presented by two journalists, Henry Fairlie in 1955 and Richard Rovere in 1961; see Walter Isaacson and Evan Thomas, *The Wise Men: Six Friends and the World They Made* (New York: Simon and Schuster, 1986), 27. Because of his pedigree, John F. Kennedy may not have been an official member of the Establishment, but he certainly interacted with it, especially in Georgetown.

37. Gregg Herken, *The Georgetown Set: Friends and Rivals in Cold War Washington* (New York: Knopf, 2014), 253–54.

38. Katherine Graham, *Personal History* (New York: Vintage Books, 1998), 259.

39. Ibid., 273.

40. Robert W. Merry, *Taking on the World: Joseph and Stewart Alsop, Guardians of the American Century* (New York: Viking, 2012), 358–59.

41. John Glenn with Nick Taylor, *John Glenn: A Memoir* (New York: Bantam Books, 1999), 79.

42. Ibid., 4–5.

43. Ibid., 5.

44. "Future High Flier: John Herschel Glenn, Jr.," *New York Times*, November 30, 1961, 20.

45. Glenn, *John Glenn*, 153–55.

46. National Aeronautics and Space Act of 1958 (Unamended), NASA, accessed August 4, 2017, https://history.nasa.gov/spaceact.html.

47. *New York Times*, April 10, 1959, 1.

48. "Space Fliers Underwent Rigid Tests before Selection," *New York Times,* April 10, 1959, 3.

49. "Future High Flier: John Herschel Glenn, Jr.," *New York Times*, November 30, 1961, 20.

50. Buck, *The Kennedy Women*, 53.

51. Peter Conn, *Pearl S. Buck: A Cultural Biography* (Cambridge: Cambridge University Press, 1998), 271.

52. Hilary Spurling, *Pearl Buck in China: Journey to the Good Earth* (New York: Simon and Schuster, 2010), 253.

53. "Pearl Buck: Banquet Speech," Nobel Prizes and Laureates, NobelPrize.org, accessed August 4, 2017, http://www.nobelprize.org/nobel_prizes/literature/laureates /1938/buck-speech.html.

54. Pearl S. Buck, *Asia and Democracy* (London: Macmillan, 1943).

55. Conn, *Pearl S. Buck*, 270–71.

56. Ibid., 71, 106.

57. Ibid., xv.

58. Buck, *The Kennedy Women*, 53.

59. Ibid., 56.

60. John English, *The Life of Lester Pearson*, vol. 2: *The Worldly Years, 1949–1972* (Toronto: Knopf, 1992), 238–39.

61. Memorandum for the President, John F. Kennedy Presidential Papers, President's Office Files, Speech Files, Remarks at Nobel Prize Winners Dinner, April 29, 1962.

62. John A. Munro and Alex. I. Inglis, eds., *Mike: The Memoirs of the Right Honourable Lester B. Pearson*, vol. 3, 1957–1968 (New York: Quadrangle/New York Times Books, 1976), 63–64.

63. Jim Coutts, "Lester Pearson: An Unlikely Leader and Bold Reformer," *The Star* (Toronto), April 10, 2013, https://www.thestar.com/opinion/commentary/2013/04/10 /lester_pearson_an_unlikely_leader_and_bold_reformer.html.

64. English, *Worldly Years*, 24.

65. Ibid., 140.

66. Lester B. Pearson, *Diplomacy in the Nuclear Age* (Cambridge, MA: Harvard University Press, 1959), 89–113.

67. Deborah C. Peterson, *Fredric March: Craftsman First, Star Second* (Westport, CT: Greenwood Press, 1996), 215–17.

68. Letitia Baldrige, *In the Kennedy Style: Magical Evenings in the Kennedy White House* (New York: Madison Press Books, 1998), 93.

69. Sarah Gibson Blanding Files, Archives and Special Collections Library, Vassar College, Poughkeepsie, New York, accessed August 4, 2017, https://specialcollections .vassar.edu/collections/archives/findingaids/president/blanding_sarah_gibson.html #doe56.

70. *Vassar Miscellany News*, May 2, 1962, Archives and Special Collections Library, Vassar College, Poughkeepsie, New York, accessed August 4, 2017, https:// specialcollections.vassar.edu/collections/archives/findingaids/president/blanding_sarah _gibson.html#doe56.

71. Ibid.

72. "Nancy Hofstadter, Widow of Nobel Laureate in Physics, Dead at 87," August 17, 2007, Stanford News Service, Stanford University, http://news.stanford.edu/pr/2007/pr -nancy-082207.html.

73. J. B. West, *Upstairs at the White House: My Life with the First Ladies* (New York: Open Road Integrated Media, 2016), 235.

CHAPTER FIVE | REDEMPTION AND PROMISE

1. Betty C. Monkman with William G. Allman, *The White House: Its Furnishings and First Families*, 2nd ed. (New York: Abbeville Press, 2014), 188–89.

2. "J. Robert Oppenheimer, Atom Bomb Pioneer Dies," *New York Times,* February 19, 1967, http://www.nytimes.com/learning/general/onthisday/bday/0422.html.

3. Ibid.

4. I. I. Rabi, "Introduction," in I. I. Rabi, Robert Serber, Victor F. Weisskopf, Abraham Pais, and Glenn T. Seaborg, *Oppenheimer* (New York: Charles Scribner's Sons, 1969), 3.

5. "The Oppenheimer Minerals," The Pauling Blog, November 19, 2009, https:// paulingblog.wordpress.com/2009/11/19/the-oppenheimer-minerals/.

6. Ray Monk, *Robert Oppenheimer: A Life Inside the Center* (New York: Anchor Books, 2014), 335–40.

7. Kai Bird and Martin J. Sherwin, *American Prometheus: The Triumph and Tragedy of J. Robert Oppenheimer* (New York: Knopf, 2005), 308.

8. Monk, *Oppenheimer,* 455.

9. Bird and Sherwin, *American Prometheus*, 249–50, 363–65.

10. Ibid., 331–32.

11. Ibid., 419–22.

12. Ibid., 333.

13. US Atomic Energy Commission, *In the Matter of J. Robert Oppenheimer: Transcript of Hearing before the Personnel Security Board, Washington, DC, April 12, 1954, through May 6, 1954* (Washington, DC: Government Printing Office, 1954), 726.

14. Bird and Sherwin, *American Prometheus*, 531–32.

15. Robert Oppenheimer, "The Tree of Knowledge," *Harper's Magazine*, October 1958, 55–60.

16. Joseph and Stewart Alsop, "We Accuse!" *Harper's Magazine*, October 1954, 25–45.

17. Bird and Sherwin, *American Prometheus*, 5.

18. Diana Trilling, "A Visit to Camelot," 60.

19. William Styron, *Havanas in Camelot: Personal Essays* (New York: Random House), 5–6. Note, however, that in a footnote to a published letter of William Styron from May 2, 1962, Rose Styron says that Schlesinger and Styron met for the first time that night. Styron also speculates in the letter that perhaps his friendship with John Marquand was a factor in his invitation, but that appears unlikely. See William Styron to William Blackburn, in Rose Styron, ed., *Selected Letters of William Styron*, 324–27.

20. Ibid., 327.

21. William Styron to William Styron Sr., September 28, 1943, in Rose Styron, ed., *Selected Letters of William Styron*, 4–5.

22. William Styron to William Styron Sr., November 23, 1943, in Rose Styron, ed., *Selected Letters of William Styron*, 5–6.

23. William Styron, Peter Matthiessen, and George Plimpton, "William Styron, The Art of Fiction, No. 5," *Paris Review*, no. 5 (Spring 1954), https://www.theparisreview.org/interviews/5114/william-styron-the-art-of-fiction-no-5-william-styron.

24. Alexandra Styron, *Reading My Father: A Memoir* (New York: Scribner, 2011), 81.

25. Information on *Lie Down in Darkness* and its success is covered in several letters in Alexandra Styron, *Reading My Father*, 100–104.

26. William Styron to Louis D. Rubin Jr., January 28, 1952, in Rose Styron, ed., *Selected Letters of William Styron*, 105, 105n.

27. Ibid., 156n.

28. "Quaker Schooling Planted Seeds for Styron's Activism," *Newnan Times-Herald*, accessed February 7, 2017, http://times-herald.com/news/2016/12/quaker-schooling-planted-seeds-for-styrons-activism.

29. William Styron to William C. Styron Sr., May 6, 1953, in Rose Styron, ed., *Selected Letters of William Styron*, 180–81.

30. William Styron to Dorothy Parker, May 25, 1952, in Rose Styron, ed., *Selected Letters of William Styron*, 131–32.

31. Rose Styron, ed., *Selected Letters of William Styron*, xxiii.

32. Styron to John P. Marquand Jr., July 22, 1960, in Rose Styron, ed., *Selected Letters of William Styron*, 301. Rose Styron had met Kennedy when she was an undergraduate student at Wellesley College.

33. Styron to William Blackburn, May 2, 1962, in Rose Styron, ed., *Selected Letters of William Styron*, 325.

34. Rose Styron, interview with the author, November 20, 2014, Cambridge, Massachusetts.

35. Styron, *Havanas in Camelot*, 6.

36. Ibid.

37. Ibid.

38. Styron to William Blackburn, May 2, 1962, in Rose Styron, ed., *Selected Letters of William Styron*, 325–26.

39. Styron, *Havanas in Camelot*, 6–7.

40. Arthur M. Schlesinger Jr., *Robert Kennedy and His Times* (New York: Houghton Mifflin 1978), 585.

41. Evan Thomas, *Robert Kennedy: His Life* (New York: Simon and Schuster, 2000), 70.

42. Thomas, *Robert Kennedy*, 57–58.

43. Ibid., 58.

44. Ibid.

45. Quoted in Pearl S. Buck, *The Kennedy Women: A Personal Appraisal* (New York: Cowles Book, 1970), 117.

46. Edwin O. Guthman and Jeffrey Shulman, *Robert Kennedy in His Own Words: The Unpublished Recollections of the Kennedy Years* (New York: Bantam, 1988), 346.

47. See Robert F. Kennedy, *Just Friends and Brave Enemies* (New York: Harper and Row, 1962).

48. Larry Tye, *Bobby Kennedy: The Making of a Liberal Icon* (New York: Random House, 2016), 262.

49. "Potted Histories: Beef Wellington," *Telegraph*, August 21, 2013, http://www.telegraph.co.uk/foodanddrink/10252209/Potted-histories-Beef-Wellington.html.

50. J. B. West, *Upstairs at the White House: My Life with the First Ladies* (New York: Open Road Integrated Media, 2016), 234.

51. Baldrige, *Kennedy Style*, 96–97; René Verdon, *The White House Chef Cookbook* (New York: Doubleday, 1967), 153–54.

52. Arthur J. Morris Law Library, Special Collections, University of Virginia School of Law, accessed February 18, 2017, http://archives.law.virginia.edu/records/rg/200–78/digital/6355.

53. Thomas, *Robert Kennedy*, 55–56.

54. Tye, *Bobby Kennedy*, 219.

55. Brian Urquhart, *Ralph Bunche: An American Life* (New York: W. W. Norton, 1993), 23–44. Weaver later became the first black cabinet member, appointed secretary of housing and urban development in 1966.

56. Ibid., 81–91.

57. Anne T. Keene, *Peacemakers: Winners of the Nobel Prize Peace Prize* (New York: Oxford University Press, 1998), 142.

58. Emily Greene Balch, John R. Mott, and the American Friends Service Committee also were awarded the Nobel Peace Prize. Linus Pauling, another guest tonight, would later receive the award, as would Dr. Martin Luther King Jr.

59. Urquhart, *Ralph Bunche*, 33.

60. Ibid., 99.

61. Ibid., 303.

62. Ibid., 340, 343, 367.

63. Ibid., 54.

64. "Unconquered Frontier," *Time*, March 1, 1954, 58–61.

65. Ibid.

66. John Nicholas Brown, Record of Conversation between Brown and President

Henry Wriston, March 27, 1953, Oppenheimer Papers, box 126, folder 2, Library of Congress, Washington, DC.

67. John Cowles to Thomas S. Lamont, May 15, 1953, Oppenheimer Papers, box 126, folder 2, Library of Congress, Washington, DC.

68. "Nathan Pusey, Harvard President through Growth and Turmoil Alike, Dies at 94," *New York Times,* November 15, 2001, http://www.nytimes.com/2001/11/15/us/nathan-pusey-harvard-president-through-growth-and-turmoil-alike-dies-at-94.html.

69. "Nathan Marsh Pusey," *Harvard Magazine,* February 2002, http://harvardmagazine.com/2002/01/nathan-marsh-pusey.html.

70. David Boroff, "Imperial Harvard," *Harper's Magazine,* October 1958, 34.

71. "William Laurence, Ex-Science Writer for *The Times,* Dies," *New York Times,* March 19, 1977, http://www.nytimes.com/1977/03/19/archives/william-laurence-exscience-writer-for-the-times-dies-william-l.html.

CHAPTER SIX | IS THAT LINUS PAULING?

1. Rose Styron, interview with the author, November 20, 2014, Cambridge, Massachusetts.

2. Thomas Hager, *Force of Nature: The Life of Linus Pauling* (New York: Simon and Schuster, 1995), 13.

3. "Cognoscenti Come to Call," *Time,* May 11, 1962, 3.

4. Hager, *Force of Nature,* 538.

5. "Ava Helen and Linus Pauling Papers, 1873–2013," Special Collections and Archives Research Center, Oregon State University Libraries, accessed February 27, 2017, http://scarc.library.oregonstate.edu/coll/pauling/timeline.html. Washington High School, which Pauling attended, eventually awarded him an unusual honorary diploma in 1962. The Portland, Oregon, high school also included chef James Beard as a distinguished alumnus.

6. Mina Carson, *Ava Helen Pauling: Partner, Activist, Visionary* (Corvallis: Oregon State University Press, 2013), 16–20.

7. Hager, *Force of Nature,* 152.

8. Ibid.; "A Lost Ally," LPP–OSUL, accessed March 2, 2017, http://scarc.library.oregonstate.edu/coll/pauling/bond/narrative/page20.html.

9. Linus Pauling Jr., phone interview with the author, June 2, 2015.

10. "The Immediate Need for Interdemocracy Federal Union and Mr. Streit's Proposed Declaration of Independence," July 22, 1940, LPP–OSUL, http://scarc.library.oregonstate.edu/coll/pauling/calendar/1940/index.html.

11. Hager, *Force of Nature,* 252–55; Linus Pauling Jr., phone interview with the author, June 2, 2015.

12. Mina Carson, *Ava Helen Pauling,* 1.

13. Linus Pauling, *No More War* (New York: Dodd, Mead, 1962), 11.

14. Cleo Trumbo to Linus Pauling, August 16, 1950, LPP–OSUL, http://scarc.library.oregonstate.edu/coll/pauling/peace/corr/corr408.6-trumbo-lp-19500816.html.

15. Hager, *Force of Nature*, 446–47.

16. Linus Pauling, *No More War* (New York: Dodd, Mead, 1962), 11–12.

17. Testimony of Linus Pauling, Senate Judiciary Committee, Internal Security Subcommittee, June 20, 1960, George Mason University Library.

18. "An Appeal to Stop the Spread of Nuclear Weapons," January 15, 1961, LPP–OSUL, http://scarc.library.oregonstate.edu/coll/pauling/peace/papers/peace5.017.4.html.

19. Linus Pauling Papers, October 18, 1961, LPP–OSUL, http://scarc.library.oregonstate.edu/coll/pauling/peace/corr/corr198.8-lp-khruschev-19611018–01-large.html.

20. Hager, *Force of Nature*, 533.

21. Linus Pauling to John F. Kennedy, January 26, 1962, LPP–OSUL, http://scarc.library.oregonstate.edu/coll/pauling/peace/corr/corr198.3-lp-kennedy-19620126.html.

22. Linus Pauling to John F. Kennedy, March 1, 1962, LPP–OSUL, http://scarc.library.oregonstate.edu/coll/pauling/peace/corr/corr198.3-lp-kennedy-19620301-transcript.html.

23. Linus Pauling to John F. Kennedy, April 9, 1962, White House Central File, box 2142, Pauling, Linus (Dr.), JFKPL.

24. Carson, *Ava Helen Pauling*, 130.

25. Stephen Kennedy Smith, "Words Jack Loved," in Stephen Kennedy Smith and Douglas Brinkley, eds., *JFK: A Vision for America* (New York: HarperCollins, 2017), 18.

26. Papers of Arthur M. Schlesinger Jr., White House Files, WH-17, JFKPL.

27. Journal notes by Ava Helen Pauling recounting her trip to the White House, April 29, 1962, LPP–OSUL, http://scarc.library.oregonstate.edu/coll/pauling/calendar/1962/04/29-xl.html.

28. Quoted in letter from Linus Pauling to Dr. Willard F. Libby, March 30, 1955, LPP–OSUL, http://scarc.library.oregonstate.edu/coll/pauling/peace/corr/corr217.2-lp-libby-19550330.html.

29. Letter from Linus Pauling to Dr. Willard F. Libby, December 21, 1961, LPP–OSUL, http://scarc.library.oregonstate.edu/coll/pauling/peace/corr/corr217.2-lp-libby-19611221–02.html.

30. Journal notes by Ava Helen Pauling recounting her trip to the White House, April 29, 1962, LPP–OSUL, http://scarc.library.oregonstate.edu/coll/pauling/calendar/1962/04/29-xl.html.

31. "Samuel I. Newhouse, Publisher, Dies at 84," *New York Times,* August 30, 1979, http://www.nytimes.com/1979/08/30/archives/samuel-i-newhouse-publisher-dies-at-84-samuel-i-newhouse-builder-of.html?_r=0.

32. "The Globe-Democrat Suit," The Pauling Blog, November 12, 2014, https://paulingblog.wordpress.com/2014/11/12/the-globe-democrat-suit/.

33. Ibid.

34. Leonard Lyons, "Lyons' Den," *Times* (San Mateo, CA), May 14, 1962, 19. Pauling denied saying this. The size of the suit is also incorrect.

35. Lee Alvin DuBridge Oral History, part 2, February 20, 1981, Archives of the California Institute of Technology, Pasadena, California, http://oralhistories.library.caltech.edu/68/1/OH_DuBridge_2.pdf.

36. "James Killian, 83, Science Advisor, Dies," *New York Times*, January 31, 1988, http://www.nytimes.com/1988/01/31/obituaries/james-killian-83-science-adviser-dies.html?pagewanted=all.

37. Pauling, *No More War*, 206–7.

38. "William L. Laurence," Atomic Heritage Foundation, accessed March 13, 2017, http://www.atomicheritage.org/profile/william-l-laurence.

39. Quoted in Bird and Sherwin, *American Prometheus*, 309.

40. "William L. Laurence," Atomic Heritage Foundation, accessed March 13, 2017, http://www.atomicheritage.org/profile/william-l-laurence. The last part of the sentence was crossed out in the existing version.

41. William L. Laurence, "Laurence Draft of Truman Speech on Hiroshima," accessed March 13, 2007, http://www.atomicheritage.org/sites/default/files/resources/Laurence%20Draft%20of%20Truman%20Speech%20on%20Hiroshima.pdf.

42. William L. Laurence, "U.S. Atom Bomb Site Belies Tokyo Tales," *New York Times*, September 12, 1945.

43. Now known as Clark Atlanta University.

44. "Norman Cousins," The Pauling Blog, accessed March 14, 2017, https://paulingblog.wordpress.com/2012/06/25/norman-cousins/.

45. Linus Pauling to Norman Cousins, March 25, 1958, LPP–OSUL, http://scarc.library.oregonstate.edu/coll/pauling/peace/corr/corr68.6-lp-cousins-19580325.html.

46. "Norman Cousins," The Pauling Blog, June 25, 2012, https://paulingblog.wordpress.com/2012/06/25/norman-cousins/.

47. Linus Pauling Jr., phone interview with the author, June 2, 2015.

48. "Pauling at Leisure," The Pauling Blog, April 7, 2009, https://paulingblog.wordpress.com/2009/04/07/pauling-at-leisure/.

CHAPTER SEVEN | "THE FIRE NEXT TIME"

1. William Seale, *The President House: A History*, vol. 1 (Washington, DC: White House Historical Association, 2008), 39–58.

2. "James Hoban Slave Payroll," White House Historical Association, accessed March 16, 2017, https://www.whitehousehistory.org/photos/photo-2–4.

3. Thomas Jefferson to John Holmes, April 22, 1820, Library of Congress, Washington, DC, https://www.loc.gov/item/mtjbib023795/.

4. Harold C. Schonberg, "Bayreuth Hears U.S. Negro Singer," *New York Times*, July 24, 1961, 16.

5. Marjorie Hunter, "Grace Bumbry Performs at a State Dinner in Honor of 3 Government Leaders," *New York Times*, February 21, 1962, 17.

6. John F. Kennedy Presidential Papers, Papers of Arthur M. Schlesinger Jr., White House Files, WH-17, JFKPL.

7. James Baldwin, "Notes of a Native Son," in *James Baldwin: Collected Essays*, ed. Toni Morrison (New York: Library of America, 1998), 9.

8. John F. Kennedy Presidential Papers, White House Staff Files of Sanford L. Fox, Social Events, 1961–1964, April 29, 1962, Dinner, Nobel Prize Winners (folder 1 of 3), JFKPL.

9. William Styron arrived separately from Paris.

10. Isabel Bayley, ed., *Letters of Katherine Anne Porter* (New York: Atlantic Monthly Press, 1990), 608.

11. Styron to William Blackburn, May 2, 1962, in Rose Styron, ed., *Selected Letters of William Styron*, 325.

12. Quoted in Bayley, *Letters of Katherine Anne Porter*, 608.

13. Ibid., 609.

14. Arthur M. Schlesinger Jr., *A Thousand Days: John F. Kennedy in the White House* (Boston: Houghton Mifflin, 1965), 961.

15. Morrison, *James Baldwin*, 9.

16. David Leeming, *James Baldwin: A Biography* (New York: Arcade Publishing, 2015), 14–20.

17. Ibid., 37–55.

18. Leeming, *James Baldwin*, 89.

19. Baldwin, "Everyone's Protest Novel," in Morrison, *James Baldwin*, 11–12.

20. Baldwin, "Many Thousands Gone," in Morrison, *James Baldwin*, 24.

21. Baldwin, "Carmen Jones," in Morrison, *James Baldwin*, 35–41.

22. Leeming, *James Baldwin*, 103–4.

23. Ibid., 128–29.

24. Quoted in W. J. Weatherby, *James Baldwin: Artist on Fire: A Portrait* (New York: Donald I. Fine, 1989), 165.

25. Leeming, *Baldwin*, 135–47.

26. James Baldwin, "The Hard Kind of Courage," *Harper's Magazine*, October 1958, 61–65.

27. James Baldwin, "Nobody Knows My Name: A Letter from the South," in Morrison, *James Baldwin*, 197–208.

28. Weatherby, *James Baldwin*, 173–75.

29. Weatherby, *James Baldwin*, 125.

30. Leeming, *James Baldwin*, 117.

31. Baldwin, "Faulkner and Desegregation," in Morrison, *James Baldwin*, 209–14.

32. Leeming, *James Baldwin*, 198.

33. Robert F. Kennedy, *The Enemy Within* (New York: Harper and Brothers, 1960), 174. Before holding a position with Senator McClellan, Robert Kennedy had worked for Senator Joseph McCarthy on the Senate Permanent Subcommittee on Investigations.

34. Pierre Salinger, *With Kennedy* (New York: Doubleday), 13–28.

35. Ibid., 155–60.

36. Ibid., 161–88.

37. Ibid., 116.

38. Diana Trilling, "A Visit to Camelot."

39. Ibid.

40. Ibid.

41. Ibid.

42. "Obituary, Catherine 'Kay' Kerr, 1911–2010," *Berkeley Daily Planet*, December 24,

2010, http://www.berkeleydailyplanet.com/issue/2010–12–22/article/37047
?headline=Catherine-Kay-Kerr-1911–2010—From-the-University-of-California-Press
-Office.

43. "Catherine Stratton, 100; Promoted Art, Humanities at MIT," *Boston Globe,*
September 28, 2014, https://www.bostonglobe.com/metro/2014/09/27/catherine
-stratton-wife-former-mit-president-promoted-art-humanities-campus/QtCcTpIRow57
NNIo1t8dRK/story.html.

44. "Alan Tower Waterman (1892–1967)," National Science Foundation, accessed
March 22, 2017, https://www.nsf.gov/about/history/waterman_bio.jsp.

45. Diana Trilling, "A Visit to Camelot."

46. "Procedure for Nobel Prize Dinner Tonight," John F. Kennedy Presidential
Papers, President's Office Files, Speech Files, Remarks at Nobel Prize Winners Dinner,
April 29, 1962, JFKPL.

CHAPTER EIGHT | A GALAXY OF GENIUSES

1. Agneta Wallin Levinovitz and Nils Ringertz, *The Nobel Prize: The First 100 Years*
(London: Imperial College Press, 2007), 5–12.

2. Bernard S. Schlesinger and June H. Schlesinger, *The Who's Who of Nobel Prize
Winners, 1901–1905* (Phoenix, AZ: Oryx Press, 1996), vii–ix. A prize for economics was
added in 1969.

3. "Theodore Roosevelt—Acceptance Speech," NobelPrize.org, accessed April 3, 2017,
http://www.nobelprize.org/nobel_prizes/peace/laureates/1906/roosevelt-acceptance
.html.

4. Eventually, ten Americans were awarded the Nobel Peace Prize; Barack Obama,
the most recent, received the award in 2009.

5. "The Nobel-Prize Awards in Science as a Measure of National Strength in
Science," *Report of the Congressional Research Service for the Task Force on Science
Policy, Committee on Science and Technology, US House of Representatives* (Washington,
DC: Government Printing Office, 1986), 123.

6. John F. Kennedy Presidential Papers, President's Office Files, Speech Files,
Remarks at Nobel Prize Winners Dinner, April 29, 1962, JFKPL.

7. Kennedy, "Address in Berkeley at the University of California," in *Public Papers of
the Presidents of the United States: John F. Kennedy, 1962,* 263–66.

8. "Glenn Seaborg," Atomic Energy Foundation, accessed April 5, 2017, http://www
.atomicheritage.org/profile/glenn-seaborg.

9. Glenn T. Seaborg, interviews with Dr. Richard G. Hewlett and Howard C. Brown
Jr., from June 11, 1964, to July 1, 1964, Oral History Program, JFKPL.

10. Ibid., 3–4.

11. Ibid., 13.

12. John F. Kennedy, "Letter to the Chairman, Atomic Energy Commission, on
the Development of Civilian Nuclear Power," March 20, 1962, in *Public Papers of the
Presidents of the United States: John F. Kennedy, 1962,* 248–49.

13. Kennedy, "Address in Berkeley at the University of California," in *Public Papers of the Presidents of the United States: John F. Kennedy, 1962*, 263–64.

14. Monk, *Robert Oppenheimer*, 676–77.

15. Wolff, *Tour of the White House*, 123–24.

16. Ibid., 127, 131.

17. Kloss, *Art in the White House*, 318.

18. Ibid., 381; Wolff, *Tour of the White House*, 129.

19. Shelton, *The White House*, 72–79.

20. "Revisiting Samuel Eliot Morison's Landmark History," *Smithsonian Magazine*, February 2011.

21. "John Fitzgerald Kennedy, A Eulogy," *Atlantic*, accessed April 5, 2017, https://www.theatlantic.com/magazine/archive/2013/08/john-fitzgerald-kennedy-a-eulogy/309491/.

22. Samuel Eliot Morison to Winthrop Aldrich, April 20, 1954, photocopied letter owned by Argosy Book Store and viewed by the author.

23. Arthur Schlesinger to Ray Helsel, May 24, 1993, letter owned by Argosy Book Store and viewed by the author.

24. John Dos Passos, "John Dos Passos, The Art of Fiction No. 44," interview by David Sanders, *Paris Review*, no. 46 (Spring 1969), https://www.theparisreview.org/interviews/4202/john-dos-passos-the-art-of-fiction-no-44-john-dos-passos.

25. "John Randolph Dos Passos," JohnDosPassos.com, accessed April 5, 2017, http://www.johndospassos.com/biography/.

26. Jay Nordlinger, "Doses of Dos Passos, Part I," *National Review*, May 2, 2016, http://www.nationalreview.com/article/434792/re-encountering-john-dos-passos-part-i.

27. "John Randolph Dos Passos," JohnDosPassos.com, accessed April 6, 2017, http://www.johndospassos.com/biography/.

28. Baker, *Ernest Hemingway*, 42.

29. Ernest Hemingway to John Dos Passos, April 22, 1925, in Baker, *Ernest Hemingway*, 157–58.

30. Baker, *Ernest Hemingway*, see, for example, 300, 331, and 335.

31. Joseph Epstein, "The Riddle of Dos Passos," *Commentary*, January 1, 1976, https://www.commentarymagazine.com/articles/the-riddle-of-dos-passos/.

32. Quoted in James McGrath Morris, *The Ambulance Drivers: Hemingway, Dos Passos, and a Friendship Made and Lost in War* (Boston: Da Capo Press, 2017), 242. Also, Ernest Hemingway to John Dos Passos, circa March 26, 1938, Baker, *Selected Letters of Ernest Hemingway*, 463–65.

33. Mary Welsh Hemingway, *How It Was*, 72.

34. Ibid., 221.

35. John Dos Passos, "John Dos Passos, The Art of Fiction No. 44."

36. Henry Allen, "Katherine Anne Porter: The Vanity of Excellence," in Joan Givner, ed., *Katherine Anne Porter: Conversations* (Jackson: University Press of Mississippi), 169. Regarding Sacco and Vanzetti and Dos Passos and Porter, each of the writers published books on the case. Dos Passos wrote *Facing the Chair: Story of the Americanization of*

*Two Foreign-Born Workmen* in 1927, and Porter wrote *The Never-Ending Wrong* fifty years later.

37. Katherine Anne Porter to Glenway Wescott, April 2, 1963, in Bayley, ed., *Letters of Katherine Anne Porter*, 607–9.

38. *Life*, May 11, 1962, 40–41; Shelton, *The White House*, 74.

39. James T. Farrell, *$1,000 A Week and Other Stories*, (Garden City, NY: Sun Dial Press, 1943).

40. C. Hartley Grattan, "James T. Farrell: Moralist," *Harper's Magazine*, October 1954, 93–98.

41. James A. Abbott and Elaine M. Rice, *Designing Camelot: The Kennedy White House Restoration* (New York: Van Nostrand Reinhold, 1998), 89.

42. Kloss, *Art in the White House*, 56–57.

43. Idid., 60–61.

44. Kloss, *Art in the White House*, 108–9; Shelton, *The White House*, 59.

45. Abbott and Rice, *Designing Camelot*, 92.

46. Kloss, *Art in the White House*, 327.

47. Ibid., 232–33.

48. Shelton, *The White House*, 56.

49. "The Albert Szent-Gyorgyi Papers," U.S. National Library of Medicine, National Institutes of Health, accessed April 7, 2017, https://profiles.nlm.nih.gov/ps/retrieve/Narrative/WG/p-nid/147.

50. Rose Styron, interview with the author, November 20, 2014, Cambridge, Massachusetts.

51. "Victor F. Hess—Biographical," NobelPrize.org, accessed April 7, 2017, http://www.nobelprize.org/nobel_prizes/physics/laureates/1936/hess-bio.html.

52. "Victor F. Hess, Physicist, Dies," *New York Times*, December 19, 1964.

53. "Harold Urey, Scientist, Dies at 87," *New York Times*, January 7, 1981.

54. "Cognoscenti Come to Call," *Life*, May 11, 1962, 36.

55. Paul O'Neil, "The No. 2 Man in Washington," *Life*, January 26, 1962, 76–92; Larry Tye, a recent biographer of Robert Kennedy has referred to a copresidency between John and Robert Kennedy, Biographers International Conference, Boston, May 20, 2017 (author present at presentation).

56. Schlesinger, *Robert Kennedy and His Times*, 623.

57. Mark K. Updegrove, *Indomitable Will: LBJ in the Presidency* (New York: Crown, 2012), 61.

58. Tye, *Bobby Kennedy*, 115.

59. Ibid., 105.

60. Diana Trilling, "A Visit to Camelot," 62.

61. "Cognoscenti Come to Call," *Life*, May 11, 1962, 38–39.

62. Rose Styron, interview with the author, November 20, 2014, Cambridge, Massachusetts.

63. Baldrige, *In the Kennedy Style*, 93.

64. Ibid., 95.

65. Abbott and Rice, *Designing Camelot*, 65.

66. Wolff, *Tour of the White House*, 78.

67. Monkman, *The White House*, 192–93.

68. Kloss, *Art in the White House*, 66–69.

69. Abbott and Rice, *Designing Camelot*, 65–75.

70. Ibid., 6.

71. Buck, *The Kennedy Women*, 55–56. *The Living Reed*, a sort of Korean equivalent of Buck's early work *The Good Earth*, was published in 1963 after the president's death.

72. Conn, *Pearl S. Buck*, 346.

73. "Pool Covering Fredric March's Reading after Nobel Prize Dinner," JFKPL.

74. Marc Cirino, "An Evening at the White House: Fredric March Performs Hemingway's Islands in the Stream," *Hemingway Review* 29, no. 2 (Spring 2010), 123–32, accessed April 8, 2017, https://muse.jhu.edu/article/384714.

75. "The Marshall Plan Speech," George C. Marshall Foundation, accessed April 8, 2017, http://marshallfoundation.org/marshall/the-marshall-plan/marshall-plan-speech/.

76. Cirino, "An Evening at the White House."

77. Ibid.

78. Styron to William Blackburn, March 2, 1962, in Rose Styron, ed., *Selected Letters of William Styron*, 324–28.

79. Rose Styron, interview with the author, Cambridge, Massachusetts, November 20, 2014.

80. Diana Trilling, "A Visit to Camelot," 62.

81. "Cognoscenti Come to Call," *Life*, May 11, 1962, 41.

82. Ibid., 37.

83. Schlesinger, *A Thousand Days*, 961.

84. *Life*, May 11, 1962, 37.

85. Styron to William Blackburn, March 2, 1962, in Rose Styron, ed., *Selected Letters of William Styron*, 324–28.

86. Diana Trilling, "A Visit to Camelot," 62.

CHAPTER NINE | AN AFTER-PARTY

1. Photograph by Robert Knudsen, accession no. KN-C29528, JFKPL.

2. Abbott and Rice, *Designing Camelot*, 143.

3. Ibid., 144.

4. Diana Trilling, "A Visit to Camelot," 63.

5. Styron to William Blackburn, May 2, 1962, in Rose Styron, ed., *Selected Letters of William Styron*, 326. The entire letter is from pp. 324–28.

6. Diana Trilling, "A Visit to Camelot," 63.

7. Styron to William Blackburn, May 2, 1962, in Rose Styron, ed., *Selected Letters of William Styron*, 326. The entire letter is from pp. 324–28.

8. Diana Trilling, "A Visit to Camelot," 63.

9. Seale, *The President's House*, vol. 1, 288–89.

10. Ibid., 412–13.

11. Elaine Rice Bachmann, "Circa 1961: The Kennedy White House Interiors," in *White House History*, collection 3, no. 13 (Washington, DC: White House Historical Association, 2003), 77–78.

12. Abbott and Rice, *Designing Camelot*, 173.

13. Sotheby's, *The Estate of Jacqueline Kennedy Onassis*, April 23–26, 1996 (New York: Sotheby's, 1996), 178. Sotheby's auction catalog.

14. Ibid., 226–27.

15. P and P Chair Company, The Kennedy Rocker, accessed April 10, 2017, http://www.thekennedyrocker.com/history.html.

16. Sotheby's, *The Estate of Jacqueline Kennedy Onassis*, 80–82.

17. Styron to William Blackburn, in Rose Styron, ed., *Selected Letters of William Styron*, 326.

18. Abbott and Rice, *Designing Camelot*, 171.

19. Styron, *Havanas in Camelot*, 9; Styron to William Blackburn, in Rose Styron, *Selected Letters of William Styron*, 326; and Diana Trilling, "A Visit to Camelot," 63.

20. Diana Trilling, "A Visit to Camelot," 63.

21. Styron, *Havanas in Camelot*, 9–10.

22. "Jean or Me?," *Newsweek*, May 14, 1962, 27.

23. Styron, *Havanas in Cuba*, 9–10.

24. Styron to William Blackburn, in Rose Styron, ed., *Selected Letters of William Styron*, 326–27.

25. Diana Trilling, "A Visit to Camelot," 63.

26. Ibid., 64–65.

27. Ibid., 65.

28. Schlesinger, *A Thousand Days*, 961–62.

29. Weatherby, *James Baldwin*, 184.

30. Styron to William Blackburn, May 2, 1962, in Rose Styron, ed., *Selected Letters of William Styron*, 325; Morison, *Vita Nuova*, 190.

31. Diana Trilling, *Beginning of the Journey*, 163.

32. Diana Trilling, "A Visit to Camelot," 65.

33. Marjorie Hunter, "49 Nobel Prize Winners Honored at White House, *New York Times*, April 30, 1962, 1, 19.

34. "Science in the White House," *New York Times*, May 1, 1962, 36.

35. Dorothy McCardle, "Kennedys Salute Nobel Winners," *Washington Post*, April 30, 1962, B5.

36. Dorothy McCardle, "49 Nobel Guests at a Notable Evening," *Washington Post*, May 1, 1962, A22.

37. See, for example, "173 Nobel Prize Winners Dinners Guests of Kennedy," *Bennington Banner* (Vermont), April 30, 1962, 10.

38. Frances Lewine, "Kennedys Are Hosts at Dinner Feting Nobel Prize Winners," *Times* (Shreveport, Louisiana), April 30, 1962, 2.

39. "Nobel Prize Winners Honored," *Logansport Pharos-Tribune* (Indiana), April 30, 1962, 5.

40. "Cognoscenti Come to Call," *Life*, May 11, 1962, 32–41.

41. "'Jean or Me,'" *Newsweek,* May 14, 1962, 27.

CHAPTER TEN | LIVES CONNECTED

1. "TV Programs," *New York Times*, April 29, 1962, sect. 2, 18.

2. Ibid., advertisement.

3. "'Man for All Seasons' Wins Tony," *New York Times*, April 30, 1962, 30.

4. Linus Pauling to Gunnar Jahn, May 8, 1962, LPP–OSUL, http://scarc.library.oregonstate.edu/coll/pauling/calendar/1962/05/9-xl.html.

5. "Statement by Linus Pauling," July 9, 1962, LPP–OSUL, http://scarc.library.oregonstate.edu/coll/pauling/peace/notes/safe2.039.138.html.

6. Linus and Ava Helen Pauling to John F. Kennedy, telegram, October 23, 1962, White House Central Name File, box 2142, Dr. Linus Pauling, JFKPL.

7. Linus Pauling to John F. Kennedy, telegram, October 27, 1962, White House Central Name File, box 2142, Dr. Linus Pauling, JFKPL.

8. "The Bomb Test Controversy and World Peace," manuscript of Linus Pauling, November 1, 1962, LPP–OSUL, http://scarc.library.oregonstate.edu/coll/pauling/peace/notes/1962s.19-ms-01-large.html.

9. "The Bomb Test Controversy and World Peace," November 1, 1962, Manuscript Notes and Typescripts, LPP–OSUL, http://scarc.library.oregonstate.edu/coll/pauling/peace/notes/1962s.19-ms-05.html.

10. Robert Dallek, *An Unfinished Life: John F. Kennedy, 1917–1963* (Boston: Little, Brown, 2003), 613–19.

11. Ibid., 620.

12. Linus Pauling to John F. Kennedy, August 1, 1963, White House Central Name File, box 2142, Dr. Linus Pauling, JFKPL.

13. McGeorge Bundy to Linus Pauling, August 7, 1963, White House Central Name File, box 2142, Dr. Linus Pauling, JFKPL.

14. "Oslo Bound," The Pauling Blog, accessed April 13, 2017, https://paulingblog.wordpress.com/tag/kennedy-assassination/.

15. "Nobel Peace Prize Award to Pauling," *Palo Alto Times*, October 10, 1963, 1; in the *San Mateo* (California) *Times and Daily News Leader* of the same date, the Associated Press story on Pauling was also on page one, and three columns over was an article entitled "Test Ban Pact Now in Effect."

16. "Response by Linus Pauling," December 10, 1963, LPP–OSUL, http://scarc.library.oregonstate.edu/coll/pauling/peace/notes/1963s.21-ts-02.html.

17. Linus Pauling to Jerome Wiesner, December 13, 1963, Correspondence, LPP–OSUL, http://scarc.library.oregonstate.edu/coll/pauling/peace/corr/safe2.039.16–02.html.

18. Robert Oppenheimer to Arthur Schlesinger, May 2, 1962, Oppenheimer Papers, box 65, folder 7, Library of Congress, Washington, DC.

19. Monk, *Robert Oppenheimer*, 680.

20. Bird and Sherwin, *American Prometheus*, 575.

21. Ibid.

22. Laurence Stern, "Scientists Seek Oppenheimer Clearance Action," *Washington Post*, April 9, 1963, A2.

23. "From Pariah to Hero," *New York Herald Tribune*, April 6, 1963; "Vindication," *Trenton Evening News*, April 8, 1963.

24. Monk, *Robert Oppenheimer*, 682.

25. Bird and Sherwin, *American Prometheus,* 576.

26. Monk, *Robert Oppenheimer*, 682.

27. "Brotherly Spirit," *Newsweek*, December 16, 1962, 54.

28. Robert Coughlan, "The Tangled Drama and Private Hells of Two Famous Scientists," *Life*, December 13, 1963.

29. Monk, *Robert Oppenheimer,* 682–83.

30. "Brotherly Spirit," *Newsweek*, December 16, 1963.

31. Arthur Schlesinger to Robert Oppenheimer, February 21, 1966, Oppenheimer Papers, box 65, folder 7, Library of Congress, Washington, DC.

32. Glenn, *John Glenn: A Memoir*, 281.

33. Ibid., 290–302.

34. Ibid., 296–99.

35. Ibid., 303–5.

36. Ibid., 320–23.

37. F. D. Reeve, *Robert Frost in Russia* (Boston: Atlantic–Little, Brown Books, 1964), 3.

38. Robert Frost to John F. Kennedy, July 24, 1962, John F. Kennedy Presidential Papers, President's Office Files, Special Correspondence, Frost, Robert, May 1961–April 1962, JFKPL.

39. Parini, *Robert Frost*, 426–34.

40. Ibid., 434–35.

41. Robert Frost to Norman Thomas, circa September 28, 1962, Lawrance Thompson, ed., *Letters of Robert Frost*, 594–95.

42. "Udall Report on Robert Frost Trip to USSR, April 1963," John F. Kennedy Presidential Papers, President's Office Files, Departments and Agencies, Interior, JFKPL.

43. John F. Kennedy Presidential Papers, President's Office Files, Speech Files, Statement on Robert Frost's death, January 29, 1963, JFKPL.

44. Alfred C. Edwards to John F. Kennedy, February 1, 1963, John F. Kennedy Presidential Papers, President's Office Files, Special Correspondence, Frost, Robert, May 1961–April 1962, JFKPL.

45. John F. Kennedy Presidential Papers, President's Office Files, Speech Files, Remarks at Robert Frost Library Ground-Breaking, Amherst College, Amherst, Massachusetts, October 26, 1963, JFKPL.

46. Leeming, *James Baldwin*, 198–99.

47. Weatherby, *James Baldwin*, 204.

48. Baldwin, *Collected Essays*, 291–95.

49. Weatherby, *James Baldwin*, 206.

50. Leeming, *James Baldwin*, 221.

51. Ibid., 222.

52. Guthman and Shulman, *Robert Kennedy in His Own Words*, 223.

53. Leeming, *James Baldwin*, 222.

54. Schlesinger, *Robert Kennedy and His Times*, 331.

55. Ibid.

56. Tye, *Bobby Kennedy*, 194.

57. Schlesinger, *Robert Kennedy and His Times*, 331–35; Morrison, *James Baldwin*, 345.

58. Guthman and Shulman, *Robert Kennedy in His Own Words*, 225.

59. Schlesinger, *Robert Kennedy and His Times*, 335.

60. Tye, *Bobby Kennedy and the Making of a Liberal Icon*, 198.

61. Schlesinger, *Robert Kennedy and His Times*, 335.

62. Taylor Branch, *Parting the Waters: America in the King Years, 1954–63* (New York: Simon and Schuster, 1988), 812–13.

63. "Radio and Television Address on Civil Rights," June 11, 1963, Papers of John F. Kennedy, President's Office Files, Speech Files, JFKPOF-045-005, JFKPL, https://www.jfklibrary.org/Asset-Viewer/Archives/JFKPOF-045-005.aspx.

64. Robert Schlesinger, "The Story Behind JFK's 1963 Landmark Civil Rights Speech," *US News and World Report,* June 11, 2013, https://www.usnews.com/opinion/blogs/robert-schlesinger/2013/06/11/the-story-behind-jfks-1963-landmark-civil-rights-speech.

65. Branch, *Parting the Waters*, 813.

66. Tye, *Bobby Kennedy*, 236.

67. Nathaniel Rich, "James Baldwin and the Fear of a Nation," *New York Review of Books*, May 12, 2016, 36.

68. Tye, *Bobby Kennedy*, 410–11.

69. Styron to William C. Styron Sr., July 21, 1962, in Rose Styron, ed., *Selected Letters of William Styron*, 337–39; Styron, "Havanas in Camelot," in *Havanas in Camelot*, 13–17.

70. Styron to William Blackburn, December 18, 1963, in Rose Styron, *Selected Letters of William Styron*, 354–55.

71. Leeming, *James Baldwin*, 185.

72. Styron to James and Gloria Jones, August 12, 1965, in Rose Styron, ed., *Selected Letters of William Styron*, 374–76; Rose Styron, interview with the author, November 20, 2014, Cambridge, Massachusetts.

73. Styron to Hope Leresche, January 14, 1965, in Rose Styron, ed., *Selected Letters of William Styron*, 365–66.

74. Rose Styron, interview with the author, November 20, 2014, Cambridge, Massachusetts.

75. Michael Norman, "Diana Trilling, a Cultural Critic and Member of a Select Intellectual Circle, Dies at 91," *New York Times*, October 25, 1996, http://www.nytimes.com/1996/10/25/books/diana-trilling-cultural-critic-member-select-intellectual-circle-dies-91.html.

76. Diana Trilling, "Mrs. Harris: The Death of the Scarsdale Diet Doctor," *Kirkus Reviews*, October 28, 1981, https://www.kirkusreviews.com/book-reviews/diana-trilling-4/mrs-harris-the-death-of-the-scarsdale-diet-doct/.

77. Diana Trilling, *Beginning of the Journey*.

78. Baldrige, *In the Kennedy Style*, 102–17. Malraux, the guest of honor, was seated next to Mrs. Kennedy in the Blue Room rather than President Kennedy in the State Dining Room; this was unusual.

79. Baldrige, *A Lady, First*, 205.

80. Jacqueline Kennedy, *Historic Conversations*, 168–70.

81. Greg Lawrence, *Jackie as Editor: The Literary Life of Jacqueline Kennedy Onassis* (New York: Thomas Dunne Books, 2011), 4.

82. William Kuhn, *Reading Jackie: Her Autobiography in Books* (New York: Anchor Books, 2011), 354–60.

83. Ibid., 85–91.

84. Anthony, *As We Remember Her*, 355.

85. *First Lady Jacqueline Kennedy Onassis, 1929–1964: Memorial Tributes in the One Hundred Third Congress of the United States* (Washington, DC: Government Printing Office, 1995), 10.

EPILOGUE | NOTHING LIKE IT SINCE

1. Rose Styron, interview with the author, November 20, 2014, Cambridge, Massachusetts.

2. Ibid.

3. Jacqueline Kennedy, *Historic Conversations*, 88.

4. John F. Kennedy Presidential Papers, President's Office Files, Speech Files, State of the Union Message, Drafts and Press Releases, January 30, 1961, JFKPL.

5. John F. Kennedy, *A Nation of Immigrants* (New York: Harper and Row, 1964), 64.

Root, Elihu, 97, 129
Rose Garden, White House, 34
Rovere, Richard, 198n36
Rowley, Edithe, 44
Rusk, Dean, 158

Sacco and Vanzetti trial, 135, 136, 208–9n36
Salinger, J. D., 47, 117; *Franny and Zoey,* 7
Salinger, Nancy Joy, 51, 136, 170
Salinger, Pierre, 51, 56, 123–27, 159
Sandburg, Carl, 47, 49, 117
SANE (National Committee for a Sane Nuclear Policy), 112
Sartre, Jean-Paul, 135
Scarsdale Diet doctor murders, 169
Schlesinger, Arthur M., Jr., xx; at after-party, 149, 150; *The Age of Roosevelt,* 106; arrivals and reception, 7–8, 10; on Baldwin, 119; on Baldwin/RFK meeting, 166; biography of Andrew Jackson, xx, 106; conversation with Ava Helen Pauling, xix, 106–8, 134, 174; on Hickory Hill, 94; as historian, 106–7, 134; letter to Oppenheimer, 161; at Malraux dinner, 170; Morison and, 134; oral history interviews, 69–70; planning for Nobel dinner, xx, 44, 46, 47, 64, 84, 91, 107, 117, 118; post-dinner party at house of, 146, 151–52, 159; William Styron and, 91, 201n19; as table host, 51; *A Thousand Days,* 172; *The Vital Center,* 106; White House entertainment schedule and, 40
Schlesinger, Marian, 10, 11, 51, 170
Schneider, Alexander, 43
Schonberg, Harold C., 43
Seaborg, Glenn T., xvi, 159–60; arrivals and reception, 5–6, 11; invitation to Nobel dinner, 45; in Kennedy administration, 131; as Nobel winner, 130–31; Oppenheimer and, 6, 86, 87, 91,

131–32, 159–60; Pauling and, 105, 157; as table host, 51, 110
Seaborg, Helen Griggs, 5, 87
September 11, 2001, 176
Shaw, George Bernard, 137
Shaw, Irwin and Marian, 92
Shaw, Maud, 147
Shepard, Alan, 61, 77
Sherman, Roger, 115
Sherman, William T., 56
Shockley, William and Jean Bailey, 99
Shriver, R. Sargent, 46, 51, 149, 171
Shriver, William H., Jr., 46, 51
Sidey, Hugh, 37
Simon, Carly, 171
Sinatra, Frank, 30
Sinclair, Upton, 47
Skakel, George and Ann, 94
slavery in U.S., 115–16, 168
Smith, Jean Kennedy, 51, 149, 150, 154, 168
Smith, Jerome, 166
Smith, Katy, 134
Smith, Reverend Robert, 2
Smith, Stephen, 51, 54
smoking, at Nobel dinner, 125–26, 144, 150
Sontag, Susan, 125
Sorensen, Theodore, 37, 38
Soviet Union: Afghanistan, war in, 176; Cold War, 1, 17, 20, 42, 60, 74, 77, 89, 131, 162–64, 183; Frost in, 58, 162–64; Khrushchev, Nikita, 17, 39, 60, 105, 124, 157, 158–59, 163, 172, 183; Nuclear Test Ban Agreement, signing of, 149, 181; nuclear tests, resumption of, 60
space program and Space Race, 22, 62, 75–78, 140, 155, 161, 172
Spanish Civil War, xvii, 135, 136
Spessot, Julius, 41
St. John's Episcopal Church, Washington, D.C., 2
Stanley, Marian, 125–26
Stanley, Wendell, 125–26

Stark, Joseph, 132

State Dining Room, White House, 11, 33, 35, 43, 50, 56, 64, 65, 72, 75, 86, 106, 114, 132

steel, rise in cost of, 61–62

Stein, Gertrude, 135

Steinbeck, John, 47, 117, 173, 194n54

Steinem, Gloria, 171

Stevenson, Adlai, 16, 106

Stokowski, Leopold, 43

Stoughton, Cecil, 11

Stover, Ralph "Smokey," 4

Stowe, Harriet Beecher, *Uncle Tom's Cabin,* 120

Stratton, Catherine, 126

Stratton, Julius A., 48, 126

Strauss, Lewis, 6, 89, 160

Strolling Strings, 114, 132, 142

Stuart, Gilbert, 36, 101, 133

Styron, Rose, xv, 92; at after-party, xii, 146, 148; arrivals and reception, 11; Baldwin, friendship with, xi, xvii, 6–7, 92–93, 118; on invitation to Nobel dinner, 201n19; Kennedy family, friendship with, xii, xviii, 7, 91, 93, 168–69, 174; on literary program, 146; on Nobel dinner, xi–xii, 4, 9, 174, 175, 181; at post-dinner socializing, 139; Szent-Gyorgyi and, xi–xii, 139, 142; table partners, xi, 86

Styron, William, 91–92; at after-party, xii, 93, 146, 147, 149–50; arrivals and reception, 11; Baldwin, friendship with, xi, xvii, 6–7, 92–93, 118, 121, 122, 169; *The Confessions of Nat Turner,* xviii, 7, 122, 168–69; *Darkness Visible,* 169; death of, 169; Dos Passos influencing, xvii, 91; invitation to Nobel dinner, 46, 91, 117; Kennedy family, friendship with, xii, xviii, 7, 91, 93, 168–69, 174; *Lie Down in Darkness,* 92; on literary program, 146; medication and alcohol affecting, xii, xviii, 93, 147, 149; on

Nobel dinner, xii, 92–93; as post-dinner socializing, 139; Schlesinger and, 91, 201n19; *Set This House on Fire,* xviii, 7, 91, 92; *Sophie's Choice,* xviii, 169; table partners, xi, xv, 91, 93, 100

Suez Crisis, 80

Sukarno (president of Indonesia), 39, 159

Swedish officials at Nobel dinner, 8, 48, 55

Szent-Gyorgyi, Albert, xi, xi–xii, xviii, 104, 139, 142

Talese, Gay, 25

Tarnower, Herman, 169

Tatlock, Jean, 88, 89

Tatum, Edward, 99, 108

Tatum, Viola, 99

Taubman, Harold, 24

Taylor, Zachary, 148

Teller, Edward, 89, 159, 160

Thomas, Evan, 94

Thomas, Helen, 145

Thomas, Norman, 163

Thompson, Alfred Wordsworth, 133, 136–37

Thorsen, Karen, 167

Three-Fifths Compromise, 115

Tolman, Ruth, 88

Travell, Janet G., 46, 149

Trilling, Diana Rubin, xvii–xviii; at after-party, 146, 147–48, 150; arrivals and reception, 7–8, 11, 29; on Johnson, 142; marriage and relationship with Lionel, 13, 18–20, 169; on Nobel dinner, 9, 28–29, 146, 152, 170; on Oppenheimer, xvii–xviii, 8, 90; post-dinner life and death of, 169–70; table partners, 125–26, 127; train journey to and from Washington, D.C., 13–15, 18, 20, 22, 26, 27–28, 152

Trilling, Lionel, xviii; at after-party, 146, 147–48, 150–51; arrivals and reception,